Capital Markets, Growth, and Economic Policy in Latin America

Edited by
Antonio Jorge, Jorge Salazar-Carrillo, and Bernadette West

Westport, Connecticut
London

Library of Congress Cataloging-in-Publication Data

Capital markets, growth, and economic policy in Latin America / edited
  by Antonio Jorge, Jorge Salazar-Carillo, and Bernadette West.
      p.   cm.
    Includes bibliographical references (p.   ) and index.
    ISBN 0–275–95975–9 (alk. paper)
      1. Latin America—Economic conditions—1982–   2. Latin America—
  Economic policy.   3. Debts, External—Latin America.   I. Jorge,
  Antonio, 1931–   .   II. Salazar-Carrillo, Jorge.   III. West,
  Bernadette.
  HC125.C317   2000
  338.98—dc21   99–17924

British Library Cataloguing in Publication Data is available.

Library of Congress Catalog Card Number: 99–17924
ISBN: 0–275–95975–9

First published in 2000

Praeger Publishers, 88 Post Road West, Westport, CT 06881
An imprint of Greenwood Publishing Group, Inc.
www.praeger.com

Printed in the United States of America

The paper used in this book complies with the
Permanent Paper Standard issued by the National
Information Standards Organization (Z39.48–1984).

10 9 8 7 6 5 4 3 2 1

Contents

Tables and Figures   ix
Preface   xiii
Acknowledgment   xv

PART I   INTRODUCTION AND OVERVIEW

1   INTRODUCTION AND OVERVIEW
      Antonio Jorge, Jorge Salazar-Carrillo, and
      Bernadette West   3

PART II   CONSEQUENCES OF THE DEBT CRISIS

2   CONSEQUENCES OF THE DEBT CRISIS IN LARGE
      COUNTRIES: THE CASE OF ARGENTINA
      A. Humberto Petrei   17

3   ECONOMIC GROWTH AND INFLATION IN COLOMBIA
      Jose Antonio Ocampo   31

4   REFLECTIONS ON THE MEXICAN CRISIS
      Julio A. de Quesada   63

5   THE FOREIGN DEBT CRISIS AND ITS CONSEQUENCES
      ON THE VENEZUELAN ECONOMY
      Antonio Casas-Gonzalez   75

PART III   GROWTH AND DEVELOPMENT PERSPECTIVES

6   THE MEXICAN CRISIS AND CARIBBEAN ECONOMIC
      GROWTH: IMPACT AND PROSPECTS
      Anthony Gonzales   93

7   A COMPARISON OF EAST ASIAN AND LATIN AMERICAN
      DEVELOPMENT: WILL LATIN AMERICA CREATE ITS
      OWN MIRACLE?
      F. Gerard Adams   103

8   THE FACTS OF ECONOMIC DEVELOPMENT AND
      VIRTUOUS CIRCLES
      F. Gerard Adams   115

9   THE CUBAN ECONOMY AS SEEN THROUGH FOREIGN
      TRADE
      Jorge Salazar-Carrillo   121

10   DEBT AND DEVELOPMENT IN LATIN AMERICA IN THE
      GLOBAL ECONOMY
      Antonio Jorge and Raul Moncarz   137

11   THE SOCIOECONOMIC IMPACT OF TOURISM IN
      BARBADOS
      Irma T. de Alonso and Jorge Salazar-Carrillo   147

PART IV   NEOLIBERALISM AND NEOPOPULISM: ADJUSTMENT AND STABILITY

12   NEOLIBERALISM VERSUS NEOPOPULISM
      John Williamson   171

13   SOME THOUGHTS ON THE ACHIEVEMENT OF SUSTAINED
      GROWTH WITH POVERTY REDUCTION IN LATIN AMERICA
      Gustav Ranis   177

14   OUTLINE FOR A SOCIOECONOMIC PARADIGM FOR POST-
      CASTRO CUBA
      Antonio Jorge   189

15   ON THE POLITICAL ECONOMY OF PENSIONS
        AND SOCIAL SECURITY
        Peter Diamond   205

16   BRIEF THOUGHTS ON THE POLITICAL ECONOMY
        OF ADJUSTMENT: INTERNATIONAL MARKETS
        VERSUS NATIONAL POLITICS
        Gerald M. Meier   211

Selected Bibliography   215
Index   219
About the Contributors   225

Tables and Figures

Table

2.1	International Reserves and Monetary Liabilities	18
2.2	Deposits in the Financial System	19
2.3	Trade and Current Account Balance	20
2.4	Gross Domestic Product, Yearly Percentage Change	22
2.5	Unemployment as a Percent of Economically Active Population	23
2.6	Yearly Inflation Rate, Based on CPI	24
A2.1	Argentina: Number of Financial Entities	26
A2.2	Argentina: Distribution of Deposits in the System	27
A4.1	Mexico: Net Flows of External Debt	69
A5.1	Venezuela: Plan Financiero 1990, Eligible Debt per Option	82
A5.2	Venezuela: Restructured External Public Debt Service Estimates	82
A5.3	Venezuela: Nonrestructured External Public Debt Service Estimates	82
A5.4	Venezuela: External Public Debt, Year-End Stock	83
6.1	Average Real GDP Growth Rates, 1980-90, 1982-92, and 1990-94	94
6.2	Actual and Expected Growth Rates, 1990-96	100
7.1	Growth Experience: Latin America and East Asia	104
7.2	Per Capita Real GNP: Latin America and East Asia	106
7.3	Inflation and Debt Burdens: Latin America and East Asia	107
7.4	Export Growth: Latin America and East Asia	109
7.5	Savings Rates: Latin America and East Asia	111
9.1	Exports by Country of Destination, 1989-95	124
9.2	Imports by Country of Origin, 1989-95	125

9.3	Commodity Exports, 1989-95	127
9.4	Commodity Imports, 1989-95	128
A9.1	Exports by Country of Destination, 1958-62	130
A9.2	Imports by Country of Origin, 1958-62	132
A9.3	Commodity Exports, 1958 and 1962	134
A9.4	Commodity Imports, 1958 and 1962	134
11.1	Selected Tourism Statistics from Barbados, West Indies	150
11.2	Estimated Average Length of Stays by Country of Origin, 1989	151
11.3	Average Daily Expenditures by Barbados Visitors	152
11.4	GDP at Factor Cost and the Value Added in Tourism	156
11.5	The Estimated Future Seasonal and Annual Expenditures of Visitors in Barbados	161
11.6	Tourism Density Ratio in Barbados, West Indies	164
11.7	Tourism Per Square Kilometer in Barbados, 1990-2000	165
11.8	Lodgings and Population in Barbados, 1990-2000	166

Figure

A2.1	Argentina: Fluctuation in Deposits and Lending Capacity	28
A2.2	Argentina: Country Risk	29
A2.3	Argentina: Exports and Imports	30
3.1	Colombia: GDP Growth, 1990 to 1998	38
3.2	Colombia: GDP Growth, 1971 to 1998	39
3.3	GDP Growth in Latin America, 1980 to 1995	40
3.4	GDP Growth and Volatility in Latin America and Selected Countries, 1970	41
3.5	Colombia: Value Added Growth by Economic Sector	42
3.6	Colombia: Value Added by Economic Sector	43
3.7	Colombia: GDP and Aggregate Demand	44
3.8	Colombia: Inflation, 1989 to 1995	45
3.9	Colombia: Investment Rate	46
3.10	Colombia: Infrastructure Investment	47
3.11	Colombia: Savings Rate	48
3.12	Colombia: Real Exchange Rate Index	49
3.13	Colombia: Balance of Payments	50
3.14	Colombia: Exports/GDP	51
3.15	Colombia: Diversification of Exports	52
3.16	Colombia: Oil Exports	53
3.17	Colombia: Nontraditional Exports Growth	54
3.18	Colombia: Current Account Balance	55
3.19	Colombia: Direct Foreign Investment in Oil/Mining and Other Sectors	56

3.20	Colombia: Foreign Debt Ratios	57
3.21	Colombia: Recent Bond Issues Spreads, November 1994 to January 1996	58
3.22	Colombia: Fiscal Surplus/Deficit	59
3.23	Colombia: M1 and M3 Growth	60
3.24	Colombia: Total Credit	61
3.25	Colombia: Real Interest Rates, 1990 to 1995	62
A4.1	Mexico: Libor Versus UMS Premium	70
A4.2	Mexico: Foreign Investment Flows	71
A4.3	Mexico: Current Account and International Reserves	72
A4.4	Mexico: Profile of External Debt	73
A4.5	Mexico: Real Exchange Rate	74
A5.1	Venezuela: Public Foreign Debt to GDP Ratio	84
A5.2	Venezuela: Foreign Debt as Percentage of Oil Exports	85
A5.3	Venezuela: Real Growth and Inflation Rate	86
A5.4	Venezuela: Fiscal Deficit and Percentage of GDP	87
A5.5	Venezuela: Revenues and Expenditures as Percentage of GDP	88
A5.6	Venezuela: Oil Industry Indicators	89
A5.7	Venezuela: International Reserves and Oil Prices	90

Preface

Since the end of World War II, the importance of trade, capital movements, and monetary transactions, relative to global output, has increased by leaps and bounds. The cohesiveness and interdependence of the world economy has been advancing *pari passu* with the sustained improvements of the means of communication, transportation, and information technology in all its diverse facets. To these material causal agents of globalization one must add the influence exerted by other intangible forces of great importance, such as politico ideological and purely economic ones.

At present, domestic or endogenous processes of modernization, growth, and development are inextricably linked with exogenous institutions and events of a transnational nature. Never were the words of Alfred Marshall—when referring to international trade as an engine of growth—more true than today.

However, globalization, or its concrete manifestation as a dense and complex system of international economic and financial interrelations, carries with it many subsidiary or secondary effects which we are only beginning to explore.

Topics in a large variety of interfacing areas in diverse fields, such as the international economy, money and finance, and the role of corresponding international and domestic institutions, will be at the forefront of the research agenda in both pure economics and political economy for years to come.

This present volume aspires to be among the initial contributions to an interdisciplinary area of momentous import to the welfare of individual nations, and regions, as well as to the course of the world economy itself. The chapters in this book were selected following two criteria. Some address general themes and issues of wider interest and application, while others circumscribe to the concrete conditions and characteristics of specific cases. We hope to have attained a good balance between the two. One that while keeping an eye on systemic and recurrent points will also not lose sight of actual events and real outcomes.

Acknowledgment

The financial help of Hamilton Bank in Miami, Florida, and particularly the support of its Chairman and CEO, Mr. Eduardo Masferrer, is gratefully acknowledged for having made possible the publication of this volume.

PART I

INTRODUCTION AND OVERVIEW

INTRODUCTION AND OVERVIEW

Antonio Jorge, Jorge Salazar-Carrillo, and Bernadette West

INTRODUCTION

This book contains a collection of chapters inspired by recent economic events in Mexico and Latin America. Many of these chapters were first presented at the Conference on International Economic and Financial Systems: The Mexican Crisis and the Latin-American Debt Redux (the Conference), held in January 1996 at the Biltmore Hotel in Coral Gables, Florida. On that important event, distinguished economists from Latin America, the Caribbean, and the United States met to discuss the 1995 Mexican crisis and the extent to which it had adversely affected these neighboring economies. By all accounts, the fallout, or so-called tequila effect, appears to have been quite extensive—seriously affecting some countries by slowing their economic growth and swelling the ranks of the unemployed. One remarkably resilient country during this episode was Colombia. Not only did it emerge relatively unscathed, but now boasts of being stronger than ever. It seems the threat posed by this crisis created a "political climate" that allowed Colombian officials to pass many needed reforms in their public and private sectors. Of course other countries also used this crisis to pass reforms of their own, but with a lesser degree of success. Their experiences are recalled here to shed new light on the effectiveness of the traditional reforms supported by the International Monetary Fund (IMF) and other international financial organizations. Through these experiences we get a better picture of what lies in store for Asia, now that it is in the midst of its own financial crisis, dubbed the "Asian contagion."

ORGANIZATION

This book is organized into four parts, including Part I, "Introduction and Overview," presenting highlights from each chapter that follows. Part II, "Consequences of the Debt Crisis," contains four chapters providing statistics and firsthand accounts of the devastating impact of the 1994 Mexican crisis on that country and its neighbors. In particular, chapter 2 looks at how the Mexican crisis affected the Argentine economy; chapter 3, the Colombian economy; chapter 4, the Mexican economy; and chapter 5, the Venezuelan economy.

Part III, "Growth and Development Perspectives," includes chapters that, together, analyze, compare, and evaluate different growth and development strategies in Latin America, East Asia, and the Caribbean. Chapter 6 begins with a discussion of how NAFTA and the 1994 Mexican crisis have forced the Caribbean islands to rethink their development strategies. Chapter 7 examines and evaluates the different development paths chosen by Latin America and East Asia through their past and current economic performances. This analysis is extended further in chapter 8 where each region's economic performance is compared with the "stylized facts" of development, to discount the doctrine of "vicious cycles of poverty." A unique view of the "elusive" Cuban economy, as seen through its trade with other nations (after the dissolution of the Soviet Union), is provided in Chapter 9. In chapter 10 we explore the relationship between debt, development, and economic growth in Latin America. Chapter 11 closes with an impact study of how tourism-based development strategies are likely to affect Barbados and other islands on the Caribbean.

Part IV, "Neoliberalism and Neopopulism: Adjustment and Stability," includes several chapters that discuss, in broad and specific terms, the political and social implications of traditional macroeconomic adjustments and reforms currently being endorsed by the IMF and World Bank. Chapter 12 opens with a philosophical discussion of what neoliberalism and neopopulism mean within Latin America's economic and political landscape, and why these seemingly opposite schools of thought now flourish side by side. Chapter 13 offers some new ideas on how to achieve both sustainable growth and a more equitable distribution of income simultaneously. In chapter 14, the social, political, and economic institutions of a centrally planned economy are compared with the economic system of "pre-Castro" Cuba to reconstruct a new economic system in which "post-Castro" Cubans can live. In chapter 15 we look at the political economy of the Social Security fund and why successful reform in this area depends ultimately on reforming the capital markets in which they operate. Chapter 16 closes the book with some brief notes and observations on the inner workings of capital markets and why volatility here is inconsistent with many economic reforms and policies aimed at encouraging international capital flows. The 1994 Mexican crisis is used here to highlight the inconsistencies and pitfalls awaiting developing countries as they try to play an ever-increasing role in the global economy.

CHAPTER HIGHLIGHTS

This section provides brief highlights from each chapter which will guide the reader to the chapter or chapters of interest. It allows a glimpse of the broad spectrum of issues and controversies being discussed.

Part II: Consequences of The Debt Crisis

Part II opens with a chapter by A. Humberto Petrei entitled "Consequences of the Debt Crisis in Large Countries: The Case of Argentina." This chapter was transcribed and edited from a video of the author's presentation at the Conference. A. H. Petrei begins his presentation by noting how detrimental the Mexican crisis was to the Argentine economy, which at the time was especially vulnerable. Argentina's economy was relying very heavily on foreign capital inflows while maintaining a monetary system with full convertibility. Under their system, an Argentine peso could be exchanged for one U.S. dollar or its equivalent in gold. However, because of Mexico's financial crisis, Argentina saw its own foreign reserves decline sharply, and given the rules of convertibility, a substantial contraction of their money stock soon followed. According to some estimates, the money supply shrank by as much as 17 percent. Rather than abandon or relax the rules of convertibility, they opted instead for several public- and private-sector reforms to address the social hardships and financial chaos that would inevitably follow a monetary contraction of this size. Petrei provides interesting data on how key macro-variables in the Argentine economy were affected. The only sector that did well during this painful episode was the external sector, which had actually generated a trade surplus. Nevertheless, as the author notes, this was expected given the size of the monetary contraction and its impact on aggregate demand. The chapter closes with some compelling arguments in favor of continuing the Argentine monetary system of full convertibility.

Chapter 3 by Jose Antonio Ocampo, entitled "Economic Growth and Inflation in Colombia," was also transcribed and edited from a video of his presentation at the Conference. In this chapter, Ocampo comments on the remarkable performance of the Colombian economy during the Mexican crisis. The only noticeable impact was an initial delay on bond offerings in the international market in the early part of 1995. Other than that, the Mexican episode had essentially left them unaffected. According to Ocampo, the crisis may even have had a positive impact on their economy. One reason is that it forced the government and the central bank to pay closer attention to the exchange rate—which at the time was moving very erratically. Fortunately, both institutions could agree on a mutually consistent exchange-rate policy. And another reason was the country's own restrictive policy on external financing, which had been in place since early 1994. According to the author, "The basis of the restrictions (and what I [author] consider an essential lesson of the crisis), is that all [external] financing should be structured with long-term loans rather than short-term loans." The author goes on to say that "today, Colombia is totally financed with long-term capital flows and will continue to be well into the future." Statistical information contained here describes the dynamic path of Colombia's main economic variables, including gross domestic product (GDP) growth rates, unemployment rates, interest rates, budget deficits, and inflation rates, before and during the Mexican crisis.

Chapter 4 by Julio de Quesada, entitled "Reflections on the Mexican Crisis," is a personal account of how Mexico's financial crisis unfolded while he was the division head of Mexico's Citibank operations. He vividly recalls December 20, 1994, the day the stock market plunged into chaos, after the government announced that its exchange rate ceiling would be raised by 15.3 percent. That announcement came without warning or explanation, leaving investors confused and in disarray. What followed, in the author's words, was "capital flight . . . hemorrhaging at alarming rates." The central bank did not have sufficient reserves to defend the new ceiling, and as investor confidence plummeted, so did the credibility of the new Mexican government. After a period of indecision and uncertainty by government officials, an emergency program was finally put in place. Strict monetary and fiscal reforms were designed to contract aggregate demand significantly and fix the economy's massive external imbalances. Fortunately, the program had an immediate and desired effect, though not without a price. The Mexican economy is now tentatively on the mend, and as the author sees it, still has a bright and exciting future.

Chapter 5 by Antonio Casas-Gonzalez, entitled "The Foreign Debt Crisis and Its Consequences on the Venezuelan Economy," recalls Venezuela's struggles during the 1980s with its massive foreign debt. In the previous decade, Venezuela had enjoyed trade surpluses that led to many ambitious investment projects, mostly financed with foreign funds. This was mainly because local reserves were not sufficient for the size of the investments planned. Unfortunately, the unusually high crude oil prices that generated Venezuela's trade surpluses in the 1970s also led to widespread inflation among the importers of crude oil, particularly in the industrialized countries. This prompted anti-inflationary measures that caused world interest rates to rise, which in turn caused Venezuela's foreign debt service to rise. When crude oil prices (and other primary good prices) dropped rapidly and unexpectedly in the late 1970s, the stage was set for the debt crisis that followed. Against this backdrop, the author discusses major agreements transacted between Venezuela on one hand, and the international banking community, the IMF, and the World Bank on the other, to help it regain access to foreign capital inflows. While some reforms and adjustments in the economy were quite restrictive, they did have their desired effect. The bad news is that Venezuela is now facing another crisis, not related to the Mexican crisis. This time it is their banking sector that is in trouble. This latest crisis began with the failure of Banco Latino in January of 1994 and has since escalated to the point that it now threatens their entire economy. Again, Venezuela's future depends on its current negotiations with the IMF, leaving the author to speculate on what types of adjustments will be required of Venezuela this time. The chapter closes with suggestions on how best to steer Venezuela on a "track of sustained growth, with price stability, and a viable balance of payments in the short and medium run."

Part III: Growth and Development Perspectives

Part III opens with chapter 6 by Anthony Gonzales, entitled "The Mexican Crisis and Caribbean Economic Growth: Impact and Prospects." Here the author assesses the impact of the Mexican crisis (and the North American Free Trade Agreement [NAFTA]), on the Caribbean's potential for future growth. This was not an easy task, given the region's diverse and varied economic structures, trading patterns, and growth experiences. Nevertheless, several key economic variables were found to have changed significantly and consistently during the Mexican crisis—the overall average economic growth rate, consumption rate, and savings rate. The author's research shows that the region started to experience sharp fluctuations around an annual growth rate of 2 percent in the early 1990s. In the previous decade, the region's average annual growth was higher, at around 2.4 percent. NAFTA was largely to blame for the slower growth rate, while the widening fluctuations around the trend emerged only after the Mexican crisis. The source of the problem is a familiar one: The Caribbean was relying too heavily on international capital inflows to supplement shortfalls in its foreign aid at the time. This led to the assignment of higher risk rates and increasing volatility in the flow of international capital. Unlike past risk-rating systems, the new rates were now being based on the ability to generate foreign exchange quickly enough to meet short-term obligations. This system does not bode well for the region, given its historically high trade deficit-to-GDP ratios and its inability to produce high-valued exports with the infrastructure currently available. According to the author, this region will see significant growth only if exports expand by at least 10 percent and domestic savings rates increase sufficiently enough to offset volatile foreign capital flows. Some studies suggest it may take as much as an 8 percent increase in the savings rate to generate at least a 2 percent increase in GDP growth. Without these changes, and others, the region's future looks even less promising than its recent past.

Chapter 7 by F. Gerard Adams is entitled "A Comparison of East Asian and Latin American Development: Will Latin America Create Its Own Miracle?" As the title suggests, this chapter focuses on the growth experiences of East Asia and Latin America. Adams' research shows that East Asia's average annual growth rate was between 6 and 7 percent during the 1980s and early 1990s, while Latin America's average was only about 2 percent. Per capita GDP was also much higher in East Asia, but with greater income disparity than in Latin America. What lies behind these major differences? The answer, suggested by Adams, lies in their different development strategies, structural changes, macroeconomic policies, and government policies where these key differences were identified:

- *Development strategies*: Both regions followed roughly the same "import substitution" strategy during the 1960s, but East Asia quickly switched to export promotion, while Latin America only recently made the switch.
- *Structural changes*: Structural changes accompanying economic development, such as rising wages, helped shift comparative advantage in East Asia toward more capital-intensive technologies. These changes were dramatic and accompanied by "linked processes" that the author describes as "production complementarity." In contrast, production linkages in Latin America appeared more "conflictive" and much less "complementary."
- *Macroeconomic policies*: Macroeconomic policies in East Asia generally focused on fiscal stability that helped them to avoid inflation. Latin America, on the other hand, pursued populist policies with inflationary consequences.
- *Government policies*: East Asia's remarkable development followed directly from government policies aimed at maintaining favorable terms of trade, economic stability, and industrialization with undervalued exchange rates. In contrast, government policies in Latin America created unstable macroeconomic environments and efforts at stabilization generally came at the expense of overvalued exchange rates.

Though Latin America is now emulating East Asia's development strategy of free-markets, export expansion, and privatization, those efforts may not be enough. To catch up with their Asian counterparts, the author also recommends strengthening production linkages, increasing savings rates, and more intraregional trade to increase the scale of production and, therefore, their international competitiveness.

Chapter 8 is also by F. Gerard Adams, entitled "The Facts of Economic Development and Virtuous Circles." This chapter begins with the "vicious circle" theory that explains why relatively poor countries are likely to remain poor. They have serious savings and investment constraints directly related to their poverty, which impedes their economic growth and development. They also face human capital constraints that limit the use of advanced technologies and relegate them to the production of primary goods that are typically demand inelastic. And they face the Malthusian dilemma of population growing more rapidly than available resources with any improvement in overall living standards. While the theory may seem logical, evidence from Latin America and East Asia points to an alternative process at work. In these relatively poor regions we have witnessed, to varying degrees, rapid and sustainable growth without abundant natural resources; accelerating export growth of all primary and manufactured goods; capital-intensive technology shifts; and increasing standards of living accompanied by declining birth rates. These facts suggest that "vicious circles of poverty" can be avoided. Adams' research points to one possibility, as suggested by the direct relationship observed between actual growth rates and anticipated growth rates in East Asia: "rational expectations." While vicious cycles of poverty exist, so do "virtuous cycles," driven by the expectations and promise of growth and prosperity in the future.

Chapter 9 by Jorge Salazar-Carrillo, entitled "The Cuban Economy as Seen Through Foreign Trade," evaluates Cuba's recent economic performance through international trade flows and the composition of imports and exports from 1989 to 1995. The analysis takes a rather unique approach—using Cuba's trading partners' statistics rather than Cuba's official trade statistics, which are considered by Salazar-Carrillo and others to be intentionally ambiguous, misleading, and rife with distortions. From the statistics provided by Cuba's trading partners, the author makes the following observations about the Cuban economy:

- Exports in 1995 were less than a quarter of their 1989 value, in real terms.
- Its main trading partner is no longer Russia, but Canada and China, in that order.
- The worst export performance on record occurred between 1993 and 1994.
- Sugar is still the main export, representing more than half of all exports.
- Massive investments in the biotechnology industry are not panning out.

Cuba's composition of exports today is not much different from 1989. One area with a noticeable change is tourism, and another is foreign investment. The number of visitors to Cuba increased dramatically during the 1990s, but so did the imports needed to satisfy them. It is not clear whether this shift toward tourism improved or worsened Cuba's balance of payments. Government officials also claim to have received large amounts of direct foreign investment, but no hard statistics are available to substantiate that claim. To the contrary, evidence suggests those investment flows from Cuba's main sources of foreign capital, namely the former Soviet bloc countries, are now virtually nonexistent. Cuba's future does not look very promising and the "window dressing" reforms imposed of late do not seem to have helped much. What the Cuban government desperately needs to do is expand privatization efforts and market reforms, and extend political and economic freedom to its people.

Chapter 10 by Antonio Jorge and Raul Moncarz, entitled "Debt and Development in Latin America in the Global Economy," provides a brief discussion of the evolution of Latin America's debt crisis and why we ought to be more concerned. Latin America has extensive external financial ties with the rest of the world. Given current demographic trends, this region is very likely to be the next largest untapped market in the new millennium. Therefore, it is in the world's best interest to find a lasting solution to the region's persistent debt problem. Some suggestions offered here by the authors can easily be extended to other parts of the world now facing similar difficulties, such as East Asia and Russia. The authors' list of suggestions includes the following:

- Examine the relationship between debt, development, and trade. Trade liberalization and labor market reforms may not always produce the growth anticipated.
- Acknowledge that external factors are also major determinants of the burdensomeness of debt and relief that can be expected.

- Hold economic summits to coordinate global policies.
- Open the region to further international trade.

And last, but not least,

- Shift the responsibility of debt management from the IMF to the World Bank, so that loans can be structured over a longer period.

Chapter 11 by Irma de Alonso and Jorge Salazar-Carrillo, entitled "The Socioeconomic Impact of Tourism in Barbados," evaluates the economic and social impact of a tourist-based development plan for the island. In particular, they examine the effect of tourism on economic indicators such as GDP, government tax revenues, foreign exchange, and the development of other sectors, which they obtain through the spending patterns of tourists. The two main spending categories in this study are "spending by stay-over tourists" and "spending by cruise ship passengers." Total impacts on the economic indicators are then calculated with the aid of multipliers that specifically reflect the Island's economy and the Caribbean tourism industry. In many ways this study is an update of an earlier one by Armstrong et al. (1968), that also analyzed the impact of the tourist industry in Barbados. Interestingly, while these studies used different theoretical approaches, the multipliers they generated would have been very similar, except for one crucial assumption: the Armstrong study found (through input-output analysis), that 40 percent of tourists spending leaks out of the island's economy as imports specifically earmarked for the tourists. In contrast, this later study assumed (based on expert opinions), that as much as 60 percent of this spending leaks out. This makes the authors' results quite different from the earlier study, as the multiplier effect is significantly weaker with the assumption of greater leakage. Despite this, the authors' still found the economic impact of tourist-based development to be beneficial. Even when weighed against the social impacts—many of which are strongly negative, such as increased traffic congestion, crime, pollution, environmental degradation, social tension, and so on. The authors' are quick to note, however, that the smaller multiplier effect means that the negative social impacts mentioned above could easily outweigh the positive economic impacts. To prevent this occurrence, the island needs to educate the population about the importance of tourism, reduce crime (especially tourist-related crime), promote understanding of the Island's unique historic and cultural heritage, and protect the environment.

Part IV: Neoliberalism and Neopopulism

Chapter 12 by John Williamson, entitled "Neoliberalism Versus Neopopulism," explains why neoliberalism and neopopulism, two seemingly opposing ideological positions, are comfortable companions in Latin America's varied political and economic landscape. The author begins this philosophical discussion by first adopting Mario Simonsen's definition of neoliberalism as "the economics of Reagan and Thatcher." Neoliberalism, like classical liberalism, regards the market as a constructive institution, but with much less emphasis on social issues. Populism, on the other hand, is defined by the author as any action undertaken for the masses, despite whether or not it benefits them. The two ideologies converge in Latin America, with "liberalism," both of the classical and neo variety flourishing alongside "populist" policies—policies that get politicians elected. Ironically, these same policies would have meant political suicide just a few years back. So what accounts for this reversal in attitude? The author explains that economists have traditionally overstated the cost of macroeconomic stability programs, particularly concerning the short-run unemployment-inflation trade-off, and this emphasis is misleading. He uses Israel as a case in point: The Israeli stabilization of 1985 showed us that anti-inflation programs can achieve macro-stabilization with economic growth. Chile had a similar experience, which led to social welfare expansion and economic expansion. The author's hypothesis is that the output costs of stabilizing rapid inflation are "prepaid." If accelerating inflation leads to decelerating output (stagflation), then the reverse should also be true—that is, decelerating inflation should lead to accelerating output. If one accepts this, then it is no wonder that policy reforms that reduce inflation through fiscal and other constraints are now politically tenable in Latin America.

Chapter 13 by Gustav Ranis, entitled "Some Thoughts on the Achievement of Sustained Growth with Poverty Reduction in Latin America," notes a reversal of attitudes and policies in Latin America regarding the relative importance of an open economy. The past decade has shown that avoiding painful policy changes does not guarantee developmental success. Nor does having ample natural resources—which, in Latin America, is blamed for stalling the implementation of crucial reforms seen as politically unappealing. The current problems now facing the region stem from a lengthy period of import substitution. Inefficiencies and distortions became entrenched over that period, leading to diminished growth, a worsening of the distribution of income, and increased poverty. Undoing these problems requires a rethinking of the role of government and the whole development process. While the new emphasis on exports may be a step in the right direction, it may turn out to be just as lopsided as import substitution because it seriously neglects the agricultural and rural sector. According to Ranis, economic growth with poverty reduction requires the following measures:

- Land reform
- More rural credit infrastructure and technology information systems
- More emphasis on indigenous applied science and technology
- Developing linkages between the formal and informal sectors of the economy
- More flexibility in labor markets
- More equitable distribution of social goods, such as education, health care, and potable water
- Encouraging repatriation of human capital
- More decentralized decision making in rural sectors, from central to local government.

Post-debt-crisis policy mixes have put Latin America on a stabilization path marked by micro structural changes, increased privatization, lower barriers of protection, and increased decentralization. But given its history of interventionism during the days of import substitution the temptation to revert to former policies in the face of external shocks is still strong. Ranis points to remnants of this type of policy thinking, such as the adherence to fixed exchange-rate stabilization strategies. However, there is cause for optimism. The proposed extension of NAFTA to the entire Western hemisphere and the creation of the World Trade Organization (WTO) should create external pressures that would prevent a return to the policies of old.

Chapter 14 by Antonio Jorge, entitled "Outline for a Socioeconomic Paradigm for Post-Castro Cuba," presents a general outline for the reconstruction, development, and desocialization of post-Castro Cuba. Jorge recommends a gradualist approach to development rather than a Big Bang approach, as was used in the former USSR. The functions and role of the state are an integral part of this discussion.

The key features of Jorge's outline for reconstructing Cuba include:

- Coordinating the means of structural change with the stabilization measures of monetary, fiscal, and exchange rate policy over a lengthy period—perhaps as long as five years
- Assigning maximum priority to agricultural diversification and rational economic self-sufficiency with emphasis on the production of basic goods for general consumption
- Assigning as a secondary priority, the development of light industry, for the production of consumer goods and intermediate manufacturing
- Establishing a system of property rights which takes into account the country's geoeconomic and political characteristics, comparative advantages, financial and other resources, and its traditional economic psychology and sociology and that of its natural trading partners
- Establishing a system of semirational prices
- Designing stabilization policies—to encompass tax reform, monetary and fiscal policy, the foreign exchange rate system, and convertibility in the money stock
- Creating a sound financial, banking, and credit system

This gradualist approach will ease Cuba's orderly transition from a collectivist, centralized economy to that of a healthy market system through spontaneous natural growth and expansion. This path is adaptable to the disastrous Cuban economy at present and its low level of development, small markets, scarce productive resources, limited available land, and current population demographics.

Chapter 15 by Peter Diamond, entitled "On the Political Economy of Pensions and Social Security,"discusses how government policies regarding pension funds affect the capital markets in which they play a large role, such as in the United States. Four motives have been identified here to justify the U.S. government's intervention in this area. *One*, there are short-run budgetary considerations stemming from the tax treatment of pension fund contributions. *Two*, the long-run financial position of the Social Security fund in the U.S. is looking somewhat ominous, as the date the fund hits zero continuously edges forward with each new projection. This realization has prompted the author and other economists to consider alternative social security systems, such as mandated individual savings (MIS), the Chilean system, and mandated universal pensions (MUPS), which was adopted in Australia in 1995. *Three*, government is looking at pension funds, and the regulation of these funds, as a possible means of improving the workings of the economy by ensuring more stable and equitable flows of income. This means that more reforms are needed in capital markets to make them "fairer, less risky, and less expensive to trade in." And *four*, governments need to respond to special interest groups that would use their influence to tilt resources in their favor. Of the many complex issues concerning Social Security reform, none may be more controversial than the coverage issue. Preferred tax treatments are designed to encourage pension fund contributions, but how wide should the coverage be? Should everyone be covered or should coverage be limited to just management and highly paid workers? The answer may appear straightforward until one considers the impact on the government's budget balance and its political significance. Limiting coverage would increase tax revenues and lessen the need for tax rate increases, but at what cost to society? Controversial issues like this are brought to light in this brief chapter, with the U.S. and Chilean experiences serving to illustrate just how complex they really are. Throughout, the author emphasizes the importance of a smooth-running capital market as a prerequisite to Social Security system reform. Without that, the success of the Chilean reform would not have been possible.

Chapter 16 is the final chapter, entitled "Brief Thoughts on the Political Economy of Adjustment: International Markets Versus National Politics" by Gerald Meier. In this chapter Professor Meier sheds light on a rather interesting dilemma facing developing countries that have come to rely heavily on volatile international capital markets for investment funds. He makes his point with the Mexican crisis, where national policies and reforms were initiated to specifically attract large international capital flows. Mexico's success, however, turned out to be short-lived as foreign capital inflows soon caused the exchange rate to appreciate, nominal interest rates to rise, and their current account deficit to widen. This in turn resulted in a higher default rate premium throughout the region, and for Mexico in particular, ultimately leading to massive capital outflows, falling reserves, and a regionwide "liquidity" crisis. Many economists are now considering ways to lessen the detrimental impact of volatile international capital markets. Meier's solution calls for the creation of a stronger international public sector that will have the muscle to "remedy international market failures as globalization occurs."

PART II

CONSEQUENCES OF THE
DEBT CRISIS

CONSEQUENCES OF THE DEBT CRISIS IN LARGE COUNTRIES: THE CASE OF ARGENTINA

A. Humberto Petrei

INTRODUCTION

The recent Mexican crisis interrupted a growth process that had begun in Argentina in 1991. Argentina was probably more affected by the Mexican crisis than any other Latin American country, barring Mexico itself. There are several reasons for this: Argentina's heavy reliance on capital inflows and its fiscal deficit, which began to surge in the second quarter of 1994, just as the Mexican crisis was beginning to unfold.

In the first quarter of 1995, the effects of the crisis brewing in Mexico had been confined mainly to Argentina's financial sector. However, it was not long before damage began to surface in the real sector. By the second quarter of 1995, and definitely by the third quarter, we see evidence of the crisis' impact on the real sector, manifested particularly in growth rates and unemployment rates. The consequences of this latest crisis will be felt for some time and all the ill effects reversed.

CONSEQUENCES OF THE MEXICAN CRISIS

At the beginning of the crisis, the Argentine authorities did not perceive the full magnitude of events. Their response was to devise measures that would create or add surplus to international reserves so as to ensure compliance with all their financial commitments in the external sector. But two months into the crisis, the authorities were finally beginning to realize that the crisis was much deeper than originally perceived and that it could affect the country much more seriously than had originally been predicted.

The authorities started to plan for a very difficult year as it came to be. They began negotiating with international financial organizations to secure their finan-

Table 2.1. International Reserves and Monetary Liabilities (billions of U.S. dollars)

Date	International Reserves	Monetary Liabilities
Dec. 31, 1994	17.9	16.3
March 31, 1995	12.5	12.4
May 31, 1995	13.5	13.5
July 31, 1995	15.1	14.6
Dec. 28, 1995	17.9	17.3

cial needs and began to think about measures that could be applied to the financial sector to supplement or fix a vacuum that had been left over from previous reforms. They also began to design important and substantial reforms for the fiscal sector.

To appreciate the magnitude of the Mexican crisis as it affected Argentina, consider these facts and figures. Let's start with its impact on international reserves, as seen in Table 2.1. International reserves are very important, everywhere, and in every country, no matter how large or small. It is one of those variables that economists watch very carefully. In Argentina, it is particularly important because of its system of exchange rates and the monetary rules it has adopted. Argentina has a very interesting, albeit restrictive, system of convertibility, where one peso equals one U.S. dollar on demand. There is no narrow band here, the relationship is strictly maintained at one-to-one. The basis of the system is to keep international reserves roughly even, or very nearly even, with the monetary base. When reserves drop, so does the monetary base of the economy. One can well imagine, under this system, the chaos that the Mexican crisis created in Argentina's banking system.

We see in Table 2.1 a sudden decrease in total reserves, which at the end of 1994 amounted to 17.9 billion. By March of 1995, these reserves had fallen to 12.5 billion—which is an extremely large decline, nearly 30 percent—in only three month's time. This sharp decline in reserves and, consequently, the monetary base, created havoc in the financial sector and left international markets with the impression that Argentina was on the verge of default.

Immediate corrective measures were called for in both the financial and business sectors of the economy. To avoid default, Argentina had to secure additional financial resources—a task made more difficult by the fact that tax collections were declining and potential deficits were rising. As it turned out, some of the resources that were prededicated or expected to be used for paying off

TABLE 2.2. Deposits in the Financial System (billions of U.S. dollars)

Date	Total Deposits
Dec. 31, 1994	43.9
March 31, 1995	37.8
May 31, 1995	38.6
July 31, 1995	41.2
Dec. 26, 1995	43.8

external debts were not available. Additional resources had to be generated immediately, and even though they could not be secured, the country still needed on top of that impossible sum, an additional $5 billion in order to feel relatively comfortable complying with all of its 1995 financial commitments.

Falling reserves, consequently, led to massive flight out of the banking system as seen by the figures in Table 2.2. Bank deposits fell by as much as 17 percent. Although not as large as the 30 percent fall in reserves, it was still significant. The upward trend in loan growth that the country had experienced prior to this crisis could no longer be maintained, and by all indicators, loan creation had fallen by as much as 5 percent.

This put tremendous pressure on the private sector, especially since it had grown accustomed to continuous growth and was planning for even further expansions. Not only would there be no more expansion, but even worse, a number of important investment projects were canceled, and in some instances loans had to be prepaid or called back because banks felt uneasy about their liquidity position.

Throughout this turmoil, there was one sector that seemed to be adjusting very well—the external sector. While the financial and fiscal sectors were going through a very difficult and painful episode, the external sector was performing quite admirably. See, for example, the export and import figures in Table 2.3. From 1992 through 1994 imports exceeded exports, coinciding with the country's rapid economic expansion over the same period. By 1994 the deficit in the trade balance had grown quite substantial, to roughly $5.8 billion. This raised serious doubts within academic circles and within the financial sector about the viability of the convertibility plan. Many contended that the policy Argentina had adopted could not be sustained because of the large deficits in the current account. Although the deficits indicated here were not comparable to the deficits that Mexico was experiencing at the time, they were, in any case, large for the size of the Argentine economy.

In 1995 and early 1996, the balance-of-trade scenario reversed itself, with

TABLE 2.3. Trade and Current Account Balance (billions of U.S. dollars)

Year	Exports	Imports	Current Account Balance
1991	12.0	8.4	-2.8
1992	12.2	14.9	-6.3
1993	13.1	16.8	-7.3
1994	15.7	21.5	-10.1
1995	20.7	19.7	-3.6
1996	22.8	22.0	-3.5

exports exceeding imports by about $1.0 billion. Several factors account for this reversal. The slowing down of the economy, precipitated by a reduction in aggregate demand, led to a reduction in imports. Also, measures that Argentina had taken before the crisis, in terms of creating conditions for improving the competitiveness of the economy, were starting to pay off. For example, in the resource market, labor-intensive training programs were introduced which increased labor flexibility in the economy, facilitating this trade event. The unwanted consequence, however, was an overall reduction in salary income of about seven percent.

There were also a number of measures taken in the financial and fiscal sectors, which I will make explicit. The decline in deposits resulted in a corresponding reduction in the banking system's lending capacity, and action needed to be taken quickly. The central bank could not expend much effort dealing with this problem as it was preoccupied with the severity of the economic contraction that would soon hit the economy. Instead it opted for a "quick fix" and lowered the reserve rate requirements, leaving the convertibility system intact. This remedy resulted in a number of bank failures, but far less than would have been the case had it done nothing.

Instead of signaling a possible change in convertibility rules, the central bank had decided to strengthen the links between the dollar and the peso. Every signal from the central bank was that convertibility would not only be maintained, but extended. For example, before the crisis, the peso and the dollar were allowed to vary within a narrow band. That band was eliminated with new convertibility rules that established a strict one-to-one relationship between the peso and the dollar.

The central bank also improved the workings of its system of interbank loans to facilitate the use of reserves so that banks could have easy access to excess reserves. This was a much welcomed move on their part. The main reform, in my opinion, however, was the creation of two fiduciary funds to alleviate the situation of those banks experiencing difficulties. One fund was to provide help to private banks and the other was to be used to privatize the provincial banks. These two funds were funded by Banco Nacion, with the legal part of its lending capacity, the treasury, which devoted some its own resources, and with loans obtained from international financial organizations, such as the World Bank and the IMF.

Looking back over this episode, these two reforms performed excellently. Through these mechanisms, Argentina had avoided paying the very high price for this banking crisis that it had paid on two previous occasions in the recent past—once during the crisis of 1982 and the other in 1989. This time, because of the measures mentioned above, the fiscal cost of the banking crisis was very small, less than 0.5 percent in terms of the number of banks that folded. Although 44 banks eventually closed, this entailed a smooth process of absorption and mergers fortified by other larger banks that were helped by the process as well. This is in stark contrast with other experiences in the region, where the fiscal costs have been extremely high.

WHO PAID FOR THE CRISIS?

Who paid for the crisis? Those who had to pay. The shareholders of the banks suffered most and, to a minor extent, the depositors of those 44 banks that went bankrupt. Otherwise, the costs of the banking crisis have been almost nil in Argentina, save for the reduction in economic activity that was related to Mexico's difficulties and not directly to the banking crisis itself.

Unfortunately, Argentina did not have in place at the time of the crisis a system of guaranteed deposits. This was probably the most important shortcoming of the reforms and was overlooked when the reforms were first being implemented. In time, however, with the actions of the central bank, a system of guaranteed deposits was finally put in place and this helped to avert an even more profound crisis.

On the fiscal side, there were some important measures enacted that exacted a cost from the population at large. For example, government expenditures were cut by approximately 10 percent, income taxes were increased temporarily, and the social security system was reformed. In addition, a new fiscal package with the provinces was forged.

The fact that Argentina was able to reform its social security system, to privatize its provincial banks, and to introduce fiscal reforms shows that Argentina took good advantage of the crisis. We all know the saying, "where there is a crisis, there is an opportunity." Well, Argentina was able to grab that opportunity and use it to introduce important reforms that otherwise would have been very difficult to pass through its congress. It was the crisis that enabled the executive branch to convince congress of the urgent need for such reforms—in particular, in the areas of social security, labor legislation, and the management of bank reserves.

TABLE 2.4. Gross Domestic Product, Yearly Percentage Change

Year	GDP Growth Rate
1989	-6.2
1990	0.5
1991	8.9
1992	8.7
1993	6.0
1994	7.4
1995*	1.0

* Projected

WHAT WERE THE LASTING CONSEQUENCES OF THE CRISIS?

Now that the crisis has passed, Argentina is better poised for growth. The economy is now stronger, and its international competitiveness vastly improved. Many enterprises, facing this difficult episode, have already made their adjustments and survived. For this reason, I believe the Argentine economy is stronger now than it was at the end of 1994. The figures in Tables 2.4 and 2.5 support this optimistic view.

According to the figures in Table 2.4, Argentina had been growing very fast over the four years prior to 1995, achieving growth rates between 6 and 9 percent annually. However, in 1995 a noticeable reduction in the growth rate occurred. A revised estimate would show an even lower rate of growth than suggested here — perhaps even slightly negative. The declining rate of growth evident here is not much different from Mexico's, falling by approximately 7 percent between 1994 and 1995.

This growth reduction was accompanied by large increases in unemployment, as shown in Table 2.5. Unfortunately, the high unemployment rates in recent years are the worst legacy of this episode. Unemployment rates over 7 percent had been unprecedented in Argentina, which had grown accustomed to unemployment rates between 6 and 7 percent. That changed in 1993 and 1994, when unemployment rates climbed to new highs of 9.9 percent and 12.2, respectively. In 1995 it soared to an incredibly high rate of 18.6 percent, which fortunately has since fallen. It had dropped to 16.4 percent as of October 1995, but even that is considered much too high for Argentina's economy.

Not all of the recent unemployment can be attributed to the Mexican crisis.

TABLE 2.5. Unemployment as a Percent of Economically Active Population

Year	April/May	October
1990	8.6	6.2
1991	6.9	6.0
1992	6.9	7.0
1993	9.9	9.3
1994	10.8	12.2
1995	18.6	16.4

A number of structural changes were taking place at the same time that share some of the blame: total privatization of state enterprises, opening the economy to foreign competition, and the intervention and change of the industrial mix. While these structural changes occurred somewhat rapidly, they cannot account for most of the unemployment that took place during this time. A large part of the blame does rest squarely on the Mexican crisis. As mentioned previously, many Argentinian enterprises were planning to expand at this time, but instead were forced to either scale back, postpone, or cancel their new projects as a result of the crisis.

ASSESSING THE MANAGEMENT OF THE CRISIS

Argentina probably could have done a better job at managing the crisis if the administration back in 1991 and 1992 had not been so enthusiastic about the growth process that had GDP growing at just under 9 percent. A more conservative use of resources at that time may have resulted in more available resources at the time of the crisis that could have been used to create additional reserves and, thus, have permitted a more comfortable mask of intervention—one that could have alleviated the banking sector immediately and not have permitted the expansion of credit that promoted the crunch in the first place. In retrospect, more supervision was needed in the banking sector to help overcome the crisis. Of course, a system of guaranteed deposits would have been extremely helpful in facilitating the management of the crisis.

CONCLUDING REMARKS ABOUT CONVERTIBILITY

There is a debate, not in Argentina, but in academic circles outside of Argentina, that convertibility is something that should be avoided. I strongly

TABLE 2.6. Yearly Inflation Rate, Based on CPI

Year	Annual Inflation Rate
1989	4900.0
1990	1300.0
1991	84.0
1992	17.5
1993	7.4
1994	3.9
1995*	3.0

* Projected

disagree with this view and am an ardent supporter of Argentina's decision to maintain convertibility well into the future. The Argentine government and the population at large are quite comfortable with convertibility and satisfied with its implementation and results. Of course, it does have its limitations.

From a theoretical perspective, when you have a system of flexible exchange rates, you have an instrument by which to isolate problems that develop externally from the inner workings of the economy. But theoretical motives are not the only description or indication of what the economy can or should do. In my opinion, policy-making considerations are equally important, as are psychological and historical factors. Argentina, in this century, has experienced three episodes of hyperinflation (the most recent in 1989-90, see Table 2.6), and no one is willing to risk the chance of that happening again. Argentinians have first-hand knowledge of hyperinflation, and remember the trauma of those episodes —especially the high cost of having to go to the bank every day (sometimes twice a day) to exchange pesos for dollars. Those painful memories help explain the widespread political support for continued convertibility in the monetary system. This support was evident in the last election, where 80 percent of the polls clearly indicated a preference for the maintenance of convertibility.

The horror of hyperinflation is deeply etched in the Argentine psyche—as was the case in Germany after World War I and in the United States during the 1930s with regard to unemployment. Consequently, Argentina will be subscribing to convertibility for sometime because it has provided a comfortable solution in the fight against inflation.

NOTE

This chapter is an edited transcription of a video of Petrei's presentation at the Conference. Given the limitations of the video (i.e. poor sound quality, etc.), some parts of the presentation were omitted.

APPENDIX TABLES AND FIGURES

The following pages contain additional information about Argentina's economy.

APPENDIX TABLE 2.1. Argentina: Number of Financial Entities

TYPE OF ENTITY	AT DEC. 31, 1994	AT MAY 1995	FLUCTUATION	
			TOTAL	%
BANKS				
National Private Banks	66	52	14	21.2
Corporations in Federal District	40	37	3	7.5
Retailers	11	11	0	0.0
Wholesalers	29	26	3	10.3
Corporations in the Provinces	26	15	11	42.3
Cooperatives	38	13	25	65.8
Foreign	31	30	1	3.2
National State-Owned Banks	4	4	0	0.0
Provincial and Municipal Banks	29	27	2	6.9
Total Banks	168	126	42	25.0
NON BANKING ENTITIES	37	31	6	16.2
TOTAL FINANCIAL SYSTEM	205	157	48	23.4

APPENDIX TABLE 2.2. Argentina: Distribution of Deposits in the System

ORDER	NOVEMBER 1994 BANK	%	MARCH 1995 BANK	%
1	Nacion	12.96	Nacion	12.84
2	Provincia De BS. AS.	9.26	Provincia De BS. AS.	10.89
3	Rio De La Plata	5.14	Galicia	5.89
4	Galicia	5.04	Rio De La Plata	5.76
5	Citibank	3.81	Citibank	4.88
6	Boston	3.37	Boston	4.08
7	Frances	2.47	Frances	3.10
8	Cuidad De BS. AS.	2.41	Cuidad De BS. AS.	2.66
9	Credito Argentino	2.34	Credito Argentino	2.59
10	Provincia De Cordoba	2.22	Roberts	2.31
First 10		49.02	First 10	55.00
10-20		15.01	10-20	14.99
First 20		64.03	First 20	69.99
20-40		13.13	20-40	13.24
First 40		77.16	First 40	83.23
Remaining Entities		22.84	Remaining Entities	16.77
Total		100.00	Total	100.00

APPENDIX FIGURE 2.1. Argentina: Fluctuation in Deposits and Lending Capacity
(millions of pesos)

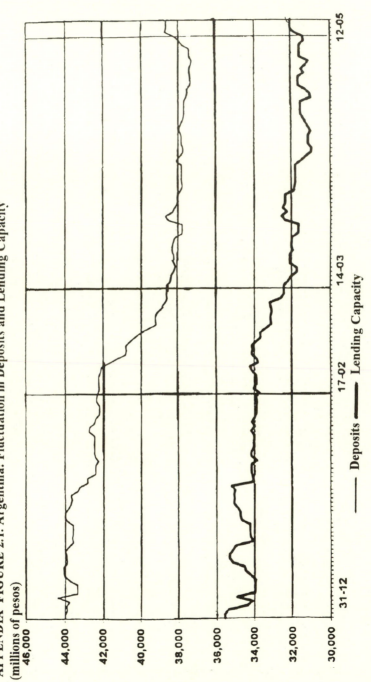

Source: Argentine Central Bank and our calculations.

28

APPENDIX FIGURE 2.2. Argentina: Country Risk

%

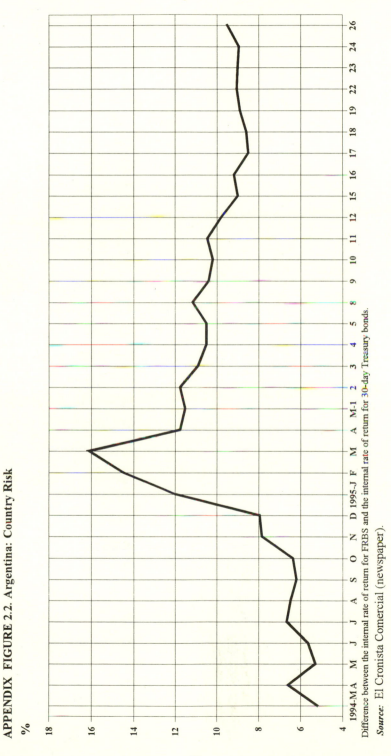

Difference between the internal rate of return for FRBS and the internal rate of return for 30-day Treasury bonds.

Source: El Cronista Comercial (newspaper).

APPENDIX FIGURE 2.3. Argentina: Exports and Imports

(US $ millions)

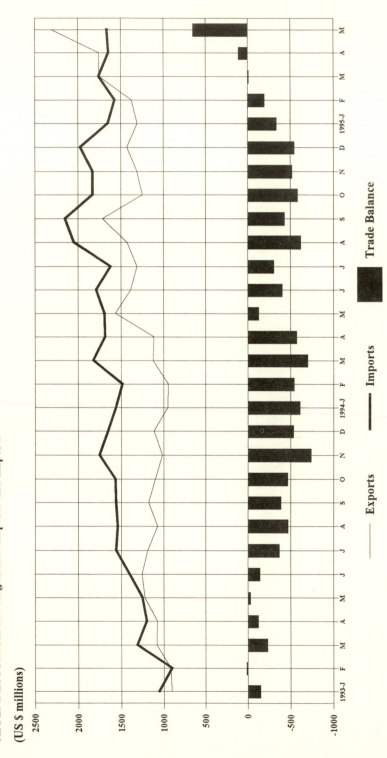

3

ECONOMIC GROWTH AND INFLATION IN COLOMBIA

Jose Antonio Ocampo

INTRODUCTION

How has the Mexican crisis affected Colombia's economy? The answer is—minimally. While there was a noticeable impact in early 1994 with some initial adverse bond ratings in the international market, that appears to have been the extent of it.[1]

An examination of Colombian bonds spreads over this period suggests that the international community has finally learned to discriminate between Colombia, Chile, and, to some extent, Peru, on the one hand, and Mexico and other Latin American countries, on the other. In this respect, I think, rather than having a negative impact, the Mexican crisis which forced international investors to discriminate in this way, may have actually benefitted the Colombian economy.

In the summer of 1994, just prior to the Mexican crisis, the new Colombian government at the time was preoccupied with its own problems—signs of disequilibria were cropping up in many important sectors of the economy. As seen in the figures in this chapter, the economy was experiencing increasing current account deficits, falling savings rates, excessive growth in aggregate demand, excessive ignorance of domestic trade, and a rapidly appreciating currency. The position of the new administration was very clearly positive—the economy should move toward an equilibrium growth path, and that transition would require modern stabilizing policies.

Fortunately, the central bank, which has been independent since 1991, was already moving toward restrictive monetary policy when the new government came to office. Both the central bank and the government were in agreement on many issues regarding the economy, with one exception: The government was not very concerned about the appreciating exchange rate at the time. But that soon changed with the onset of the Mexican crisis.

One of the great, although peculiar, outcomes of the Mexican crisis was that it forced government officials to reconsider the country's exchange rate policy and take steps toward radical reform. The problems encountered in the second semester of 1994 convinced central bankers and the rest of the economy that it was time to abandon the characteristically erratic path of exchange-rate appreciation/depreciation and seek a more stable path. This most important lesson has ultimately led to the healthier and more stable economy of today.

What follows now is a brief discussion of the country's main economic variables and their dynamic paths at the time of the Mexican crisis and other important international events.

ECONOMIC GROWTH AND INFLATION

The Colombian economy experienced accelerating growth between 1991 and 1994 as seen in Figure 3.1 (all figures are at the end of the chapter). Shortly after 1994, however, there was a moderate decline in GDP growth of about 0.7 percent. The slowing of the GDP growth rate was the result of moderate aggregate demand growth at the time. As a whole, projections for 1996 suggested further slowing of the economy by 0.9 percent to an estimated growth rate of 4.9 percent.

The economy was expected to pick up by 1997-98 because of increased oil and food exports. Average growth rates at the time were expected to climb as high as 5.5 percent. This is higher than the 4.2 percent that was the average for the period between 1991 and 1994, and absolutely close to the historical record for the country.

Figure 3.2 provides an historical view of growth rates dating back to 1971. The horizontal lines show the average growth rate per period. With this longer view we see that the average growth rate for 1991-94 is just below the average for the late 1980s. Also note that the projected average growth rate for the late 1990s is closer to that of the 1970s.

In Figure 3.3, we see a comparison of average growth rates across several Latin American countries, for the period 1980 to 1995. The overall average for this period was 1.76 percent. Chile was the fastest growing economy at almost 4.5 percent, followed by Colombia at 4 percent, Ecuador at 2.5 percent, and Brazil at 2 percent. The remaining countries—Mexico, Argentina, and Venezuela—had roughly the same growth rate of about 1.25 percent.

Perhaps more important than the actual growth rate was the volatility of that growth rate through time. Figure 3.4 compares the volatility of Colombia's GDP growth with that of other major countries and regions of the world. Relatively speaking, Colombia's economy experienced more stable growth between 1970 and 1992 than any other Latin American country over this same period. Interestingly, it also appears that Colombia has had more stable growth than South East Asian countries and the more industrialized countries. From this perspective, we can say that Colombia has a very stable economy.

The policy measures implemented since mid-1994 not only slowed the growth rate of GDP but also changed the pattern of growth. Recall from Figure 3.1 that the economy was rebounding around 1991 after a period of declining growth in the late 1980s (see Figure 3.2). In Figure 3.5, we now see that much of this growth spurt was due to growth in the nontradeable sectors, such as construction and services, while the tradeable sectors actually tended to slowdown, remaining very "undynamic" through 1994. From that point on we see a slowing down of the growth rate of nontradeables and an acceleration in the growth rate of tradeables. Given the trajectories in Figure 3.5, the two growth rates were expected to coincide in 1996 at 5 percent and then to continue along the same growth path until 1997, when the tradeable sectors would likely experience faster growth than the nontradeable sectors.

In Figure 3.6 we find statistics on value added growth rates by sector within the tradeable and nontradeable categories of the previous figure. From here we notice a dramatic decline in the growth rate of coffee (a tradeable), from -4.3 percent over the 1991-94 period to -11.8 percent in 1994, and at the same time a rapid increase in the growth rate of construction (a nontradeable), from 6.0 to 11.3 percent, respectively. Note that the growth rates for 1996 suggested more balanced but moderate growth across all sectors.

At more or less the same time that these structural changes were unfolding in the tradeable and nontradeable sectors, there was a strong pickup in aggregate demand growth, as indicated in Figure 3.7. The growth rate of aggregate demand over the period 1991 through 1993 was approximately 12 percent in real terms, but has since slowed to between 5.0 and 5.5 percent. Interestingly, during this period of phenomenal growth in aggregate demand, the inflation rate actually decelerated (see Figure 3.8). Inflation picked up only briefly between mid-1993 and early-1994 but since then had continued to decline.

SAVINGS AND INVESTMENT

One important success of the mid-1990s economic policies was the strong recovery of private investment spending to such an extent that we now have the highest investment rate, in constant terms, since the 1950s (see Figure 3.9). We are currently enjoying not only one of the strongest runs in investment spending, but also one of the longest runs in over 50 years.

In these new policies, strong emphasis was placed on increasing the country's infrastructure. According to Figure 3.10, if we include the participation of private-sector spending on infrastructures of all sorts, particularly with public spending on energy and transportation, we see another important success story emerge: an increase of about 632 million (in Colombian pesos) or roughly 18 percent in infrastructure investment between 1994 and 1995. This represents significant growth in the investment of real infrastructures. And more important, over 80 percent of the increase is associated with private investment, particularly foreign private investment.

The savings rates presented in Figure 3.11 show that we have been confronting a serious problem in the early 1990s, a very slow reduction in the savings rate for the economy. Compared with the historical savings rates of the 1970s and 1980s, which averaged around 20 percent each, savings rates since 1991 have fallen gradually to about 15 percent as of 1995. Most of this decline is attributed to a reduction in private-sector savings rates, although public-sector savings rates have also fallen somewhat. With respect to public-sector savings rates, the reductions indicated here represent a gradual return or convergence to an historical rate of about 5.0 to 6.0 percent (see Figure 3.11, public savings in the 1970s and 1980s). Fortunately, with respect to private-sector savings rates, it now appears that the downward trend has been stopped, another success for our economic policies. We are now beginning to see a moderate climb in the evolution of savings rates for 1996 and beyond.

REAL EXCHANGE RATES AND THE BALANCE OF PAYMENTS

The policy of the early 1990s, as it relates to the balance of payments, was one of depreciating/appreciating exchange rates. When this process first began in the early part of 1991 (see Figure 3.12), no one was really worried about the appreciating exchange rate because it was widely agreed that it was undervalued at the time.[2] However, as this process continued unchecked, it became a major source of concern. Fortunately, the policies carried out during the 1994-98 administration have more or less put a halt to the exchange-rate appreciation. The exchange rate over the later part of 1995 is considered very competitive, from an historical perspective, and one we think can be maintained in the future.

The opening-up of the economy and the falling savings rate is reflected in the deterioration of the current account (see Figure 3.13). However, this is not as serious as what Mexico and Argentina in particular experienced, where they also saw a significant drop in foreign investment. In contrast, and this should be emphasized, Colombia enjoyed a tremendous foreign investment boom associated with oil, infrastructure investments, and investments in other sectors of the economy. Bearing this in mind, it is prudent to discount the effects of what appears to be falling direct foreign investment (see Figure 3.13) and instead focus on the debt-financed deficit portion of the current account. This represents debt that has to be financed with international debt or with foreign international reserves. The debt we incurred with the opening of the economy in 1991 was heavy, but is now stabilized at around 2 percent of GDP. As can be seen in Figure 3.13, this is consistent with Professor Campos' notion of "targeting" the debt ratio. I would like to add that in the case of Colombia, what should be targeted at 2 percent or less is the debt-financed deficit of the current account.[3]

In Figure 3.14 we see the path of exports-to-GDP, originating back to the 1950s and up through 1998.[4] Clearly there has been a remarkable turnaround in this ratio, which began rising in the late 1980s and has continued to rise through the present. This ratio is expected to stabilize at around 25 percent of GDP.

An investigation into exports reveals a dramatic increase in diversification, particularly away from coffee, which used to be the main export, and into manufacturers and oil and derivatives. In Figure 3.15 we see that coffee exports represented over half (52%) of all exports in 1980, followed distantly by manufactures (27.7%). Oil and derivatives amounted to no more than 2 percent. In 1995, however, a much different distribution emerges, with manufactures now the leading export at roughly 45 percent, and with coffee and oil trailing at 18.4 and 18.7 percent, respectively. It is interesting to point out here that oil and coffee are now roughly equal in importance.

Oil exports will be an important source of economic growth for the economy in years to come due to discoveries made in 1992 in Colombia's oil fields. Although oil exports have been dropping every year since 1990, this trend is not expected to continue. In fact, we have already experienced our first major increase in oil exports in 1995, where exports rose from roughly $1.3 billion in 1994 to $2.2 billion (see Figure 3.16). Due to transportation constraints at the time, oil exports in 1996 did not rise significantly over the 1995 level. Most of the increases were likely to occur in 1997 and 1998, where oil exports are expected to be as high as $3 billion and $4.4 billion, respectively.

Another view of exports is presented in Figure 3.17. Here we see how the policies of the 1994-98 government affected the growth of nontraditional exports. In mid-1994 there was a marked acceleration in the growth of nontraditional exports, and in mid-1995 that growth increased to around 25 to 30 percent. This increase, along with the projected increase in oil exports, are just some of the reasons why we expect economic growth to pickup in the next few years.

Figure 3.18 presents an important picture of the current account deficit and the country's financing requirements. The line above the horizontal axis represents the current account deficit. In 1994 we see that all of the financing came from direct foreign investment (which is the lower bar) and long-term foreign indebtedness. Short-term debt in 1994 was in excess of financing requirements due to a significant reduction in short-term capital flows between 1993 and 1994, and an even further reduction in 1995. The reasons for this are partly due to international events, but more important, to the restrictions on short-term capital flows that were put in place in the early part of 1994. The basis of the restrictions (and what I consider an essential lesson of the crisis), is that all financing should be structured with long-term loans rather than short-term loans. Today, Colombia is totally financed with long-term capital flows and will continue to be well into the future. This strategy is consistent with several important studies undertaken by investment bankers in the early part of 1995, which questioned whether Colombia would find itself in crisis after the Mexican and Argentinian crises. The basic conclusion reached was that Colombia would not be seriously impacted due to the structuring of its external financing.

Figure 3.19 shows the pattern of direct foreign investment in oil/mining and other sectors of the economy during the 1990s. In 1991 the combined total of direct foreign investment in both categories was less than 0.6 percent of GDP but has been climbing steadily ever since. In 1995 direct foreign investments totaled about 2.7 percent of GDP. Because of booming oil exports, they were expected to rise to roughly 4 percent of GDP in 1996 with the oil/mining sectors accounting for roughly 1.5 percent of GDP and all other sectors accounting for about 2.5 percent.

At the same time that direct foreign investment was rising (beginning in 1991), foreign debt-to-GDP and foreign debt-to-exports were falling,(see Figure 3.20. This pattern is expected to continue through the end of 1999. The foreign debt-to-GDP ratio in late 1997 was less than 30 percent, which was the lowest in all of Latin America. Also note the foreign debt-to-exports ratio was at an all time low of 1.8 percent, down from more than 3 percent in 1990.

The graph in Figure 3.21 represents a market simulation of bond spreads over treasuries through 1995 that compares the spread of Colombian bonds with those of Argentina and Mexico. We see that with the Mexican crisis the spreads in all three countries widened significantly, particularly in Argentina and Mexico. Colombia also saw a widening spread of about 150 to 160 points in November of 1994 (just before the crisis), to an average of about 240 points for the first half of 1995, with some peaks well above that. However, since the beginning of 1996, the spread seems to have stabilized at a level slightly higher than before the crisis, at 160 to 180 points. Argentina's and Mexico's spreads also fell sharply—particularly Argentina, which returned to its pre crisis level with a lower spread than Mexico.

ECONOMIC POLICY OBJECTIVES: MACROECONOMIC POLICY

In this last section I would like to finish with some points regarding Colombia's macroeconomic policy. As seen in Figure 3.22, the economycontinued to experience problems in the fiscal area, particularly associated with the social programs of the past,a tendency toward ever-increasing social security entitlements, and laws that were issued in 1993. Still, we consider the overall fiscal situation of Colombia to be healthy, although it has deteriorated slightly in recent years. If we exclude expenditures related to privatizations, we see fiscal equilibrium essentially since 1990, with a small surplus in 1994. But since the recession in 1995, the deficit has been increasing. In 1995 it represented about 1 percent of GDP, and in 1996, about 1.25 percent of GDP. In terms of gross privatizations, we see a significant increase in 1994, as a percent of GDP, and a general slowing since then.

Monetary policy over this period is reflected in the growth of M1 and M3, as shown in Figure 3.23. In the fiscal area, we have adopted a series of policies that adjust to a new fiscal reality. These policies include tax reforms passed by congress, a reduction in current expenditures in the public sector as of the second quarter of 1996, and new laws that will dictate the level of transfers to the regents. We see quite clearly a slowdown of monetary growth in recent years. It is apparent that monetary growth was excessive before the 1994-98 administration came to office, and that this administration has been in agreement with the central bank to slowdown the growth of M1 and M3.

Figure 3.24 shows a reduction in the aggregate growth of domestic credit. Again, we see a growth of more than 50 percent in nominal terms. In real terms, this represents about 20 to 24 percent, which, given Colombia's situation, is extremely rapid. The significant slowdown we see since 1994 represents policy measures introduced by the central bank and government jointly. The growth rates of M1 and M3 are now 30 to 35 percent less than in 1994.

Monetary policy over this period (from 1990 to 1995) was wholly reflected in interest rates. The low deposit rate, in real terms, from 1992 to 1994 (see Figure 3.25), is one reason for the slower growth rates. There was also some disagreement between the central bank and the government regarding the high interest rates in late 1994 and early 1995 and how to bring them down. But an agreement was reached in mid-1995 to target the interest at between 6 to 8 percent in real terms on the deposit side, and at 15 percent on the credit side, which is very appropriate by international standards.

SUMMARY

In summary, I would like to say that the Colombian economy behaved very flexibly during the 1995 Mexican crisis. Domestic events, rather than events in Mexico, were the leading force in the evolution of the economy in recent years. Although there was a slowdown in economic growth at the onset of the crisis that continued into 1996, we see this as a healthy accommodation of the economic aggregates to a level now sustainable in the long run.

NOTES

1. This chapter is an edited transcription of a video of Ocampo's presentation at the Conference. Given the limitations of the video (i.e. poor sound quality, etc.), some parts of the presentation were omitted.

2. An increase in the exchange-rate index represents a depreciation while a decrease in the exchange-rate index represents an appreciation.

3. This reference is to a comment made by Roberto Campos, a senator from Brazil, who attended the Conference.

4. 1997 and 1998 figures are projections.

FIGURE 3.1. Colombia: GDP Growth, 1990 to 1998

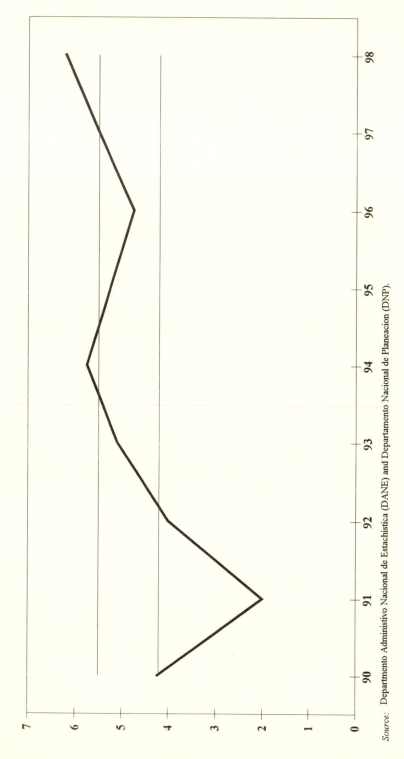

Source: Departmento Administivo Nacional de Estachistica (DANE) and Departamento Nacional de Planeacion (DNP).

FIGURE 3.2. Colombia: GDP Growth, 1971 to 1998

%

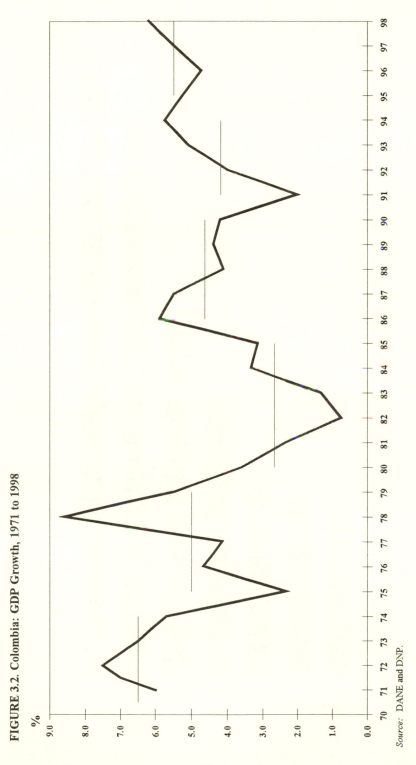

Source: DANE and DNP.

39

FIGURE 3.3. GDP Growth in Latin America, 1980 to 1995

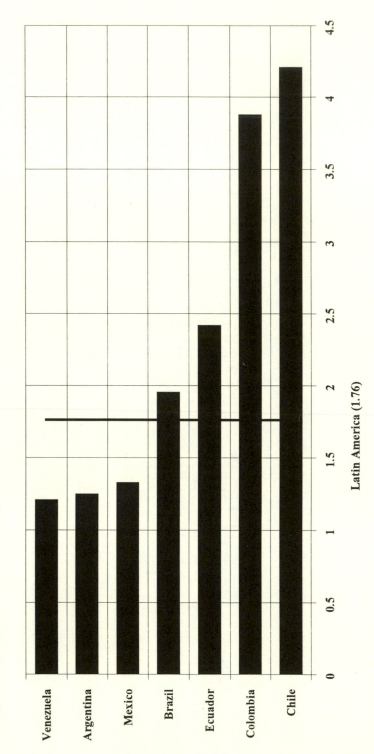

FIGURE 3.4. GDP Growth and Volatility in Latin America and Selected Countries, 1970

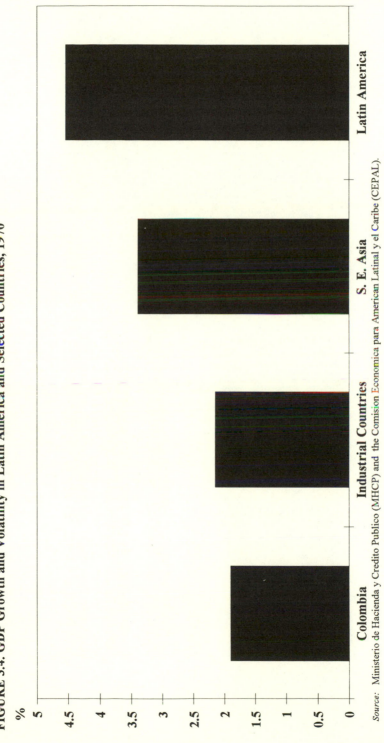

Source: Ministerio de Hacienda y Credito Publico (MHCP) and the Comision Economica para American Latinal y el Caribe (CEPAL).

FIGURE 3.5. Colombia: Value Added Growth by Economic Sector

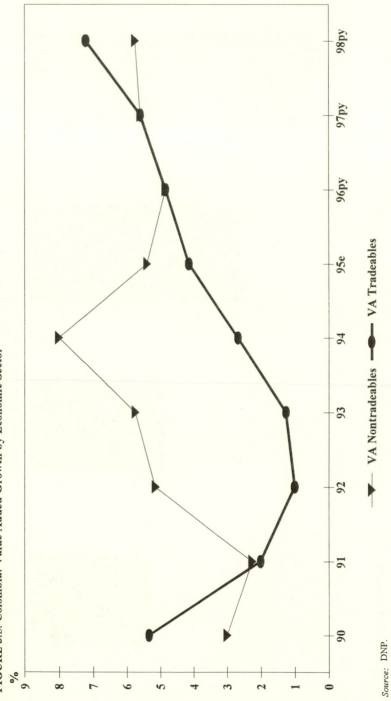

VA Nontradeables ◆ VA Tradeables

Source: DNP.

42

FIGURE 3.6. Colombia: Value Added by Economic Sector (growth rates)

	1991-94	1994	1995	1996
VA Tradable	1.5	1.8	4.2	4.7
Agriculture	2.1	3.3	4.9	5.0
Mining	-2.2	0.2	17.2	9.4
Industry	3.2	4.2	2.7	3.9
Coffee	-4.3	-11.8	-4.3	1.6
VA Nontradable	5.3	8.0	5.4	4.9
Construction	6.0	11.3	5.2	7.0
Services	5.2	7.8	5.5	4.7

FIGURE 3.7. Colombia: GDP and Aggregate Demand (growth rates)

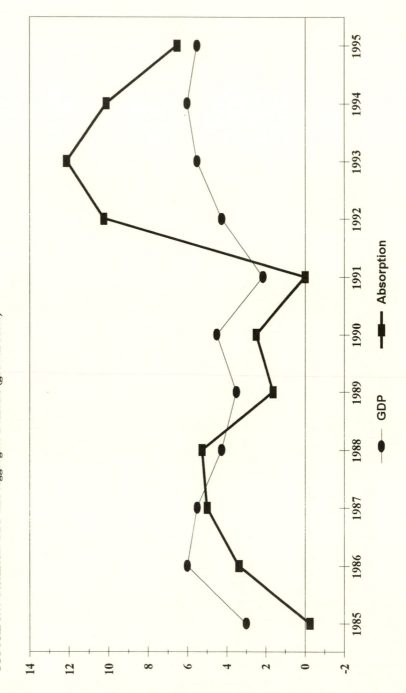

FIGURE 3.8. Colombia: Inflation, 1989 to 1995

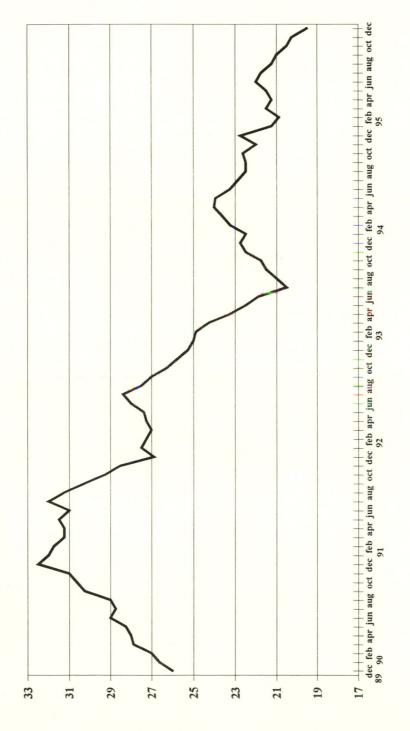

FIGURE 3.9. Colombia: Investment Rate (share of GDP)

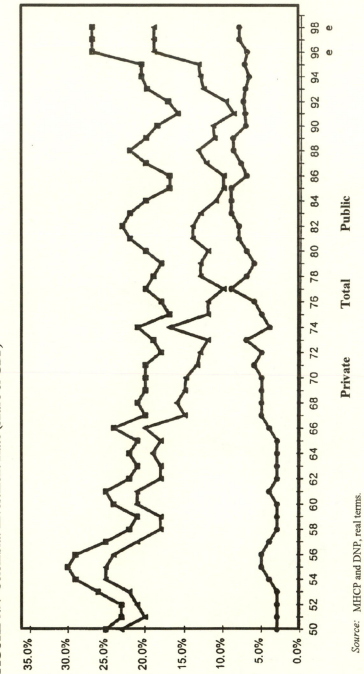

Source: MHCP and DNP, real terms.

46

FIGURE 3.10. Colombia: Infrastructure Investment (billions of 1995 Colombian pesos)

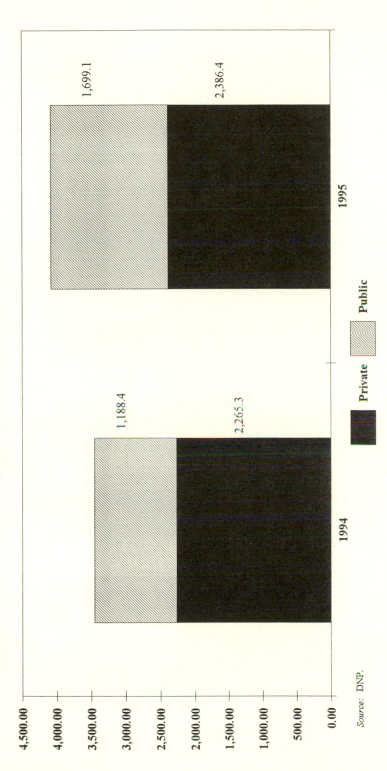

FIGURE 3.11. Colombia: Savings Rate (share of GDP)

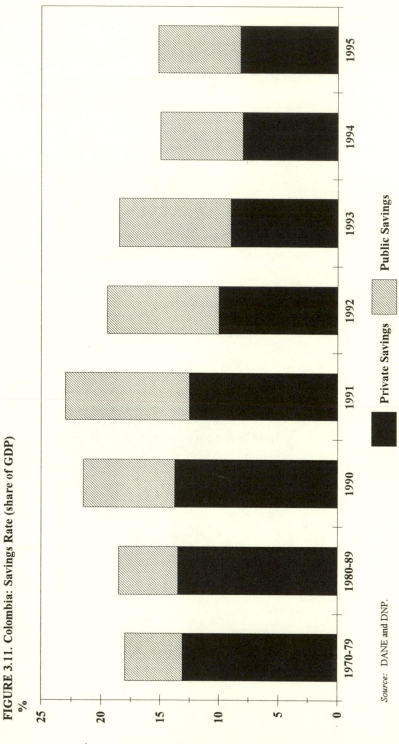

Source: DANE and DNP.

48

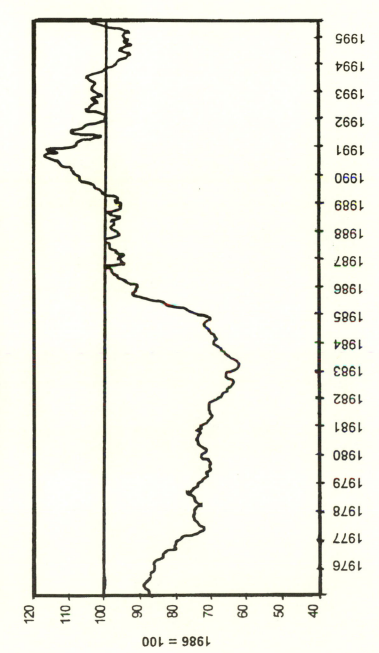

FIGURE 3.12. Colombia: Real Exchange Rate Index (monthly average)

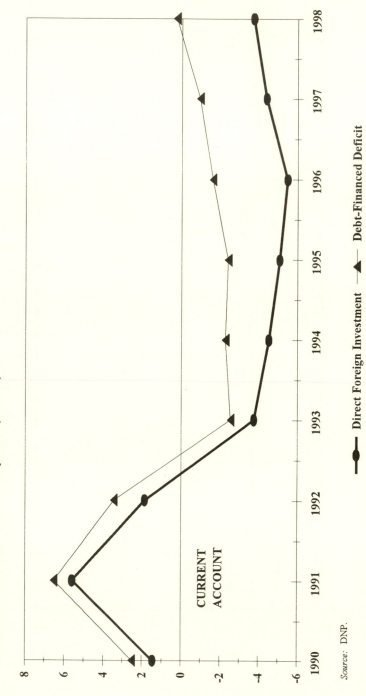

FIGURE 3.13. Colombia: Balance of Payments (% GDP)

CURRENT
ACCOUNT

Direct Foreign Investment ——— Debt-Financed Deficit

Source: DNP.

FIGURE 3.14. Colombia: Exports/GDP

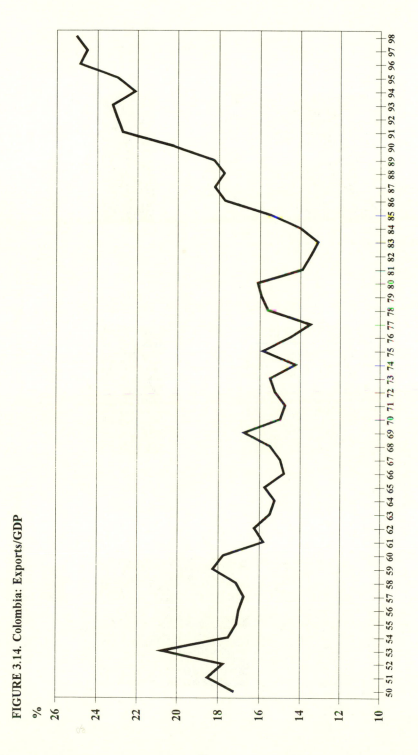

FIGURE 3.15. Colombia: Diversification of Exports

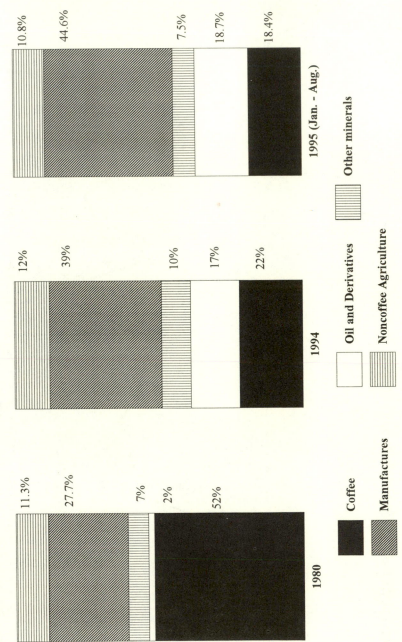

1980

1994

1995 (Jan. - Aug.)

11.3%
27.7%
7%
2%
52%

12%
39%
10%
17%
22%

10.8%
44.6%
7.5%
18.7%
18.4%

Coffee

Manufactures

Oil and Derivatives

Noncoffee Agriculture

Other minerals

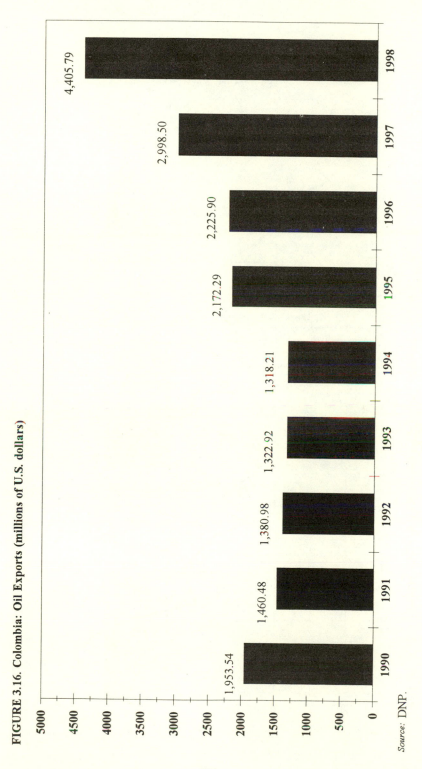

FIGURE 3.16. Colombia: Oil Exports (millions of U.S. dollars)

1990: 1,953.54
1991: 1,460.48
1992: 1,380.98
1993: 1,322.92
1994: 1,318.21
1995: 2,172.29
1996: 2,225.90
1997: 2,998.50
1998: 4,405.79

Source: DNP.

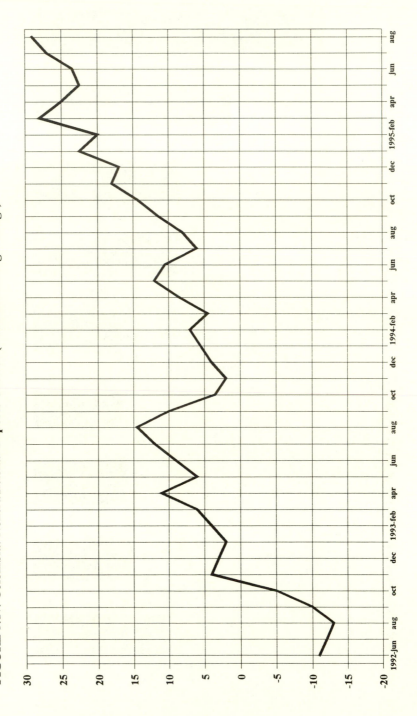

FIGURE 3.17. Colombia: Nontraditional Exports Growth (6-month moving average)

54

FIGURE 3.18. Colombia: Current Account Balance (% PIB)

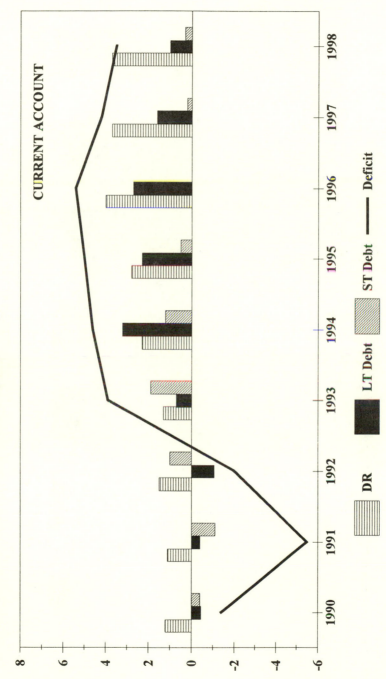

CURRENT ACCOUNT

DR | LT Debt | ST Debt | Deficit

55

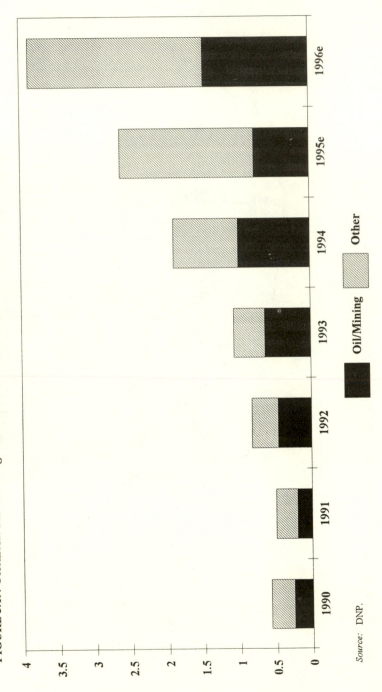

FIGURE 3.19. Colombia: Direct Foreign Investment in Oil/Mining and Other Sectors (% of GDP)

Other

Oil/Mining

Source: DNP.

56

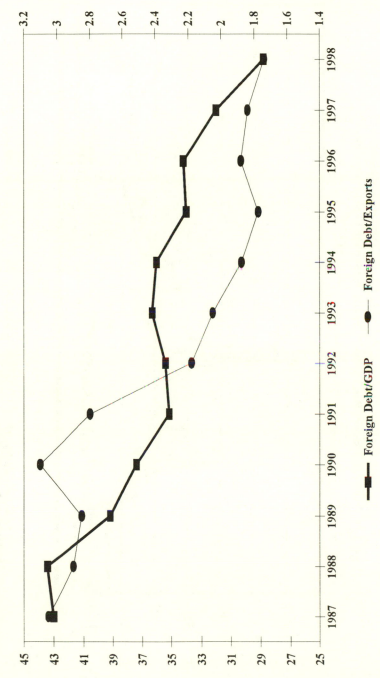

FIGURE 3.20. Colombia: Foreign Debt Ratios

■ Foreign Debt/GDP   ● Foreign Debt/Exports

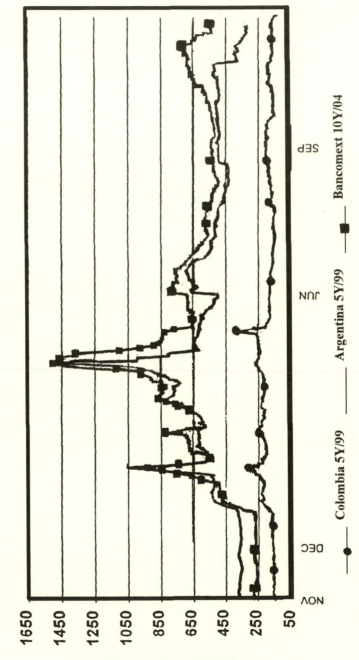

FIGURE 3.21. Colombia: Recent Bond Issues Spreads, November 1994 to January 1996

SPREAD OVER TREASURY

— Colombia 5Y/99   —— Argentina 5Y/99   —— Bancomext 10Y/04

58

FIGURE 3.22. Colombia: Fiscal Surplus/Deficit

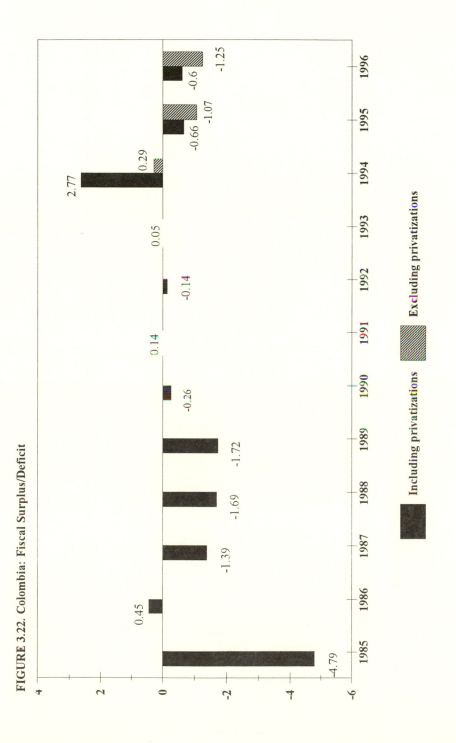

Including privatizations

Excluding privatizations

FIGURE 3.23. Colombia: M1 and M3 Growth

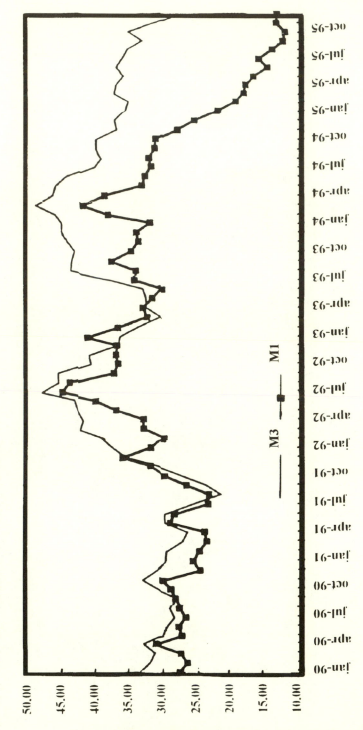

FIGURE 3.24. Colombia: Total Credit

%

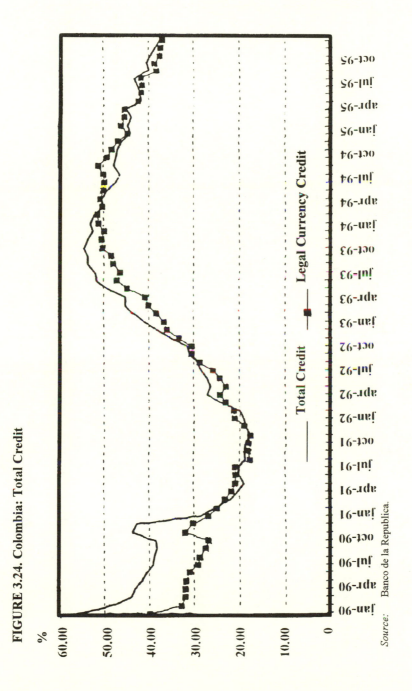

Source: Banco de la Republica.

FIGURE 3.25. Colombia: Real Interest Rates, 1990 to 1995

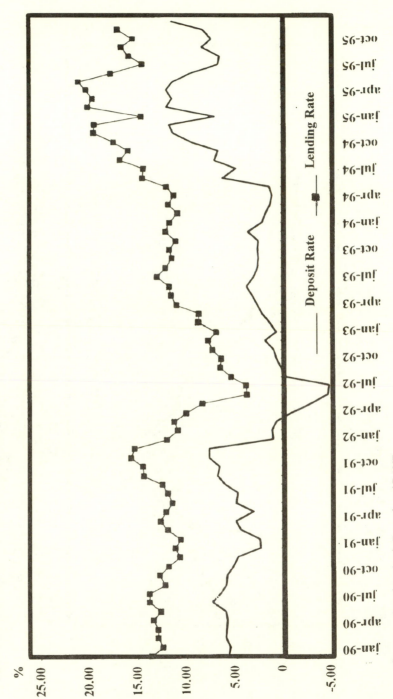

Source: Superintendencia Bancaria and DANE.

REFLECTIONS ON THE MEXICAN CRISIS

Julio A. de Quesada

INTRODUCTION

I recall one morning over breakfast, President Vartan Gregorian explaining to a group of us the value of an education within Brown University's liberal academic curriculum. Well, I can certainly attest to the value it had in helping me cope with the Mexican crisis—especially those courses in religion and philosophy.[1]

To put this discussion into its proper perspective, let me first provide some background on Citibank's operation in Mexico. Back in 1994, I arrived in Mexico as the new head of Citibank's 65-year-old operation there. Prior to that, I had been the county manager for Citibank in faraway, troubled, and often volatile Pakistan. Ordinarily, this would have been a good career move—to come to a more stable, modern, Organization for Economic Cooperation and Development (OECD) economy that was being propelled into the 21st century by NAFTA. In spite of the political shocks of 1994, the country—guided by the dream team of President Carlos Salinas and Finance Minister Pedro Aspe—was destined, eventually, to take its place among the industrialized economies of the world.

The August 1994 election results and the general perception that the voting process was clean served as confirmation that there was no stopping Mexico's economic progress. A Citicorp vice chairman, who was also a trustee of Brown University, called me to say I was the luckiest guy in this Bank—all I needed to do was put it on autopilot and our business in Mexico would flourish.

Sure there was a large and growing current account deficit and excessive dependence on short-term portfolio capital flows to finance this deficit. A few even dared say that the peso was overvalued. I was witness to several instances where these concerns were brought up with Aspe, Manuel Mancera (governor of Banco de Mexico), and even President Salinas, and the response was always very confident: the current account deficit is a result of the country's success in attracting capital inflows. In other words, why criticize success. If there ever came a time when these inflows diminished, the current account deficit would self-adjust.

Somehow the markets believed this. President Salinas was leaving the presidency as one of the most popular presidents in Mexico's history, and the top job at the World Trade Organization (WTO) was his for the taking. Prestigious U.S. corporations and academic institutions were lining up to convince him to join their boards and advisory committees. At the October 1994 Mexican Banking Conference in Cancun, Aspe was given a 15-minute standing ovation as the architect of the modern Mexican economy by Mexican and foreign bankers alike. At a breakfast hosted by Citibank at this Conference, the representatives of some of the most powerful international financial institutions lined up to receive the authorizations to establish local subsidiaries from this giant of finance, like eager children waiting to receive their school diplomas.

IT WAS GREAT TO BE A BANKER IN MEXICO!

So what happened? Modern Mexico surely had seen major devaluations and crises before. Large devaluations had taken place in 1976 and 1982, both presidential election years. It had not happened in 1988, partly because it had already occurred the previous year. It is well known that high budget deficits, rapid growth in public external debt, high inflation, capital flight, and an overvalued peso had led to a major devaluation at the end of the Luis Echeverria administration, with Jose Lopez Portillo already at the helm as president-elect. The Lopez Portillo scenario began with the IMF-imposed austerity program of 1977. Once this crisis was "resolved" the country again fell prey to inadequate economic policies with an overdependence on oil exports, which resulted in mushrooming public external debt to cover a large external deficit once oil prices dropped. Again, inflation, capital flight, and an overvalued currency led to a major devaluation on February 17, 1982, only a couple of weeks after Lopez Portillo had promised to defend the peso como un perro (English translation, "like a dog"). This time the banks panicked and asked for payment—leading to another major crisis. History repeated itself with the incoming president, Miguel de la Madrid, who had to start his administration with an IMF austerity plan.

WHY SHOULD THE SALINAS-ZEDILLO HANDOFF BE ANY DIFFERENT?

Why should the Salinas-Ernesto Zedillo handoff be any different? After all, there had been significant structural reforms during the Salinas administration, inflation was low and declining, the budget was balanced, and non-oil imports were increasing at a rapid rate. The opening up of the economy had forced Mexican industry (which for decades had been protected by the government), to modernize and become competitive.

I reflect back on that clear, pleasant morning of December 19, 1994, when my wife and I began what had been a long-awaited Christmas vacation (with the transfer to Mexico we had not taken any vacation the entire year). We had plans to fly for a day to the Chiapas region to see the Mayan ruins of Palenque and then return to Mexico City that same evening so we could catch the morning flight to Miami to spend Christmas with the family. During our trip to Palenque we witnessed massive military troop and hardware movements, which led me to the conclusion that the government was expecting major trouble on the anniversary of the zapatista uprising on January 1. I remember telling my wife that I wanted to postpone the Miami trip to monitor developments. At 6 a.m. on the morning of December 20, I received a call from Pepe Madariaga, the president of the Mexican Bankers Association, to tell me that the government had decided to widen the exchange rate band by moving the ceiling up 15.3 percent. We had been advocating something like this during the last couple of months of the Salinas administration, but the government had said there was no need. Now there is this announcement, out of the blue with no explanation. Needless to say, December 20 was a day that will live in infamy. The initial market reaction was positive—boost to exports, but panic started to set in when no explanation was given by the government, and investors did not know who to turn to.

Capital flight, which had started in earnest in September through December (President Zedillo officially took over on December 1), was now hemorrhaging at alarming rates and on December 22 the central bank did not have sufficient reserves to defend the new ceiling—the peso had to be allowed to float.

The rest is history. We saw a country going from extreme optimism to hopeless negativism and despair. President Salinas' reputation changed from "admired world statesman" to "opportunistic ill-intentioned politician" overnight—both in the eyes of the Mexican people and the foreign investor community. Who was to blame for the "December accident" as it became popularly known? Was it the Zedillo team, which bungled the "management" of the devaluation? Was it the Salinas team, which had pursued the wrong economic policies? Was it the result of the political shocks of 1994? Was it the fault of fickle foreign investors who would abandon a country at the slightest sign of trouble? Or was it merely the resulting pains from a country in political and economic transition?

Before giving my observations on these, I would just like to repeat what Michel Candessus of the IMF said in a recent speech. He said that the Mexican crisis was the first crisis of the 21st century in that the massive capital flows coming from pension and mutual funds which left Mexico as easily as they entered, would characterize the world financial scene for years to come. The amounts at stake are much higher than in the banking crisis of the 1980's and the players are faceless. This crisis also played out at high speed with the information technology available today. As a result of the Mexican crisis, many countries are having second thoughts about becoming hostage to foreign portfolio investment. They have seen the effects of huge hot-money tides on the national economy.

In retrospect we have important lessons to learn from this latest Mexican crisis. There is no question that the devaluation was mishandled by the Zedillo team. The new team was barely in place so there was the issue of credibility. There was a degree of arrogance and the government did not see a need for explanations. There was no announcement of an accompanying set of economic policy measures. They failed to see a need to, *a priori*, organize some type of backup fund to reassure overseas investors that there would be sufficient funds to meet the Tesobono maturities. Tesobonos are Mexican treasury bills denominated in U.S. dollars. Even after the announcement, authorities displayed indecision and uncertainty. There were considerable delays in announcing new policy measures to restore confidence.

However, the crisis was not the result of one single "accident." The problem was much more complex and deep rooted. In spite of all the reforms undertaken by the Salinas team, the focus was on inflation and the budget deficit, ignoring the external balance. There was too little currency depreciation relative to the rate of inflation, resulting in an overvalued currency. This, along with the opening of the economy, led to a large external deficit that was financed primarily by portfolio money; direct foreign investment accounts for only a quarter of the financing. This large external deficit was an invitation for serious problems if the financing should vanish—and that of course is what happened.

Finance had been given the upper hand over a sustainable development strategy based on internal savings and investment. As a matter of fact, with the more open economy and the increased availability of consumer credit, there was actually a decline in private saving. The country needed (and still needs) high rates of investment and more of the investment needs to be financed by national savings rather than foreign savings. There was little economic growth and a large and growing current account deficit—not a reflection of high investment, but rather a decline in saving, both private and public.

It seemed as if the Salinas team did not learn from the exchange rate crises in the European Monetary System (1992-93), which revealed a number of valuable lessons about quasi fixed exchange rate regimes, all of which are applicable to Mexico.

- Weak currency countries maintain their bands through high interest rates, this attracts disproportionate amounts of portfolio capital flows—once commitment is no longer credible then you have disproportionate outflows.
- Target zones are vulnerable to speculative pressures—one-way bets, foreign exchange reserves insufficient.
- The market must be made to believe that once currency is devalued that there will be no further devaluations—"undervalued" versus "overvalued."

The Salinas team through arrogance or sheer political motivation refused to heed the warning signs and refused to make any adjustments to their economic policy during 1994, when it would have been much easier to sell it to the market. Instead a *pactum* with unrealistic goals, (4 percent growth, 4 percent inflation, balanced budget), was concocted and the hot potato of dealing with nervous short-term portfolio investors was left to the new Zedillo administration, which naively walked into a minefield.

The emergency program put in place on March 9, 1995, with its strict monetary and fiscal policies had as a primary goal to fix the external imbalances by significantly contracting aggregate demand. A floating peso would allow the currency to be valued so as to give competitiveness to Mexican exports. A tight monetary policy would limit the inflationary effects of the devaluation. The external assistance provided by the U.S. and the IMF was essential to guarantee the commitment of the government to comply with all its financial obligations ($29 billion in Tesobonos in 1995), and stop the run on Mexican assets.

The adjustment program began to have almost an immediate effect on the trade balance with a likely drop in the current account balance deficit from $29.2 billion in 1994 to just $1 billion for 1995. No doubt a success story, but it has not come without a price.

The resulting contraction in economic activity (which reached a negative 10.5 percent in the second quarter and a negative 9.6 percent in the third quarter of 1995), has caused high levels of unemployment, bankruptcies to small and medium-sized companies, and a substantial increase in loan delinquencies to an already troubled banking sector. Debtor groups which began to organize at the start of the crisis have grown increasingly militant in spite of the government-subsidized debt restructuring programs for individual debtors and small companies.

MARKET REACTION

The banking sector, which had been brought to its knees by the economic austerity measures, was supported through a series of capitalization programs. Dollar liquidity was provided at the beginning of the crisis to prevent defaults. Foreign investment limits for the Mexican banking sector had disappeared as the authorities encouraged foreign capital and know-how to help revive the more severely affected banks. But it was indeed a difficult balancing act: continuation of restrictive economic policies which further debilitated an already fragile banking sector.

As the external accounts improved, the markets began to react favorably, and both the month-to-month inflation and interest rates began to decline. The goal was to have economic activity recover as interest rates fell, capital markets opened up, and exports grew faster than imports. This works in theory. In practice, however, the markets, which had originally focused on the external accounts situation and the country's ability to meet its foreign currency obligation (including the dollar-indexed Tesobonos), now shifted their focus to how and when economic activity would revive. Surely, the adherence to restrictive monetary policy, which is one of the cornerstones of the adjustment program and one the central bank is unlikely to abandon, would not allow for a reactivation of the economy.

The market reaction was swift, putting renewed pressure on the peso and causing interest rates to sky rocket. The general perception was that the government did not have a credible plan to reactivate the economy in the short term and that it certainly did not have longer term policies directed at generating employment and sustainable growth. Announcements regarding the privatization of the pension fund system to stimulate internal savings and the speeding up of the privatization of key sectors of the economy did not impress the markets.

CONCLUDING REMARKS AND OBSERVATIONS

Should monetary policy have been relaxed to accommodate a turnaround in economic activity? Should the government have focused less on inflation and more on growth? What will it take to regain the confidence of the markets? Is it merely a question of clear and evident leadership?

There are probably more questions than answers. Mexico has been a victim of unrealistic expectations both from the foreign investment community and its own people. The real Mexico lies somewhere in the middle of the surrealistic optimism that prevailed before the crisis and the extreme pessimism that we experienced at that moment. Mexico was not the trumped-up OECD economy it was made out to be at the height of Salinas' popularity, nor is it the high-risk, hopeless economy that it is made out to be today. No doubt there are major challenges ahead not only on the economic front, but also in the political, education, and socioeconomic realms. Yet Mexico with its young and energetic population, natural resources, proximity to the largest market in the world, and strong and proud sense of nationhood is an emerging market with high potential. A nation that, I am convinced, has a bright and exciting future. A nation that with time, hard work, and the lessons learned from this crisis will one day claim its rightful place among the world's modern economies.

NOTE

1. This breakfast was held in honor of the Thomas J. Watson Jr. Institute for International Studies, Brown University.

APPENDIX TABLE AND FIGURES

The following pages provide facts and figures about the Mexican economy just prior to and including its most recent crisis.

APPENDIX TABLE 4.1. Mexico: Net Flows of External Debt, (billions of U.S. dollars)

Debt Outstanding	1989	1990	1991	1992	1993	1994	1995
International Financial Institutions	16.1	21.2	22.7	21.9	21.3	22.0	34.4
Official Bilateral Creditors	10.6	12.6	13.4	15.2	15.2	16.9	29.5
Commercial Banks	65.7	62.4	64.0	60.5	61.9	65.2	64.4
Other Creditors (Portfolio)*	7.0	9.4	22.0	35.7	55.0	59.0	42.5
Total External Debt	99.4	105.6	122.1	133.3	153.4	163.1	170.8
Net Flows	1989	1990	1991	1992	1993	1994	1995
International Financial Institutions	--	5.1	1.5	(0.8)	(0.6)	0.7	12.4
Official Bilateral Creditors	--	2.0	0.8	1.8	--	1.7	12.6
Commercial Banks	--	(3.3)	1.6	(3.5)	1.4	3.3	(0.8)
Other Creditors (Portfolio)*	--	2.4	12.6	13.7	19.3	4.0	(16.5)
Total	--	6.2	16.5	11.2	20.1	9.7	7.7

Note: *includes portfolio investment in debt securities and investments in local currency securities.

APPENDIX FIGURE 4.1. Mexico: Libor Versus UMS Premium

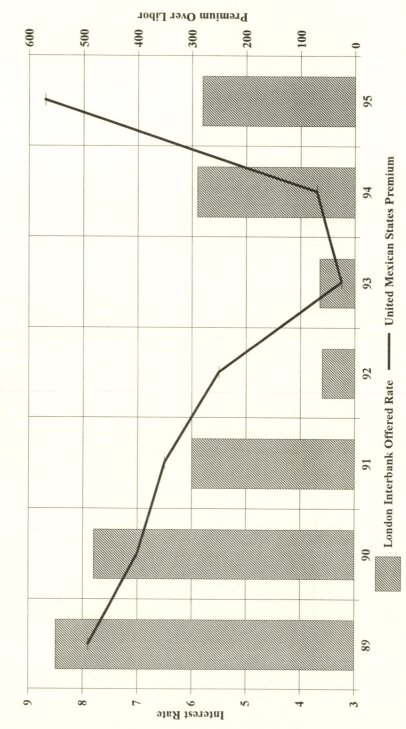

Premium Over Libor

Interest Rate

London Interbank Offered Rate ▬▬▬ United Mexican States Premium

APPENDIX FIGURE 4.2. Mexico: Foreign Investment Flows

US $Billions

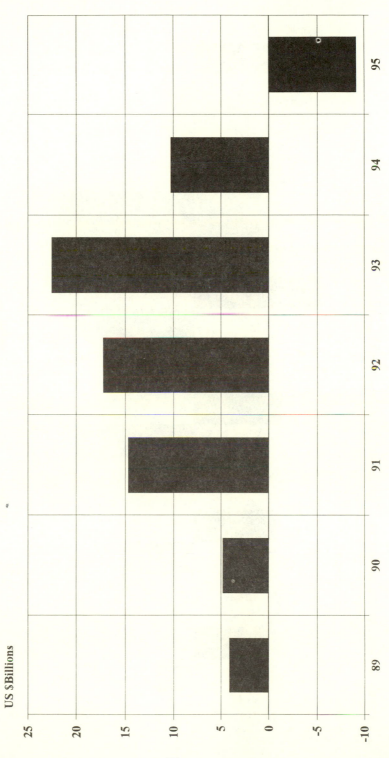

APPENDIX FIGURE 4.3. Mexico: Current Account and International Reserves

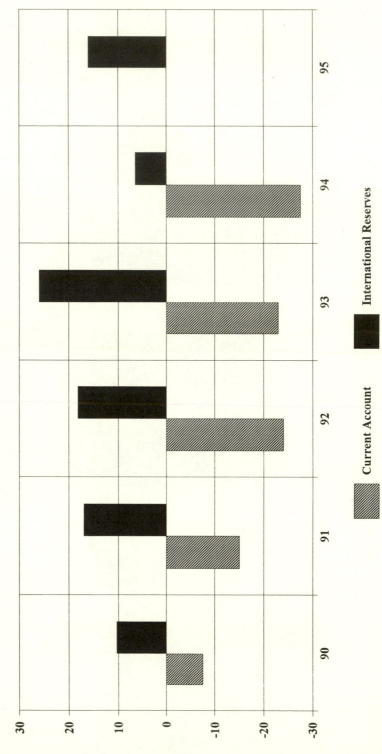

Current Account

International Reserves

APPENDIX FIGURE 4.4. Mexico: Profile of External Debt

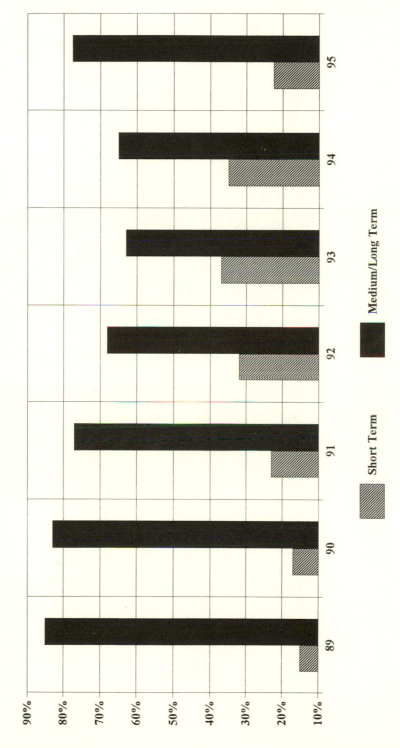

Short Term

Medium/Long Term

APPENDIX FIGURE 4.5. Mexico: Real Exchange Rate (1986=100)

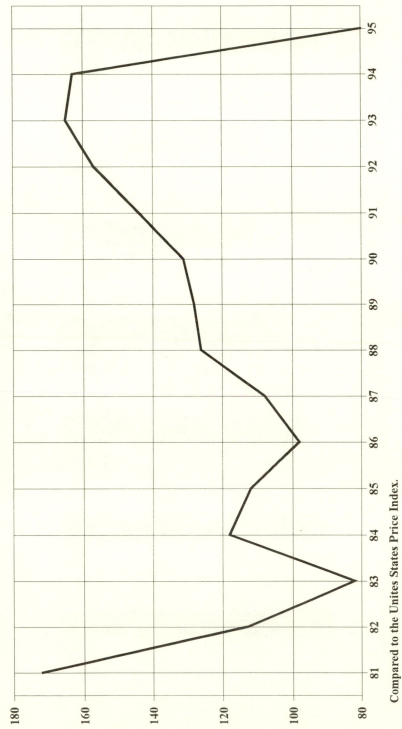

Compared to the Unites States Price Index.

5

THE FOREIGN DEBT CRISIS AND ITS CONSEQUENCES ON THE VENEZUELAN ECONOMY

Antonio Casas-Gonzalez

BACKGROUND

The foreign debt crisis that swept across Latin America in the 1980s had a strong impact on the Venezuelan economy, as it did on other indebted countries in the region, generating a series of negative effects on their balance of payments, their exchange rates, and their levels of domestic economic activity that ultimately resulted in a drop in their standard of living.

Following World War II, a group of international financial mechanisms and institutions were put in place to facilitate the channeling of resources to those countries that faced balance-of- payments problems and required funds to finance productive activities. Institutions such as the World Bank and the International Monetary Fund directed resources toward these countries through medium- and long-term fixed-rate credits for the development of specific projects, or through special arrangements to cover negative balances on international accounts. On a regional level, similar institutions were established such as the Inter-American Development Bank, the Andean Development Corporation, the Fondo Latino-americano de Reservas, and others in Latin America.

The increase in the price of oil and other raw materials early in the 1970s brought about a change in the pattern of indebtedness across nations. The rapid increase in oil prices, in particular, created balance-of-payments problems for exporting nations (surpluses) as well as for importing nations (deficits). The scale of the foreign surpluses that the oil exporting countries recorded, including Venezuela, surpassed the absorption capacity of those economies. As a result, these surpluses were placed as deposits with the international banking community, or channeled to other types of investments by the same institutions which were called "the funds recycling mechanisms." At the same time, Venezuela, as well as other surplus countries, decided to undertake ambitious investment projects, which led to the increased use of the foreign financing as, in many cases, local reserves were insufficient for the size of the new investments. In the case of Venezuela, investment plans were undertaken in basic industries (iron and aluminum) and in the area of electric energy generation. These activities required a high component of material and imported capital goods, which explains in good measure the high increase in imports, which rose from $2,626 billion in 1973 to $13,584 billion in 1982.

The foreign financing that the economy required was obtained primarily from the international banking community, with variable interest rates and short-term maturity basis, both of which signified a change in the pattern of foreign indebtedness. Likewise, it must be pointed out that this increased lending took place under circumstances in which the international banking community was in a position of excess liquidity, because of the recession that spanned the industrialized world. Those resources were channeled broadly and hastily to lesser developed nations, and frequently creditors overestimated the capacity of the projects so financed to generate foreign exchange in the short term and did not adequately evaluate the possibility of recovering the credits granted.

In this context, the process of Venezuelan indebtedness started to accelerate sharply in 1977, when the level of foreign debt reached close to$11,000 billion, an increase of almost $7,000 billion over the level existing at the end of 1976. This process continued progressively and quickly until it reached levels of about $30,000 billion in 1983, a year in which the crisis in the balance of payments occurred and which ended the long period of exchange stability in Venezuela.

THE DEBT CRISIS

The beginning of the foreign debt crisis for many developing countries started early in the 1980s when the price of oil and other prime materials dropped sharply. This resulted in a reduction in export-related income for the producer countries at a time when they had to cover the servicing of growing foreign debt. At the same time, the adoption of restrictive anti-inflationary policies in the United States caused a substantial rise in the level of real interest rates, which made the servicing of foreign debt more difficult. In this context, starting in 1981, the major debtor nations began to delay capital amortization payments, which in turn caused a progressive suspension of the granting of new loans on the part of the international banking community, including refinancing. This situation reached a crisis in August 1982 when the government of Mexico announced a moratorium on the payment of capital totaling approximately $20 billion dollars scheduled for 1982 and 1983. This resulted in a complete suspension of new loans to indebted nations, placing a heavy burden on those countries in Latin America where almost 50 percent of worldwide debt was concentrated. The closure of international financing sources obliged the debtor nations, including Venezuela, to adopt adjustment policies that had a severe recessionary impact. Against this background, the Venezuelan government and the central bank agreed, in February 1983, on the establishment of a foreign exchange control system based on differential exchange rates. This allowed the granting of foreign exchange for basic imports and debt servicing at a preferential exchange rate, while the other transactions were directed toward the free market where the exchange rate was progressively devalued. The goal of these measures was to protect international reserves and to decrease aggregate demand, reduce consumption and investment expenses, while generating exchange savings that would permit servicing the foreign debt. These policies, however, affected the potential earnings and future possible consumption by the population.

Therefore, it was necessary to arrive at an agreement with international creditor banks regarding the refinancing of public-sector foreign debt, to achieve an important reduction in the servicing burden. The Venezuelan government began contacts with the banking community in 1983, and in 1986 a restructuring agreement was signed. This had to be modified in 1987 due to the fall of oil prices, but this proved to be only a transitory solution until a new restructuring agreement was designed in 1990 in accordance with the Brady Plan mechanism.

In this regard, it should be pointed out that 1988 ended for Venezuela with mounting pressures in the foreign exchange market and an increasingly adverse economic outlook. The presence of negative real interest rates gave rise to the inefficient allocation of resources and an accelerated capital flight. As a result, and in spite of existing exchange controls, net international reserves fell steadily and in amounts that fluctuated between $ 926 million and $4,900 billion between 1986 and 1988.

Additionally, in 1988, the fiscal deficit as a percentage of GNP reached 7.4 percent and the inflation rate surpassed 30 percent, which was the highest level reached in Venezuela until that time. Unfortunately, the inflation rate became even worse in 1989, when it reached 80.1 percent, the highest registered until now.

THE 1990 RESTRUCTURING AGREEMENT

For the purpose of guaranteeing the viability of the economic adjustment and reform program adopted in 1989, it was essential to resolve the problem of servicing the public-sector foreign debt. The servicing of such debt on average represented almost 40 percent of the value of oil exports between 1982 and 1988, while the interest payments represented slightly more than 20 percent of the total fiscal expenses between 1987 and 1988.

These overseas payments, in the absence of new financing, had the double effect of reducing international reserves and negatively impacting the total savings of the economy. This was an important impediment to improving the standard of living of the population. To this effect and in the framework of the Brady Plan, the Venezuelan government began negotiations with creditor banks in 1989 with the goal of reaching an agreement that would fulfill three objectives:

- To realize a permanent and stable solution to the problem of the public-sector foreign debt.
- To assure an important reduction in the debt and the servicing.
- To normalize relations with commercial banks and to reestablish the flow of financing from banks, bilateral and multilateral institutions.

The plan offered to the banks (the Plan Financiero 1990) envisioned the voluntary participation of creditor banks and the free selection of distinct financial mechanisms incorporated in the negotiation agreement. It also incorporated two important elements. First, all of the restructured debt was converted into market obligations (bonds) negotiable in the secondary market. And second, the nation offered guarantees or collateral for the payment of principal and interest of the new debt instruments, consisting of sovereign obligations of the creditor nations ("zero coupon" type) that would be acquired with resources that the IMF and the World Bank would furnish for the purpose.

Nevertheless, it should be pointed out that to create the full collateral amount ($2,593 billion) the central bank of Venezuela contributed approximately $2.300 billion in credits. These were granted to the republic, in accordance with the Constitutional Law that authorized the Executive Body to achieve the operations foreseen in the Plan Financiero 1990. The options that this plan offered to the banking community envisioned the following alternatives:

- Full repurchase of the debt at a discount for those banks that would prefer to exclude Venezuelan debt from their portfolios. In this case the restructured debt was replaced by short-term registered notes (91 days) issued by the central bank of Venezuela at a discount of 55 percent of the principal amount.
- To broaden the long-term financial relationship with the nation through the delivery of new funds. This alternative envisioned the issuance of New Money Bonds and Debt Conversion Bonds.
- Intermediate operations that envisioned the reduction of debt, through the permanent reduction of capital and interest and the temporary reduction of interest payments. For this purpose Capital Discount Bonds, Par Bonds, and Temporary Reduction of Interest Bonds were issued.

Regarding the various options, the creditor banks showed a preference for the Par Bonds with discounted interest (38 percent of the total) and the Conversion and New Money Bonds (30 percent). The negotiations resulted in a financial package that included the refinancing of $19,014 billion in debt, with the gross debt reduction of $1,956 billion (10 percent). Likewise, the total debt service, based on the renegotiation agreement of 1986, was reduced by more than 50 percent, using as a reference point the payment estimate anticipated for 1991.

The debt restructured through Par Bonds and Discount Bonds (46 percent of the total) has the full guarantee of payments of principal falling due in the year 2020. This is why this option does not generate amortization payments, but only payment for servicing of the resources requested as loans to create collateral. On the other hand, of the total debt refinanced ($19,014 billion) approximately 55 percent is represented by fixed-interest bonds, which significantly reduces the variability of debt service.

In addition to these benefits, the 1990 plan established the basis for a permanent solution to the foreign debt problem, and had the additional effect of reopening the international financial markets to Venezuelan debt, as well as credit from bilateral and multilateral institutions. This helped the government to make use of a great amount of resources to stimulate modernization programs in the economy, as well as to balance in good measure the adjustment costs to the most vulnerable sectors of society.

CURRENT SITUATION AND OUTLOOK

Since 1994 the development of the Venezuelan economy has been influenced by two fundamental elements. First, the presence of a high fiscal deficit, with the related financing difficulties in using orderly market mechanisms. This generated inflationary pressures and instability in the foreign exchange market. Second, the country experienced a major crisis in the financial system, which led to an increase in capital flight and an important drop in the demand for money. All of this took place well before the Mexican crisis late in 1994 and so cannot be ascribed to the "tequila effect."

The banking crisis that began in January 1994 with the failure of Banco Latino ended up by requiring the indirect assistance of the central bank to the financial system, in an amount equal to 9.0 percent of GNP during the course of 1994. This, in turn, brought about a monetary expansion that had to be absorbed by the central bank through open market operations resulting in a cost to the institution of 2.4 percent of GNP in the same year.

Moreover, in order to deal with the outflow of capital, to protect international reserves and to cause a return to normalcy in the exchange market, the government and the central bank of Venezuela agreed, after the fall of eight more banks, to establish an integral exchange control system beginning in July 1994 with a fixed exchange rate set at 170.0Bs./US$.

Although the exchange control allowed the level of international reserves to recover by December 1994, the high and growing level of the domestic inflation rate in the context of a fixed exchange-rate regime resulted in a progressive appreciation of the official exchange rate. This, in turn, fostered the increase in imports which, together with the adverse expectations created by the lack of an economic program, resulted in new pressures in the exchange market and a declining trend in international reserves during a good part of 1995.

Making a difficult situation worse, the effectiveness of monetary policy has been limited due to the absence of adequate open market instruments, because the central bank has had to carry out such operations with its own securities. As these instruments mature, there has been the creation of an increasing level of domestic liquidity, which is contrary to the original restrictive intentions of the central bank. Also, it is important to note that this process has involved a high cost for the central bank because of the need to issue these instruments with a high nominal interest rate. This means that the central bank has to make available different kinds of instruments from other sources, to avoid the high cost and the inefficiencies that take place when it depends totally on its own open markets instruments.

Not surprisingly, the fiscal deficit has increased as a result of the costs of the financial crisis as well as of the running expenses of the public-sector. In particular, interest payments on the public sector foreign debt have absorbed an average of 14 percent of the total expenses during the last six years. Moreover, the instability shown by the international oil market since 1991 has contributed to the falling trend of fiscal income from the petroleum sector which, despite efforts made to diversify and boost other revenues, continues to represent almost 50 percent of the total fiscal income in Venezuela.

Another problem has been the orderly financing of the high level of the fiscal deficit as domestic financing is limited by the absorption capacity of the market and the acceptability of government securities on the part of investors, who are demanding higher returns and shorter maturities.

Moreover, the possibility of gaining access to foreign financing has been adversely affected by the perception that some investors have of the Venezuelan economy, although the Venezuelan government recently issued a three-year note for DM 500 million in the German market. Also, it is certainly reasonable to hope that when the government reaches an agreement with the International Monetary Fund on the foundation of a logical and credible adjustment program, it will be possible for Venezuela to fully return to the international markets.

The need to arrive to an agreement with the IMF is all the more important because under the 1990 debt restructuring agreement, the amortization of foreign debt principal will begin in 1997. This means that, including payment of interest, debt expenditure will be on the order of $1,970 billion per year for the period 1997-2001, the years in which the greatest volume of payments are concentrated. To these outlays must be added the costs of servicing of nonrestructured public-sector foreign debt, which is estimated to reach on average $1,690 billion per year during the same period.

Fortunately, and while the outlook for servicing the Venezuelan public-sector foreign debt may appear daunting, some initiatives have been taken lately to address the existing macroeconomic disequilibria. For example, important advances have been made in increasing the collection of non-oil fiscal income through a specialized new body called SENIAT. At the same time, Petroleos de Venezuela, S.A. has announced an ambitious investment plan known as the *apertura* which relies on a large participation of foreign capital in exploration and production activities. This plan will generate investments of approximately $11,000 billion in seven years. In addition, regulations have been eased for the export of gold, which should be helpful for gold production, the official exchange rate was devalued to 290Bs./US$ in December 1995: and very importantly the elimination of the exchange control system is foreseen for the first half of this year.

Additionally, advances have been made in the normalization of the financial system and the mechanisms of banking control and supervision have been strengthened, relying on the technical advice of experts from the World Bank and the IMF. One of the major banks intervened by the state, Banco de Venezuela, was privatized in 1996. Likewise, in the framework of a national agreement, the government approved a new system for social services for workers and pension funds through which a good part of the inflationary pressures arising from the labor market will be reduced and thus stimulate savings through public and private mutual funds.

The adoption of these measures combined with a successful outcome of negotiations with the IMF should create a favorable framework from which to face the servicing of the foreign debt in the coming years. It will also allow Venezuela to return to the track of sustained growth, with price stability and a viable balance of payments in the short and medium terms.

APPENDIX TABLES AND FIGURES

The following pages contain supporting data about Venezuela's economy.

APPENDIX TABLE 5.1. Venezuela: Plan Financiero 1990, Eligible Debt per Option (Millions of US dollars)

1. Short-term Note	1,410.6
2. Debt Conversion and New Money Bonds	6,027.4
3. Discount Bonds	1,810.0
4. Par Bonds	7,470.3
5. Interest Reduction Bonds	3,036.0
Total*	19,754.3

Note: *This amount was reduced to$19,014 million as a result of the operations considered in the Plan Financiero 1990.

APPENDIX TABLE 5.2. Venezuela: Restructured External Public Debt Service Estimates (Millions of US dollars)

	Principal	Interest	Total
1996	0.00	1,269.77	1,269.77
1997	580.07	1,256.35	1,836.42
1998	890.09	1,207.99	2,098.08
1999	890.09	1,141.20	2,031.29
2000	890.09	1,075.09	1,965.18
2001	890.09	1,007.60	1,897.69
2002	890.09	940.80	1,830.89
2003	890.09	875.06	1,765.15

Source: Ministerio de Hacienda.

APPENDIX TABLE 5.3. Venezuela: Nonrestructured External Public Debt Service Estimates (Millions of US dollars)

	Principal	Interest	Total
1996	1,551.77	762.95	2,314.72
1997	988.07	685.23	1,673.30
1998	1,376.57	675.35	2,051.92
1999	1,030.06	578.40	1,608.46
2000	1,199.89	514.83	1,714.72
2001	982.84	423.48	1,406.32
2002	846.33	357.49	1,203.82
2003	961.56	293.95	1,255.51

Source: Ministerio de Hacienda.

APPENDIX TABLE 5.4. Venezuela: External Public Debt, Year-End Stock (Millions of US dollars)

Creditors	1988	1989	1990	1991	1992	1993	1994	1995*
Nonrestructured Debt	7,262.00	8,123.00	7,745.00	8,408.00	9,098.00	9,334.00	9,423.00	8,520.00
Commercial Banks	2,378.00	2,121.00	759.00	726.00	665.00	462.00	273.00	232.00
Bilateral Inst.	799.00	1,385.00	1,488.00	1,874.00	1,883.00	2,351.00	2,786.00	2,693.00
Multilateral Inst.	199.00	550.00	1,588.00	2,132.00	2,715.00	2,817.00	2,955.00	2,824.00
Bonds	2,680.00	2,692.00	2,537.00	22,413.00	2,419.00	2,898.00	2,692.00	235.00
Suppliers	1,286.00	1,375.00	1,372.00	1,263.00	1,417.00	805.00	717.00	416.00
Restructured Debt	19,324.00	18,920.00	18,664.00	17,787.00	17,551.00	17,474.00	17,559.00	17,559.00
Commercial Banks	19,324.00	18,920.00	0.00	0.00	0.00	0.00	0.00	0.00
Bonds	0.00	0.00	18,664.00	17,787.00	17,551.00	17,474.00	17,559.00	17,559.00
Total	26,586.00	27,043.00	26,409.00	26,195.00	26,650.00	26,807.00	26,981.00	26,079.00

Note: *September 30 figures.
Source: Ministerio de Hacienda.

APPENDIX FIGURE 5.1. Venezuela: Public Foreign Debt to GDP Ratio

(*) Preliminary figures

84

APPENDIX FIGURE 5.2. Venezuela: Foreign Debt as Percentage of Oil Exports

(*) Preliminary figures

APPENDIX FIGURE 5.3. Venezuela: Real Growth and Inflation Rate

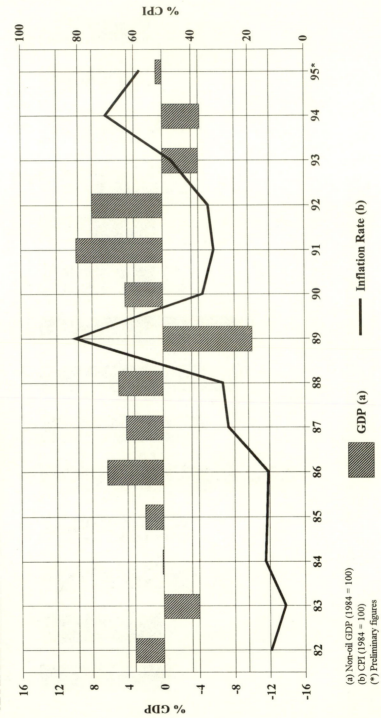

(a) Non-oil GDP (1984 = 100)
(b) CPI (1984 = 100)
(*) Preliminary figures

GDP (a)   —— Inflation Rate (b)

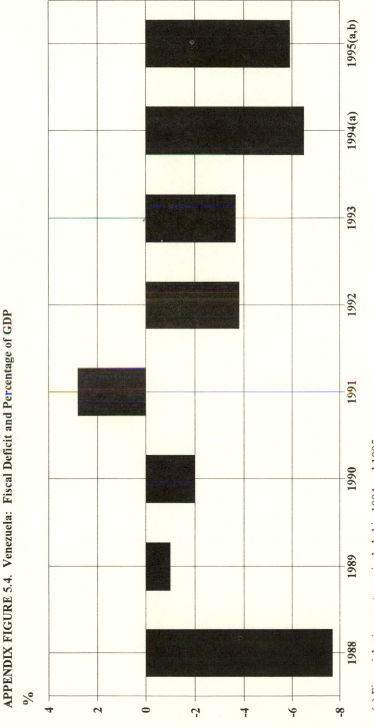

APPENDIX FIGURE 5.4. Venezuela: Fiscal Deficit and Percentage of GDP

(a) Financial crises costs are included in 1994 and 1995.
(b) Preliminary figures

87

APPENDIX FIGURE 5.5. Venezuela: Revenues and Expenditures as Percentage of GDP

(*) Preliminary figures

Oil Revenue   Non-Oil Revenue   Domestic Expenditures

APPENDIX FIGURE 5.6. Venezuela: Oil Industry Indicators

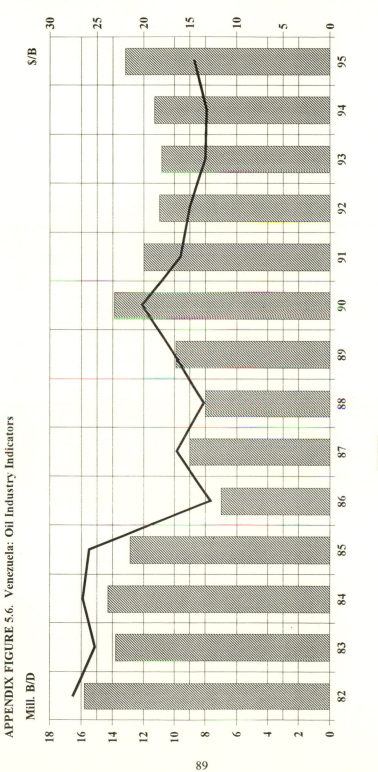

Mill. B/D $/B

Exports ▨   Price ━━━

APPENDIX FIGURE 5.7. Venezuela: International Reserves and Oil Prices

(*) Preliminary figures
Net Int'l Reserves in months of imports

Net International Reserves   Price

PART III

GROWTH AND DEVELOPMENT PERSPECTIVES

THE MEXICAN CRISIS AND CARIBBEAN ECONOMIC GROWTH: IMPACT AND PROSPECTS

Anthony Gonzales

GROWTH PERFORMANCE

In assessing the impact of the Mexican crisis on growth prospects in the Caribbean, it is essential to note that the growth experience in the region is characterized by significant variation due to differences in economic structure, degree of integration into the world economy, and policies pursued.

At the start of the Mexican crisis four key features reflected growth in the period 1990-94 as compared to the decade of the 1980s (see Table 6.1).

- The overall average growth rate fell below 2 percent compared to 2.4 percent in the 1980s.
- The high growth rates of more than 6 percent that we saw in the 1980s, and that were particularly associated with the smaller countries of the Organization of Eastern Caribbean States (OECS), dropped on average to below 4 percent in the 1990s. With the exception of Guyana and possibly Belize, no other countries in the region managed to achieve an average growth of 5 percent in that period.
- Some countries, in particular Guyana, Trinidad and Tobago, and Suriname, which consistently were experiencing negative growth rates in the 1980s, now began to record positive rates in the 1990s. Barbados, with a negative growth rate (-1.24 percent), was the only country to join Haiti which continued into the 1990s with a high negative growth rate by the end of 1994.
- In terms of strong and sustainable growth, the best performers in the 1980s were Antigua, the Bahamas, Belize, Dominica, Grenada, St. Kitts-Nevis, St. Lucia, and St. Vincent (see Table 6.1). These countries all had average growth rates exceeding 3.5 percent. In the 1990s, the high growth performers (3.5 percent or more) were Guyana along with Belize, St. Kitts-Nevis, St. Lucia, and St. Vincent. Antigua, Dominica, and Grenada experienced only modest to low growth (positive but less than 3.5 percent) as did the Dominican Republic, Jamaica, Suriname, and Trinidad and Tobago. The non-performers were Haiti and Barbados, both with negative growth rates.

TABLE 6.1. Average Real GDP Growth Rates, 1980-90, 1982-92, and 1990-94
(in percent)

Country	1980-90	1982-92	1990-94
Antigua	5.2	6.7	2.98
The Bahamas	3.6	1.9	
Barbados	1.7	1.3	-1.24
Belize	5.3	6	4.7
Dominica	4.3	2.9	3.18
Dominican Rep.	1.9	1.8	1.88
Grenada	5.8	4.7	2.2
Guyana	-2.7	-1	5.48
Haiti	-0.4	-1.5	-6.48
Jamaica	0.7	2.7	1.96
St. Kitts-Nevis	4.8	5.9	3.9
St. Lucia	6.3	7.3	3.68
St. Vincent and the Grenadines	6.9	6.1	3.66
Suriname	-2.6	-0.5	0.7
Trinidad and Tobago	-4.3	-2.7	1.1
Overall Average	2.4	2.8	2.0
Standard Deviation	3.60	3.25	2.99
Average (excl. Haiti)	2.64	3.08	2.44
Standard Deviation	3.77	3.29	1.89

Source: Compiled from World Bank, Caribbean Development Bank, Inter-American Development Bank, and national data.

This description reflects a shift from that of the 1980s, when the main driving force of growth was the rapid expansion of nonfactor services, in particular tourism, which grew from about 39 percent in 1980 to 49 percent of exports in 1990. In terms of its contribution to GDP, it increased from 15 percent to 28.5 percent during this same period. This allowed the Dominican Republic, the OECS,

Belize, and Jamaica to achieve better growth rates. It was certainly the most dynamic sector in virtually all the high-performers of the OECS. Other factors in these countries which accounted for a strong performance in this period were a sound macroeconomic framework, human resource development, and exports to niche markets.

The macroeconomic fundamentals were regarded as weak in most of the other countries and accounted for their poor performance. In general, in most of these countries the increase of consumption impacted negatively on growth. As a whole, during the 1980s and in the 1990s, gross national savings fell short of investment needs in 11 of the 14 countries examined in each year, and in the remaining three countries, for many of these years.

The national savings rate, on average, was between 11 and 24 percent of GDP. This savings effort falls well below that of the high-performing developing countries, where gross national savings, on average, was around 35 percent of GDP in 1990. Public-sector savings were particularly weak, and average foreign savings were extremely volatile, ranging from 2 percent to 30 percent. In some cases, as in Trinidad and Tobago, Suriname, and Barbados, foreign savings were negative.

Direct foreign investment (DFI) was low relative to total investment and focused mainly on tourism-related activities outside of the energy sector in Trinidad and Tobago. Manufacturing in Jamaica and the Dominican Republic had also attracted foreign investment during the second half of the 1980s. The four high-performers received DFI of more than 10 percent of GDP per annum, on average. Between 1980 and 1990, investment efforts increased mainly in the OECS and Belize. These higher investment efforts were financed with increased national savings as well as increased foreign savings.

In terms of the sources of growth, 32 percent of real GDP growth is attributable to factor accumulation and 68 percent to total factor productivity growth.[1] Forces driving such changes are greater openness, investment, (important in the Dominican Republic and Jamaica), and labor force growth (particularly in Guyana, Trinidad and Tobago, and Haiti). External debt had a negative impact on growth, especially in Guyana and Jamaica.

IMPACT OF THE MEXICAN CRISIS AND GROWTH PROSPECTS

The Mexican crisis occurred at a time when Caribbean states were being heavily pushed into the international capital market, after years of strong dependence on official aid flo. Although there has been some increase in private flows, the extent to which they have offset the decline in official flows is not yet clear.

Caribbean states are not recipients of portfolio capital in any significant way. They do not have the absorptive capacity for such investment. The potential for equity capital is, however, good, particularly if there is a friendly institutional and regulatory environment and provided the policy framework is conducive to creditworthiness and growth. DFI has now assumed a much larger portion in capital flows along with private borrowing (Eurobonds) and remittances from abroad.

International investors reacted to the Mexican crisis by withdrawing funds throughout the area. Countries which in 1993-94 were favored by international investors, suddenly came to be considered high-risk borrowers as fears of the debt crisis grew.

The fallout has affected the Caribbean insofar as higher rating requirements in the Eurobond market. For small countries, which have the additional burden of smallness in achieving high credit ratings, this is a real challenge.

Foreign investors will also be looking beyond the macroeconomic fundamentals. It is generally assumed that the "cake will continue to rise" if the macro-fundamentals are strong. In terms of investment, production, and exports, not much more needs to be done to obtain the required growth. Furthermore, there seems to be even some complacency and satisfaction with existing growth rates that are below 6 percent. From an international perspective, however, more policy guidance and initiatives are needed.

Over the last year the euphoric mood about market reforms at the international level has given way to a new look at performance that emphasizes caution. We are no longer in a situation where markets will provide capital simply because we have adopted market-oriented reforms. The Mexican crisis has shaken the confidence of investors and they are now looking beyond merely the fundamentals. A sound fiscal policy is no longer a condition for solid creditworthiness. In addition, three or six months' import cover is no longer regarded as a sign of balance-of-payments health. Even without being exposed to short-term capital movements, no restrictions on the capital account and such thin domestic capital markets seem to require a much higher ratio, probably about 10-12 months at least. We are now in what is called the "reality check" era, where hard evidence of vigorous growth is expected. Higher risk rating requirements are now in force since the Mexican crisis has made access to capital more difficult, even for the leading market-oriented reformers. Rating agencies are now focusing on the ability of countries to generate, in a timely way, the foreign exchange required to meet contractual payments to investors.

The question as to whether growth can be jeopardized as a result of the Mexican crisis must first be answered by looking at the state of the current account balance. In the Mexican case, an unsustainable current account deficit reaching about 8 percent of GDP accounted for the crisis.

How sustainable is the current account deficit in the region? Ten of the 14 countries have had consistent current account deficits over the 1990-94 period. The largest deficits can be found in the Dominican Republic, Jamaica, the Bahamas, and Guyana. On a per capita basis, some members of the OECS, such as St. Kitts-Nevis, St. Vincent and the Grenadines, and Antigua, had a much larger deficit. The best performers were Trinidad and Tobago, Barbados, and St. Lucia. Guyana and Haiti were particularly vulnerable due to the large share of GDP that their current account deficits represent.

Small current account deficits, however, are no indication of lack of vulnerability. They must be related to external debt service, personal savings, the efficiency of investment, the potential to attract capital inflows, the capacity for export growth, and the desired rates of growth.

While debt service ratios have been on the decline in some countries, such as the Dominican Republic, Jamaica, and Trinidad and Tobago, and are now in the vicinity of 20 percent of exports, they still remain high. A country like Guyana is among the world's most seriously indebted countries and is particularly vulnerable with an unsustainable debt service ratio.

In making some projections of long-term growth in the Latin America and the Caribbean, one study[2] sets a target of 6 percent for 1998-2003 and suggests that savings must be taken to 28 percent, up from 19-20 percent. Private savings in particular must move from 13.8 percent to 19.5 percent and public savings from 2.2 percent to 6 percent of GDP. This would allow a level of gross investment of 28 percent, if foreign savings goes up to 2.6 percent. With an increase of savings and investment by eight percentage points, an additional two percentage points on the rate of growth can be expected. How attainable are these goals in the Caribbean? National savings are currently between 11 and 24 percent of GDP. This falls way below the 38 percent for the newly industrialized countries (NICs) of Asia. Public-sector savings are particularly weak. In most Caribbean countries, low national savings calls for an important tightening of fiscal policy to increase savings through higher tax revenues or reduced expenditure. The above targets seem particularly challenging for countries such as Jamaica and Guyana, where the fiscal account deteriorated in 1995 though not to the same degree in both cases.[3]

Regarding external financing, there is currently a high dependence on such funding due to low national savings and high import dependence. In the Caribbean, this dependence is expressed in a higher-than-average ratio for Latin America and the Caribbean mentioned above. The Mexican crisis has caused an increase in the spreads for the two (or three) recent entrants to the Eurobond market (Trinidad and Tobago and Barbados). Capital from this source will be harder to source in the future. Only about three Caribbean countries satisfy the required rating criteria.

Reaching a higher target for foreign savings would also mean attracting much higher levels of direct foreign investment. While DFI flows have become a bit more diversified in terms of sectors and sources, doubt persists as to whether this target is attainable in light of the increased competition for DFI and the relative decline of the Caribbean Basin Initiative (CBI) vis-à-vis NAFTA as a trading regime. DFI flows can be affected particularly to the Dominican Republic, Haiti, and Jamaica—countries most likely to be affected by Mexico's entry into

NAFTA and the peso devaluation. Trinidad and Tobago seems the only country likely to achieve the higher target, given present interest and investment trends in the energy sector. Of course, the service sector in the region does hold some promise for DFI in the future, but it is difficult to speculate on how sizable this would be.

In examining the outlook for 1996, some broad international trends which could impact negatively on the regions economic performance must be borne in mind. Essentially these are the following:

- More competition in the North American market will come from Mexico as NAFTA barriers are phased-down further and the Mexican economy reacts to the appreciable peso devaluation. What is more important, investment will shift to Mexico to benefit from the dynamic gains from NAFTA (economies of scale; further vertical integration between Mexican, US and Canadian industry; etc.). Caribbean trade and investment strategy is largely premised on the need to broaden market access, especially in this hemisphere. The NAFTA option is now out and would seem to be not on the cards for the remainder of this century given the current U.S. disappointment with developments in Mexico, its concern with potential job losses, as well as its ability to compete with lower-wage countries. Since the FTAA (Free Trade Area of the Americas) process involves a much slower track, chances for increasing intraregional and hemispheric trade through enlarged market access are not likely to be increased in the short-to-medium term.

- While growth in Latin America and the Caribbean was forecasted to increase at around 3 percent in 1996, in terms of its composition, it is not evenly distributed, with some of the main regional trading partners likely to experience much lower rates. Slower growth is expected in the OECS due to problems with the restructuring of bananas and the recent climatic effects on tourism. Besides, regional trade in Caricom is virtually stagnant, hovering around peak levels reached since the early 1980s. The economic outlook for Venezuela, another main regional trading partner, continues to remain dismal. Regional trade prospects thus appear uncertain if not dim. All of this is further compounded by increasing protectionism in the markets of developed countries as a result of overemphasis on environmental and labor standards as well as the implementation of the results of the Uruguay Round, which is whittling away the preferential access enjoyed in traditional markets;

- The increasing competition for global efficiency investment that is coming from the stepped-up pace of investment liberalization in most developing countries is another factor that must be of some concern to the region. The inability to rapidly build locally competitive conditions in order to attract this type of investment must be underscored in this regard. The battle is being lost because of the failure to capture production-sharing operations at the higher-valued ends (motor vehicle parts, electrical goods, etc.). The requirements of such an investment strategy include adequate export processing zones (EPZs) and/or appropriate temporary admission systems, massive training programs, and training subsidies.

- All of the above suggests that reform must be an ongoing exercise and policy makers must remain permanently vigilant to changes in the external environment. Deepening the reforms must involve raising domestic savings, encouraging more private investment in infrastructure, restructuring labor codes and the education system,

- deregulating and debureaucratizing lower levels of government, reducing poverty and inequality, accelerating privatization plans, boosting fiscal accounts, fine-tuning the foreign-exchange regime, further promoting exports, and strengthening private banks and other financial institutions. This is the surest way to increase growth in the medium and longer term.
- The belief that private capital can further increase if there is a more friendly institutional and regulatory environment and a good policy framework may now be valid only at the margin. Caribbean countries have already gone some distance in this regard by adopting new liberal investment laws that incorporate more stable, less discretionary, and predictable rules as well as less bureaucracy and the granting of national and most-favored-nation treatment to U.S. investors. Despite this, there has been, on average, no significant acceleration in the flow of investment.
- In this same context, it should be noted that the Caribbean is not very efficient in transforming capital. The Incremental Capital Output Ratio (ICOR) is high. At 20 percent of GDP in investment, growth rates have been too low as compared with other regions with the same level of investment. The problem is particularly acute in Jamaica. The high cost of infrastructures in the region may to a significant degree account for this situation.

To attain higher growth rates, exports must increase by twice the growth rate. On average it means that exports should grow in real terms at least 10 to 12 percent annually. For exports to increase at that rate, international competitiveness must increase through productivity improvements, which in turn would depend heavily on further reforms mentioned above. Factors that will work against the achievement of this target are the erosion of preferential margins resulting from the Uruguay Round, the expected loss of preferences in the traditional markets of the North Atlantic countries, and slower growth in the region.

For the Caribbean, prospects for 1995 already show a slowdown. Forecasts for 1996 for some countries (see Table 6.2) put rates above those for 1995, indicating that the economies will emerge from the present crisis and a faster growth will resume. The idea that further deepening reforms and increasing domestic savings in particular could further boost growth in the years ahead seems attractive, especially for those countries whose reforms have slowed. At the same time, it is not clear how much further and faster reforms have to go. Free market policies have not generated the kind of explosion of activity, new industry, and exports that had been anticipated, even though some gains have been reaped.

Changes in domestic savings, education, and infrastructure could further add to growth. There may not be much to be gained from labor market reform, a more liberal foreign investment, and greater trade openness and deregulation. A low savings rate is probably the most serious constraint faced by the region in its effort to accelerate growth. One cannot rely on foreign savings either as a viable long-term source of funds or as a substitute for domestic savings. A target of at least 25 percent for aggregate savings by the turn of the century should be set. Higher public savings is one way to raise domestic savings. Thus, in-so-far as projected fiscal surpluses are attainable, aggregate savings should increase (a 1 percent in-

TABLE 6.2. Actual and Expected Growth Rates, 1990-96

Country	Forecast 1996	1990-94	1994	1995
Barbados		-1.24	4	1
Dominican Republic	3.5	1.88	4	2.5
Guyana	5	5.48	8.5	5
Jamaica	3.5	1.96	0.8	-0.05
Trinidad and Tobago	2.5	1.1	4.7	4.5

Source: Compiled from World Bank, Caribbean Development Bank, Inter-American Development Bank, and national data.

crease in public savings is believed to increase total savings by 0.5 percent). A real effort in this direction would have to come largely from a reduction of expenditure rather than an increase in taxes.

Another lesson the Mexican crisis has taught us is that we must start to prepare for adverse shocks. It is foolhardy to say that in-so-far as we do not have a widening current account deficit or significant short-term debt we would be spared from a Mexican-type crisis. The region is susceptible to adverse terms of trade shocks (sudden drops in export earnings) and capital flight. How resilient are we to a reduction of capital inflows? Do we have the economic fundamentals and quality management to deal with these potential risks and disruptions? At present even those countries that enjoy a trade surplus are threatened by increasing imports. Reliance on DFI and some international borrowing may not be sufficient to see us through such a crisis given our level of foreign reserves and low rate of domestic savings. DFI inflows generate strong flows of profit remittances. The assumption that they are more stable and reliable than portfolio equity inflows may not be entirely correct. While DFI has been seen as an alternative to lower domestic investment and the higher costs of borrowing, caution must still be exercised in our macroeconomic management of DFI.

In addition, a more precise notion is needed of what surplus on the trade account or balance on the capital account is sustainable in the medium and long term. On that basis a judgment can be made as to whether higher public-sector savings to control the current account are needed. Such a judgment would have to take into account the fact that the consumption and import boom that normally follows successful stabilization seems to be upon us in some cases.

CONCLUSION

The Mexican crisis has served to highlight some deficiencies in the growth strategies of Caribbean states. One important weakness is that, since the behavior of capital flows cannot be anticipated based on economic fundamentals and savings remains low, there is the real threat of an imbalance which will have to be financed by foreign reserves leading to tighter monetary and fiscal policies with implications for higher interest rates and a lower level of economic activity.

The challenge that faces the region is how to accelerate growth to at least 6 percent and ensure that it is better distributed. Exports need to grow faster in real terms as well as become more diversified if growth is to accelerate. The policy instruments would have to seriously address these issues if the reform process is not to be eventually derailed.

NOTES

1. See World Bank (1994), p. 13.
2. See World Bank (1995).
3. See UN ECLAC (1995), p. 7.

REFERENCES

Burki, Shahid Javed and Sebastian Edwards. (1995). "Latin America After Mexico: Quickening the Pace." Mimeo. Washington, DC: World Bank Current Issues Paper, August.

Faust, Joerg. (1995). "The Mexican Crisis and Its Regional Implications." Aussenpolitik, Vol. 4.

Gonzales, Anthony. (1996). "The 1996 Budget: An International Perspective." Mimeo. St. Augustine: University of West Indies, January.

Harris, Donald. (1996). "Finance, Investment and Growth: Economic Policy for Caribbean Economies in the Next (Quarter) Century." In Keith Worrell and Anthony Gonzales (Eds.), *Whither the Caricom Region: Whither the CDB in its Support?* Barbados: Caribbean Development Bank.

UN ECLAC. (1995). "Caribbean Economic Performance-Synopsis For 1995." Mimeo. LC/CAR/G.465. December, p. 7.

UN ECLAC. (1994). "Summary of Caribbean Economic Performance for 1994 and Overview of Economic Activities for 1993." Mimeo. LC/CAR/G.432. December.

World Bank. (1994). *Coping with Changes in the External Environment.* Washington, DC: World Bank, Caribbean Division, Country Department. Report No. 12821 LAC, May.

World Bank. (1995). "Long-Run Prospects For LAC: Rapid Growth Is Possible." Mimeo. LA-ACCE, May.

7

A COMPARISON OF EAST ASIAN AND LATIN AMERICAN DEVELOPMENT: WILL LATIN AMERICA CREATE ITS OWN MIRACLE?

F. Gerard Adams

INTRODUCTION

Looking back to the 1950s, Latin America was full of promise while East Asia was largely poor and undeveloped. In more recent years, the development experiences of East Asia and Latin America have been very different. East Asia underwent a transformation, resulting in what the World Bank has termed the "East Asian Miracle" while Latin America, clobbered by a debt crisis, had "lost a decade." Only now are we seeing a significant turnaround in Latin America, though all is not well yet.

In this chapter, I will compare the growth experience of these different regions of the world and use that information to appraise the future of Latin America.[1] Can we expect, in Latin America, the same burst of growth that we had in Asia prior to 1997?

A COMPARISON BETWEEN EAST ASIAN AND LATIN AMERICAN GROWTH

It is easy to compare growth in broad terms across these two regions. As shown in Table 7.1, real GDP in East Asia grew at a fairly steady rate between 6 and 7 percent a year from 1980 to 1993. Until recently, growth rates had remained high. Of all the countries examined, China stands out as having one of the fastest growth rates, especially in recent years. But China's statistics should be taken with a grain of salt. Other countries in the region have also experienced very rapid growth rates, some even exceeding the 7 percent threshold, which means their incomes will be doubling every ten years if that trend continues.

In contrast, Latin America's experience has been much less impressive. Stumbling on excessive debt and inflation, Latin America has grown very slowly,

TABLE 7.1. Growth Experience: Latin America and East Asia (as a percent of GDP)

	1970-80	1980-93	1995	1996-99
United States	2.8	2.7	2.1	2.4
Japan	4.3	4.0	0.4	3.0
East Asia				
Hong Kong	9.2	6.5	5.0	5.0
Singapore	8.3	6.9	8.2	8.0
S. Korea	10.1	9.1	9.3	7.2
Indonesia	7.2	5.8	7.3	6.9
Malaysia	7.9	6.2	9.7	7.7
Philippines	6.0	1.4	5.3	5.4
Thailand	7.1	8.2	8.7	8.2
China	5.5	9.6	10.2	9.4
Average for *East Asian LDCs*	6.8	6.7	8.0	7.2
Latin America				
Argentina	2.5	0.8	-3.5	4.5
Brazil	8.1	2.1	4.2	5.0
Chile	1.8	5.1	8.5	5.6
Colombia	5.4	3.7	5.3	5.0
Ecuador	9.5	2.4	2.3	4.0
Mexico	6.3	1.6	-6.9	5.0
Peru	3.5	-0.5	6.9	4.5
Uruguay	3.1	1.3	-2.5	3.0
Venezuela	3.5	2.1	2.2	3.6
Average for *Latin America*	4.8	2.0	1.8	4.5

only about 2 percent a year on average from 1980 to 1993. That growth rate is only slightly higher than the region's population growth rate for that period. However, recent signs indicate an improvement in their growth performance as Latin American countries engage in privatization, liberalization, and restructuring. Compared to East Asia, though, which has shown relatively little cyclical variation, Latin American economies are still quite volatile as seen by their reaction to recent international financial shocks—such as the "tequila effect" and the restructuring policies—which resulted in substantially negative growth. To illustrate the significance, I will comment on the experience of four major countries in the region; Mexico, Brazil, Argentina, and Chile.

Mexico
The financial firestorm that hit Mexico at the end of 1994, which was the result of a sudden reversal of short-term capital flows (some belonging to Mexican nationals), caused the peso to collapse. While bankruptcy was averted, the economy was driven into severe recession. Optimists now see a bottoming out, in real terms, but not without severe social costs—a sharp reduction in real incomes, the undermining of the middle class, and the destruction of many small enterprises. On the positive side, foreign direct investment has continued, and the hope is for a gradual recovery and perhaps even moderate growth throughout the remainder of the decade.

Brazil
The Brazilian experience is slightly more positive. Efforts to limit runaway inflation seem to have succeeded and the economy grew moderately, in real terms, early in the 1990s. Privatization and liberalization are now under way, but there is little chance the economy can repeat the income doubling growth rates of the 1960s and 1970s.

Argentina
Argentina, like Brazil, has also undertaken vast economic policy reforms which have opened and privatized the economy and stabilized their monetary and fiscal policies. Nevertheless, their reliance on an exchange rate anchor to hold down inflation resulted in an overvalued currency and recession, though, as with Mexico, a modest recovery is now forecasted for the remainder of the decade.

Chile
Chile may be the only real success story in Latin America. Beginning in the late 1970s, the Chilean government instituted conservative restructuring and open trade policies. These policies have since been moderated, and now Chile's economy is far more integrated than others in the region—a feat accomplished by exploiting their advantage as a temperate southern hemispheric country.

Table 7.2 compares per caput real GDP across regions. The figures in the first column are based on an exchange-rate conversion to U.S. dollars. The second column, which is more realistic, presents the same indicators in terms of purchasing power parity—or in other words, in real purchasing power. Since the currencies of low income countries tend to be undervalued relative to the dollar,

TABLE 7.2. Per Capita Real GNP: Latin America and East Asia

	GNP per capita Exchange Rate $ 1993	GNP per capita PPP $1993	PPP/$ Ratio
United States	24,740.0	24,740.0	1.0
Japan	31,490.0	20,850.0	1.5
East Asia			
Hong Kong	18,060.0	21,560.0	0.8
Singapore	19,850.0	19,510.0	1.0
S. Korea	7,660.0	9,630.0	0.8
Indonesia	740.0	3,150.0	0.2
Malaysia	3,140.0	7,930.0	0.4
Philippines	850.0	2,670.0	0.3
Thailand	2,110.0	6,260.0	0.3
China	490.0	2,330.0	0.2
Average for East Asian LDCs	6,612.5	9,130.0	0.4
Latin America			
Argentina	7,220.0	8,250.0	0.9
Brazil	2,930.0	5,370.0	0.5
Chile	3, 170.0	8,400.0	0.4
Colombia	1,400.0	5,490.0	0.3
Ecuador	1,200.0	4,240.0	0.3
Mexico	3,610.0	6,810.0	0.5
Peru	1,490.0	3,220.0	0.5
Uruguay	3,830.0	6,380.0	0.6
Venezuela	2,840.0	8, 130.0	0.3
Average for Latin America	2,844.0	5,871.0	0.4

the lower income countries have higher purchasing power than the exchange rate-based figures would suggest.

Overall, per capita GDP in East Asia is now much higher than in Latin America. In fact, some East Asian countries have already reached per capita GDP

TABLE 7.3. Inflation and Debt Burdens: Latin American and East Asia

	Inflation		Debt Service (% of exports)
	1970-1980	**1980-1993**	**1993**
United States	7.5	3.8	na
Japan	8.5	1.5	na
East Asia			
Hong Kong	9.2	7.9	na
Singapore	5.9	2.5	na
S. Korea	19.5	6.3	9.2
Indonesia	21.5	8.5	31.8
Malaysia	7.3	2.2	7.9
Philippines	13.3	13.6	7.9
Thailand	9.2	4.3	18.7
China	0.6	7.0	11.1
Average for			
East Asian LDCs	10.8	6.5	10.8
Latin America			
Argentina	134.2	374.3	46.0
Brazil	38.6	423.4	24.4
Chile	186.2	187.1	59.4
Colombia	22.3	20.1	23.4
Ecuador	13.8	24.9	29.4
Mexico	18.1	40.4	25.7
Peru	30.1	57.9	31.5
Uruguay	63.7	316.1	58.7
Venezuela	14.0	66.7	27.7
Average for			
Latin America	54.2	153.5	34.9

levels comparable to those in the industrial world. Yet, strikingly, other East Asian countries show levels that remain relatively low. Income disparity in East Asia appears to be much greater than in Latin America, with the advanced countries much farther ahead than their lower income counterparts. For example, we see, based on purchasing power parity, Hong Kong with the highest per caput GDP at $21,560, and China with the lowest at $2,330. In comparison, we find in Latin America, Chile with the highest per-capita GDP at $8,400, and Peru with the lowest at $3,220.

Table 7.3 compares inflation and debt burdens across regions. Again, the comparison is striking. Inflation rates in Latin America have been much higher than in Asia, reflecting a lack of fiscal discipline and control. (It is hoped that they have overcome this situation.) The differences are equally great with respect to debt burdens. More than a decade after the debt crisis, debt burdens in Latin America, relative to exports earnings, are still three times higher than in East Asia.

In Table 7.4, we find measures of export growth. Again, East Asia's performance during the earlier period of 1970 to 1980 and more recently, that of 1980 to 1993, is strikingly better than Latin America's.

Finally, in Table 7.5, we examine savings rates. During the 1970s, the savings rates in both regions were roughly comparable (21.4 percent in East Asia compared to 20.2 percent in Latin America). However, more recently, 1993 for instance, we find the phenomenal savings rate of East Asia now more than double that of Latin America, at 34.3 percent compared to 15.5 percent. Statistics like these fuel professional debates over whether increased savings cause growth or whether growth causes increased savings. Undoubtedly, the causation runs both ways.

WHAT LIES BEHIND THE DIFFERENCE IN GROWTH PERFORMANCE?

The different growth performances of East Asia and Latin America have been attributed to their different development strategies. Latin America's growth performance reflects its inward-oriented, input-substitution, protected industrialization policies of the past, while East Asia's reflects its outward-oriented, export-promotion, search for foreign investment, and technology policies of the present. The literature dealing with these development issues contains many such elaborate comparisons of Latin America and East Asia (see for example Adams and Davis, 1994). It should be noted, however, that both regions have experimented with these different development strategies at one time or another. Clearly the move toward outward orientation came much earlier and more definitively in East Asia than in Latin America. Much of the industrialization of Latin America, until the late 1970s, was the result of their import substitution policies. Manufacturing efforts at that time focused on secondary and capital goods used in the production of goods for domestic consumption. Development policy in Taiwan, Korea, and Singapore (though not in Hong Kong) also relied initially on import substitution

TABLE 7.4: Export Growth: Latin America and East Asia

	Export Growth Rates	
	1970-80	**1980-93**
United States	7.0	5.1
Japan	9.2	4.2
East Asia		
Hong Kong	9.9	15.8
Singapore	na	12.7
S. Korea	22.7	12.3
Indonesia	6.5	6.7
Malaysia	3.3	12.6
Philippines	7.2	3.4
Thailand	8.9	15.5
China	8.7	11.5
Average for *East Asian LDCs*	8.4	11.3
Latin America		
Argentina	8.9	3.2
Bolivia	8.6	5.2
Brazil	-4.0	1.7
Chile	9.6	6.6
Colombia	-3.9	2.1
Ecuador	0.1	3.4
Mexico	5.5	5.4
Peru	5.0	-0.3
Uruguay	5.2	2.6
Venezuela	-6.8	1.7
Average for *Latin America*	2.8	3.2

but quickly shifted toward export promotion. Exports of manufactured goods in-creased dramatically here from the mid-1960s through the mid-1980s—at approximately twice the growth rate of Latin America. Not surprisingly, Latin America, in recent years, has shifted its policy toward export promotion as well, but export growth of manufactured goods still lags far behind East Asia.

Why is export-oriented industrialization superior? Outward-looking policies overcome the limitations of domestic markets. The potentials of export markets are larger and grow more rapidly than domestic markets. Export-oriented policies also promote efficiency because exports must be competitive in terms of costs, product specification, and quality.

A characteristic feature of export-oriented industrialization is the structural change that occurs as productivity and real wages rise, shifting comparative advantage from labor-intensive to skill- and technology-intensive industries. The flying geese's pattern of industrial development has been conspicuous in East Asia. This is not just a pattern of leadership by the head "goose," usually represented by Japan, but rather, a linked growth process. The linkage is first to the market, the United States, the European Community, and increasingly of late, Japan. But also, and more important, the linkage is between the East Asian countries themselves. As advancement occurs in one country, its competitive advantage changes as does its industrial mix. Such advancements generally result in industrial activity being passed from the advanced countries to those farther down the development ladder. The gradual shift of labor-intensive industries, such as apparel, from Japan to Taiwan, and then to China and Vietnam, is one example of this process. More advanced countries, like South Korea, Singapore, and Taiwan, are now rapidly turning to capital-intensive, technology-intensive industries. These linkages are much less pronounced in Latin America, where they appear to be more competitive and less complementary.

Macroeconomic policy is another area where clear differences between Latin America and East Asia emerge. One key factor in the economic growth of East Asia is that policy makers have made fiscal stability a priority. East Asian countries have, in general, avoided inflation and have had resources available that allowed increased spending on investment as needed. In Latin America, except Chile, populist governments introduced policies with an inflationary bias that ultimately scaled back private as well as public investment spending.

The monetarization of large public deficits in Latin America was responsible for excess demand inflation. Given the region's existing wage escalation mechanisms, the inflation that resulted desensitized the economy to efforts aimed at reducing aggregate demand. In comparison, Asian countries were more willing to accept the short-run deflationary effects of stabilization policy, except the Philippines—which was much less successful at controlling inflation and consequently growth. Also, East Asia was better able to deal with the debt problem that cost Latin America dearly in the 1980s.

TABLE 7.5. Savings Rates: Latin America and East Asia

Savings Rate (as a percent of GDP)		
1970-80	**1993**	
United States	18.0	15.0
Japan	40.0	33.0
East Asia		
Hong Kong	25.0	31.0
Singapore	18.0	47.0
S. Korea	15.0	35.0
Indonesia	14.0	31.0
Malaysia	27.0	38.0
Philippines	22.0	16.0
Thailand	21.0	36.0
China	29.0	40.0
Average for		
East Asian LDCs	21.4	34.3
Latin America		
Argentina	23.0	na
Bolivia	20.0	21.0
Brazil	24.0	6.0
Chile	20.0	24.0
Colombia	18.0	18.0
Ecuador	14.0	22.0
Mexico	19.0	16.0
Peru	17.0	16.0
Uruguay	10.0	14.0
Venezuela	37.0	18.0
Average for		
Latin America	20.2	15.5

THE ROLE OF THE STATE

Many economists would argue that a critical difference between the performance of Latin America and East Asia lies in the role of the state. One view is that East Asia's remarkable development followed directly from for-ward-looking government policies aimed at favorable terms of trade, economic stability, and industrialization. Scholars, like Robert Wade (1990), have written about the "developmental state" and the use of explicit industrial policies to build the industries that would be the mainstays of industrialization—Japan and South Korea are two such examples. But in other successful countries, the hand of government has been less intrusive, supporting the neoclassical view that all that is really needed is to "get prices right." This view seems to be gaining support around the world as more and more countries lean toward liberalization of markets and non-intervention—a trend more visible in Latin America than in East Asia.

While the debate about government industrial intervention remains unresolved, we do know that in Latin America such direct interference has often backfired—Pemex for example.[2] The welcome news is that privatization and liberalization are proceeding rapidly.

A clear distinction between Latin America and East Asia is with respect to macroeconomic stability. The Asian countries have maintained a stable macroeconomic environment, with a conceptual undervalued exchange rate. In contrast, Latin America has had a very unstable macro environment. In Latin America, present efforts at stabilization are doing so only at the cost of overvalued currencies (in Brazil and Argentina), and/or recession (Mexico).

THE FUTURE

What about the future? Now that Latin America is finally aboard the free market, export oriented, privatization bandwagon, can we expect a pattern of growth as in East Asia? Latin America will find it difficult to match the spectacular strengths of Asia, which has experienced continued growth of about 7.2 percent per year. I have noted that in Asia there is a linked process, with the more advanced countries helping those that are still behind. There is a tradition of export markets to the United States and now to Japan. Such markets are no longer available to South America. Finally, in East Asia there are phenomenal saving rates unmatched anywhere else in the world.

Though the main Latin American countries still have substantial adjustment problems, I am moderately optimistic (see Table 7.1). Growth of GDP for the rest of the decade is projected at 4.5 percent annually. This is almost as good as the 1970-80 period and much better than in the recent past. The trend toward privatization and competition, particularly the move away from inefficient state-owned enterprises, will help. The opening of markets to each other—the Mercosur[3] group is a good example—and to Europe and North America will increase scale of production and competitiveness. Conservative fiscal and monetary policies have already had a significant impact in reducing inflation rates. These are all positives.

Latin America will need to make its own miracle, focusing on domestic as well as foreign markets. That is the challenge for the 21st century.

NOTES

1.This chapter is part of a collaboration between the University of Pennsylvania and the International Center for the Study of East Asian Development (ICSEAD), Kitakyushu, Japan.

2. Pemex (Mexico's state-run petroleum monopoly) is suspected of having generated large fortunes for its managers, union leaders, and private contractors through mismanagement, corruption, and theft. An official at Pemex estimated that 15,000 barrels of fuel were stolen daily through clandestine taps along company's pipeline.

3. Mercosur (the Common Market of the South) includes Argentina, Brazil, Paraguay, and Uruguay.

REFERENCES

Adams, F. G. and I. Davis. (1994). "The Role of Policy in Economic Development: comparisons of the East and Southeast Asian and Latin American Experience." *Asian Pacific Economic Literature*, Vol. 8, no. 1 (May).

Wade, Robert. (1990). *Governing the Market: Economic Theory and the Role of Government in East Asian Industrialization*. Princeton, NJ: Princeton University Press.

8

THE FACTS OF ECONOMIC DEVELOPMENT AND VIRTUOUS CIRCLES

F. Gerard Adams

INTRODUCTION

In response to the question, "What Have We Learned?," I would like first to summarize some stylized facts illustrated by economic development in Latin America and East Asia. I then would like to present a rather different hypothesis. An hypothesis where there are virtuous circles in economic development as well as the traditional vicious ones, and where these virtuous circles account for the spectacular growth that we observe in some parts of the world, but not in others.

THE FACTS OF ECONOMIC DEVELOPMENT

Forty years ago, when I was a graduate student, development economics was assuredly the dismal science. The poor countries had little chance for development because of the vicious circles that dominated their economic evolution. These can be summarized as:

- The poverty problem: poor countries cannot afford to save and invest.
- The human capital/technology problem: poor countries have little human capital and cannot use advanced technology.
- The Malthusian problem: rise in living standards increases population pressure on fixed resources.
- The primary commodity problem: the principal product of developing countries was primary commodities with a low demand elasticity. The more they produced, the less they earned.

These problems meant that poor countries would have great difficulty improving their living standards unless they had aid from the more advanced industrial world or unless it was possible to assure them of reasonable and stable prices for their primary commodity exports (hence the UN Program for Commodities). Paradoxically, some of these vicious circles contain the germ of virtuous circles which can advance economic development.

First we need to consider some long-term economic history. Perhaps the perception that the developing countries would find it difficult to develop reflects some of the old biased stereotypes of Western people with regard to the Third World. The fact is that all the industrial countries were once poor countries reliant on subsistence agriculture. How did they advance themselves to high income levels? Admittedly, some had advantages of abundant resources—the United States, Canada, Argentina—and others may have gained by exploiting their colonial empires. But many of the growth experiences represent what I am going to call "internally generated growth."[1] In Central Europe and Japan, the growth process was largely fueled from within, though obviously there were foreign influences and linkages to neighboring countries that should not be disregarded. In this light, the economic development of East Asia (prior to 1997) and Chile command a rational explanation. The East Asian miracle is miraculous not in the fact that it has taken place, but in the fact that the East Asian countries have accomplished in one or two generations what elsewhere has taken one or two centuries.

Can the experience of East Asia and Latin America be summarized by some stylized facts on which most economists, today, would agree? The most obvious conclusions are:

- Rapid sustained economic growth is possible, even for poor countries without natural resources.
- The engine of growth in Asia has been exports, and certainly outward orientation. A consistently undervalued exchange rate has been useful to maintain external competitiveness.
- But internal development has played an important, if not dominant, role with high rates of domestic saving and the development of internal markets.
- Technology shifts have contributed to rapid growth in the developing countries. The argument about whether there have or have not been gains in total factor productivity is a red herring.[2] Obviously, production in advanced countries is different from less developed countries. Whether the calculation assigns technological change inside or outside the assumed production function is not, after all, a significant consideration.
- The maintenance of economic stability has been an essential ingredient for the sustainability of the growth path. Even for countries that have had the best prospects, domestic or international disequilibria have had damaging consequences.
- As countries mature, coming closer to the technological frontier, even the most successful countries experience slower growth.

There remains considerable disagreement, however, on the role of government. It has been argued that a development policy consistent with anticipated comparative advantage has helped some countries.[3] Others, however, have pushed for privatization and free markets as the essential criteria (Hughes [1980]; World Bank [1993]). There is also disagreement on whether democracy is compatible with rapid sustained growth. Does development require "strong," sometimes thought to be totalitarian, government? In my view, with respect to growth, what counts is what government does, not know what it is!

VICIOUS AND VIRTUOUS CIRCLES

These facts do not suggest that vicious circles prevented economic development either in Latin America or East Asia, though they may well still operate in other parts of the world like Africa. On the contrary, for some periods virtuous circles appear to have benefitted development, though the contrast between East Asia and Latin America points starkly to the need to maintain economic stability.[4]

We suggest here some thoughts on what has been going on in the development process. A striking observation is that the most rapidly growing countries of Asia are also high saving countries. The classic internal and external constraints of Chenery and Strout (1966) still apply. But much less so than if the saving rate were low as in the more mature countries. How can a high savings rate in poor countries be justified? Recourse to the life-cycle hypothesis suggests that the aggregate saving rate is closely related to the anticipated rate of growth. Adams and Prazmowski (1995) show that the anticipation of rising incomes, and presumably consumption standards, will cause increases in the savings rate.[5] The consequence is that in place of low income-low savings, so long as we have anticipated growth, we have low income-high savings rates and rapid growth.

This view also accounts for some of the problems of the stop-go economies. If the expectation of rising incomes is interrupted, so is the need to support rising living standards in the future with high levels of savings today. A stop-go pattern of development is less conducive to savings than a credible sustainable growth pattern.

Another example involves the Malthusian constraint to growth. Traditionally, the assumption is that higher income yields higher birth rates and greater population growth, depressing income per capita in view of a resources constraint. In practice, rising living standards have translated into declining birth rates. The success at reducing birth rates, with improving expectations about income per capita and with urbanization, has been widely noted. It is not only the result of campaigns or government regulations. Initially, declines in death rates more than offset the decline in birth rates, but eventually population equilibrium tends to be reestablished as birth rates decline. The result is that growth yields lower population pressure and greater opportunity for further growth.

Still another phase relates to the transfer of technology between countries during the process of economic advancement. As the mature countries advance and their comparative advantage fades in manufacturing, direct foreign investment and outsourcing transfers their industries to less advanced countries where labor is still cheap. This process has been observed in East Asia, from Japan and, in North America, from the U.S. to Mexico. It depends on the linkages between advanced and less advanced countries like those observed in East Asia. There are similar opportunities in Latin America, but they are not as marked.

The development of human capital also involves some positive feedbacks. Human capital constraints and the lack of skilled labor and management have become apparent in some of the developing countries more quickly than had been anticipated and have driven up wages of skilled workers. Higher income and the expectations of needs for more skilled workers are being met, partially at least, by organizing more advanced education. This is clearly a challenge for the public sector, since private education can go only partway in meeting these needs.

CONCLUSION

The facts of economic development suggest that there are virtuous circles as well as vicious ones. The sustained growth process in East Asia is a reflection of the operation of these mechanisms. They operate in Latin America as well, but they have been interrupted or offset by the domestic and international disequilibria that were allowed to develop in that part of the world.

NOTES

1. I do not mean to link this term firmly to the theories of endogenous growth of Romer (1986), Barro (1991), et. al. While these theories may be useful to explain the growth process, here we mean simply that growth is animated and supported by internal rather than external forces.
2. See Young (1995), Krugman (1994), and Chow (1993).
3. See Wade (1990) and World Bank (1993).
4. See Adams and Davis (1994).
5. Moreover, young countries, that are not yet at age distribution equilibrium, must save in the aggregate since the dependency ratio is still rising.

REFERENCES

Adams, F. G., and I. Davis. (1994). "The Role of Policy in Economic Development: Comparisons of the East and Southeast Asian and Latin American Experience." *Asian Pacific Economic Literature*, Vol. 8, no. 1 (May).

Adams, F. G. and P.A. Prazmowski. (1995). "Why Are Saving Rates in East Asia So High? Reviving The Life Cycle Hypothesis." Presented at the ICSEAD Conference, Kitakyushu, Japan, July.

Barro, Robert J. (1991). "Economic Growth in a Cross Section of Countries." *Quarterly Journal of Economics*, Vol. 106. No. 2: 407-43.

Chenery, H.B. and A. Strout. (1966). "Foreign Assistance and Economic Development." *American Economic Review*, Vol. 56: 679-733.

Chow, Gregory C. (1993). "Capital Formation and Economic Growth in China." *Quarterly Journal of Economics*, Vol. 108: 809-41.

Hughes, H. (1988). *Delivering Industrialization in Asia*. Cambridge: Cambridge University Press

Krugman, Paul. (1994). "The Myth of Asia's Miracle." *Foreign Affairs*, Vol. 73 (November/ December): 62-78.

Romer, Paul M. (1986). "Increasing Returns and Long-Run Growth." *Journal of Political Economy*, Vol. 94, no. 5:1002-37.

Wade, Robert . (1990). *Governing the Market: Economic theory and the Role of Government in East Asian Industrialization*. Princeton, NJ: Princeton University Press.

World Bank. (1993). *The East Asian Miracle: Economic Growth and Public Policy*. New York: Oxford University Press.

Young, Alwyn. (1995). "The Tyranny of Numbers: Confronting the Statistical Realities of the East Asian Growth Experience." *Quarterly Journal of Economics*, Vol. 110, no. 3.

9

THE CUBAN ECONOMY AS SEEN THROUGH FOREIGN TRADE

Jorge Salazar-Carrillo

INTRODUCTION

It is well known that the communist economies consider information of crucial importance during the early stage of the dictatorship of the proletariat. In order to achieve the paradisiac final period of communal bliss, the development and control of the polity is required for what appears to be a number of decades.[1] As a result, statistics on economic matters tend to be restricted in these societies, and when they are published or disseminated in other fashion (as in speeches), they tend to be thoroughly massaged. The objective is to give the impression of continued success in the building of socialism, and to impress foreign investors who might be attracted to provide hard currency investment that may be needed by the system.

In the case of Cuba these traits have been taken to extremes, especially during the decade of the 1990s, after the disappearance of the Soviet bloc in 1989. In fact, that year was the last that the country's statistical abstract (*Anuario Estadistico de Cuba*) was published by the government. The yearly reports of the Cuban central bank (Banco Nacional de Cuba) to its international creditors have also disappeared, even though of restricted circulation to begin with. Apparently to commemorate its 45th anniversary the institution published in August 1995 an *Economic Report, 1994*, which is so difficult to obtain that it almost constitutes a clandestine operation, although it seems to be addressed to the lenders from whom Cuba is requesting a rescheduling of its massive debt.

In addition, it has been shown that Cuba has been particularly prone to be evasive about the economic information that it publishes or spreads about, to fulfill whichever purposes it might have at the moment.[2] And given that Cubans emphasize that it is going through a "Special Period,"[3] which has heightened its paranoia with respect to the fragility of its economy, it can be expected that the mendacity of the minuscule information provided by the Island is at its high point.

A cherished exercise of international economists becomes very useful under such circumstances: the continuous checking of the international trade statistics depending on the country originating the information. In order to establish true intercountry flows it is useful to parse the reports of both the exporting and importing countries to insure that the statistics match. Of course, care has to be exercised on the comparability of the flows being examined, as points of origin express their values in terms of FOB, while destinations value at CIF levels. Generally it is accepted that the reliability of the statistics is higher in those countries having the most advanced economic and political systems. This leads to the placing of a higher confidence in the numbers obtained from the developed countries. This approach fits well the purpose of enlightening the black hole of Cuban foreign trade statistics, which, whenever emitting some light waves of information, has to be suspected of distorting self-interest in order to present the best color possible.

For the purpose at hand the recently issued publication *Cuba: Handbook of Trade Statistics, 1996* (from now on referred to as the *Handbook*) published by the Directorate of Intelligence of the Central Intelligence Agency, in November 1996, will be utilized. As the publication states, its purpose is to compile "statistics on Cuban trade for the period 1990 through September 1996 . . . from the data of Havana's trade partners. This handbook provides a detailed substitute for the official statistics that the Cuban Government published yearly before 1990 in its Anuario Estadistico de Cuba."[4] Given that for practically all countries in the world there is no interest in mal- or misreporting their international trade statistics, it would seem that this approach would allow us a glimpse of Cuban trade relations, on which to base an analysis that would indirectly indicate the status of this economy.

The country characteristics of Cuba's international trade flows will be examined first, followed by its commodity composition. Finally the total numbers for exports and imports will be addressed, and an analysis of the Cuban economy through its external sector will end the study. Generally the period covered is that of 1989 to 1995, and in some cases 1996, although the last two years are consecutively estimated and projected.

It should be underlined that other sources of foreign trade statistics were considered to verify the accuracy of the *Handbook* used as a basis for this chapter. Particularly the *Direction of Trade Statistics Yearbook* published quarterly and annually by the International Monetary Fund was the most reputable (see Appendix Tables 9.1 and 9.2). It was found, however, that, like similar sources from other world bodies (United Nations, GATT, etc.), they lacked in in their reflection of trade among Cuba and the former Soviet Union and other CMEA (Council of Mutual Economic Assistance) countries of Central and Eastern

Europe. Not only did the *Handbook* include this information, but it was more conservative in the numbers attributed to Cuban trade in goods—by this meaning that the numbers are higher than those reported in *Direction of Trade Statistics Yearbook*. Finally, the country shares and the trade flows are quite similar on both sources.

CHARACTERISTICS OF GEOGRAPHICAL TRADE FLOWS

The total exports of goods of Cuba to different countries of the world by major geographic areas are listed in Table 9.1. Only the most important nations are depicted, for the period 1989 to 1995. As can be seen, Cuban exports imploded in between these two years. The latter values represent only 30 percent of the earlier. But if we consider that the U.S. dollar lost 23 percent of its value to inflation[5] during this span, in real terms 1995 exports represent only 24 percent of the 1989 figures.

Russia is no longer still the principal country of destination six years after the drastic political and economic realignment of the world, which led to the breakdown of the Soviet Union into many independent states. The 1989 to 1991 Russian data are not available but between 1992[6] and 1995 the export of Cuban goods to that country fell by close to 70 percent in nominal terms, with no other country taking up the slack.

The principal market for Cuban goods has become Canada, which has multiplied its imports in current terms by six. However, the absolute gain is from a very small base ($52 million (U.S.) in 1989) so that the absolute increase was only $182 million in nominal terms, equivalent to $148 million if discounted by price increases. The second largest taker of Cuban exports is China. Yet, compared with 1989 the values show a slight decline in current terms (see Table 9.1).

A similar depiction can be obtained from Table 9.2, where the values of imports of goods are shown. The decline in total imports has been slightly less than with exports, with the former falling to 35 percent of its 1989 nominal values, and 28 percent in real terms. But here it is possible to envisage that Russia has been supplanted by Spain and Mexico as the principal Cuban suppliers.[7] There has been a diversification of imports away from the old Soviet world, which appears to be more drastic when contrasted with the picture that emerged for exports. This applies even to China, another old communist country, which has become a less significant supplier as well (compare Table 9.2).

If we look at the trade statistics reported by other countries for Cuba, they appear to show that economic activity in the Island, which is closely tied to exports and imports,[8] hit rock bottom in 1993-94 (which are practically the same in real terms), and to have shown a discernible rise in 1995.

TABLE 9.1. Exports by Country of Destination, 1989-95 (in millions of US$)

	1989	1990	1991	1992	1993	1994	1995
TOTAL	5,392	4,910	3,550	2,030	1,275	1,385	1,600
Europe							
Finland	18	19	19	18	18	21	N.A.
France	61	52	61	44	39	44	57
Germany	21	23	19	21	14	25	36
Italy	45	52	48	51	33	50	53
Netherlands	26	22	40	26	25	24	42
Portugal	23	19	18	27	35	48	24
Russia	N.A.	N.A.	N.A.	632	436	301	196
Spain	91	80	91	85	65	78	96
United Kingdom	56	54	32	23	13	16	13
Near East/ Asia							
China	229	306	202	183	74	121	214
Japan	133	95	142	115	51	63	89
Americas							
Brazil	32	102	28	16	10	57	N.A.
Canada	52	112	133	212	132	142	234
Mexico	21	53	13	7	4	12	6
Venezuela	26	9	18	20	3	5	2
Africa							
Algeria	81	70	53	54	49	31	N.A.
Libya	3	56	29	0	0	0	N.A.

Source: CIA, *Handbook*, 1996.

N.A. = not available

TABLE 9.2. Imports by Country of Origin, 1989-95 (in millions of US$)

	1989	1990	1991	1992	1993	1994	1995
Total	8,124	6,745	3,690	2,235	1,990	2,025	2,825
Europe							
Belgium/ Luxembourg	35	45	40	22	52	33	N.A.
France	49	69	63	90	127	133	148
Germany	124	100	123	59	40	41	70
Italy	81	108	158	102	65	63	81
Netherlands	38	38	36	42	55	50	71
Russia	N.A.	N.A.	N.A.	N.A.	249	237	N.A.
Spain	216	303	285	199	191	289	395
United Kingdom	87	67	50	50	21	40	30
Near East/ Asia							
China	212	272	224	200	177	147	146
Japan	54	73	36	18	18	24	19
Americas							
Argentina	187	163	99	63	72	48	N.A.
Brazil	62	85	66	17	19	25	N.A.
Canada	132	133	114	100	107	84	200
Colombia	27	20	20	14	20	35	18
Mexico	108	103	106	117	188	269	353
Venezuela	15	464	49	79	120	90	38

Source: CIA, *Handbook*, 1996.
            NA = not available

THE COMPOSITION OF COMMERCE IN GOODS

If attention is focused on the value of commodity exports as depicted in Table 9.3, it is clearly seen that sugar and its derivatives still account for well over one half of total Cuban exports, notwithstanding the crisis affecting this sector. This makes evident the weakness of the other export activities of Cuba. It is remarkable that after promising to repay Cuban loans to the European countries and Japan in the early to middle 1980s on the strength of nontraditional exports, after about ten years these are still weak. So much investment in biotechnology was to the detriment of other alternatives that could have brought relief to the basic necessities of the people, only to reap an average of $78 million a year in the exportation of these goods between 1991 and 1995. Yet this is the only sector showing expansion. After many years of hearing about Canadian investments in nickel, it is found that it only accounts for $220 million of exports in 1995 (down from $485 million in 1989). Finally, tobacco exports have remained stagnant in value terms, which implies reduction in volumes given the steep rise in cigar prices. In sum, the composition of Cuban exports is practically unchanged since 1989, with heavy concentration on sugar and a primary commodity bent, in contrast with developing economy trends.

In Table 9.4 the commodity composition of import values is shown. The principal item in this list is fuels, which represents 30 percent of the total value. The importation of this essential component of energy supply has shrunk to 32 percent of what it was in 1989. It is well known how much this reduction straightjackets the performance of the Cuban economy, but its substantial dependence on food imports from the outside world is not as well understood. This is highlighted by the statistics showing that this category is second in importance, representing over 20 percent of imports. Of the rest, machinery represents the most crucial, since it reflects future levels of production. It is shocking to realize that at $360 million in 1995, these essential import have slid dramatically, and now represent 19 percent of the level attained in 1989. (The same trends are shown by transport equipment, although this category partly represents consumption.) In addition, they constitute a minuscule share of Cuban importation (less than 13 percent).[9] As a proxy for overall investment in small open economies like Cuba, this bodes ill for future economic growth in the Island, which is devoid of a capital-goods-producing sector.

TOURISM AND FOREIGN INVESTMENT

A rather desolate panorama of Cuban economic activity emerges from the trade in goods reported by its trading partners. The bleakness is underlined if other traits of the external sector of the Cuban economy are brought to bear. To wit, there has been an expansion in the number of tourists who have visited the Island. Even though reliable statistics, as have been presented here, are not available, re-

TABLE 9.3. Commodity Exports, 1989-95 (in millions of U.S.$)

	1989	1990	1991	1992	1993	1994	1995
Total Exports	5,392	4,910	3,550	2,030	1,275	1,375	1,600
Sugar, molasses, and honey	3,959	3,690	2,670	1,300	820	785	890
Fish	127	125	115	120	90	110	115
Fruit	139	150	100	50	50	80	35
Tobacco	85	95	100	95	75	80	90
Nickel	485	400	245	200	120	110	220
Med. Products	58	130	50	50	20	110	125
Other	473	320	270	235	100	110	125

Source: CIA, *Handbook*, 1996.

ports from Western observers in Cuba and travel agents abroad attest to a significant rise in visitors during the 1990s. Yet this activity is necessarily accompanied by an increase in imports dedicated to feed, house, entertain, and otherwise service this enclave sector. Once account is taken of the value of such imported goods, the fall of Cuban imports for internal consumption and production since 1989 would loom even larger.

Another claimed characteristic of the Cuban economy during the 1990s is an increase in foreign direct investment. If this were believable, our depressing picture of a total collapse of the Cuban economy would be even sorrier. Once again, no hard statistics are to be found on this matter, so no discounting of imports really directed to a foreign company enclave can be safely done.[10] This is supported by the statistics presented here showing that very little of Cuban imports have been under the category of machinery and transport equipment. If anything, all indications are that Soviet bloc direct investments in the Island were much higher up to the very early 1990s, and have now virtually vanished.

The latter point portends a worsening of the future performance of the Cuban economy, adding to the litany of negative factors exposed in the foreign trade numbers during the first half of the 1990s. Even though the tables have covered both exports and imports of goods, the latter have been emphasized because they provide the best indirect measurement of production and internal consumption in Cuba. The availability of fuels and foodstuffs, jointly representing over half of total importation, in addition to essential intermediate products, provide the most reliable estimates of what is happening to the gross domestic product of the Island.

TABLE 9.4. Commodity Imports, 1989-95 (in millions of U.S.$)

	1989	1990	1991	1992	1993	1994	1995
Total Imports	8,124	6,745	3,690	2,235	1,990	2,055	2,825
Food	1,011	840	720	450	490	430	605
Raw materials	307	240	140	40	35	25	90
Fuels	2,598	1,950	1,240	835	750	750	835
Chemical products	530	390	270	170	150	180	285
Semifinished goods	838	700	425	195	180	220	390
Machinery	1,922	1,790	615	350	235	240	360
Transport equipment	609	590	170	125	80	110	100
Consumer goods	276	225	90	50	50	80	130
Other	33	20	20	20	20	20	25

Source: CIA, Handbook, 1996.

Although exports did arrest their decline in 1994, and managed an almost 16 percent growth over the 1994 figures, they still cannot provide but one-fourth of their foreign exchange earning power in 1989. With less room to continue financing trade deficits[11] of over $1 billion a year, like that experienced in 1995, it is difficult to envisage an upturn in imports in the near future. Thus, the much-reported recovery of the Cuban GDP will probably be short-lived.

CONCLUSION AND POLICY IMPLICATIONS

Imports and exports of Cuba in 1995, in real terms, stand at implosion levels when compared with those of 1989.[12] The Cuban level of GDP at constant prices bears a similar historical relationship of particularly mimicking import trends. There is not much hope for a turnaround of the economy of Cuba given the evident low levels of investment, and the economy's bent on yesterday's traditional pattern of export specialization.

The window-dressing reforms of the Cuban economy are evidently not helping. Unless some profound changes are implemented, Cuba cannot expect to turn around its economic performance and make up for the slump that has afflicted its economy since 1989, cutting it by more than one-half.[13] The economy has to be increasingly privatized, and economic freedoms and market processes instituted, before domestic and foreign economic agents feel secure to invest in the future. This, together with decisive trade liberalization, are the only roads that would lead to the Island's participation in the subcontracting and partial assembly activities of the world global manufacturing factory, leading the country toward the increasing abandonment of its retrograde primary-product pattern of exports.

APPENDIX: A RECONSTRUCTION OF CUBAN TRADE PATTERNS BASED ON HISTORICAL RECORDS

Although the *Handbook* used to explore Cuban trade patterns is only concerned about recent trade, the International Monetary Fund's *Direction of Trade Statistics Yearbook* has covered intercountry commerce for many years. First it was a supplement to that organization's *International Financial Statistics*, published originally as an annual, covering several years. Later it became a stand-alone *Yearbook*. Lately, it also comes out as a quarterly periodical. As in the Central Intelligence Agency's publication, the statistics reflect the value of trade in nominal (not adjusted for inflation) dollars. However, this source is not as complete, detailed, and reliable as the *Handbook* for the 1990s, while being largely consistent with it, particularly if trade with the former Soviet bloc is excluded.

In Appendix Table 9.1 the exports of Cuba, by country of destination, are shown for the years 1958 to 1962. The most remarkable figures in the table have to do with total exports, which drop from $732 million in 1958 to $402 million in 1962. This represents a drop of 45 percent in four years, which was less steep than the drop of 76 percentage points between 1989 and 1993. The earlier drop was all accounted for by the breaking of diplomatic relations with the United States, which brought about a drop of exports from Cuba of $484 million. The more recent decline has to be due to the change in economic system in the USSR, which opened those markets to competition, and as a result made them accessible to the products of other nations. However, detailed data on the USSR and Russian imports from Cuba are not available to factually substantiate what appears to be a safe conclusion.

In the main text it has been established that foreign trade statistics can be considered the most reliable instrumental variable for total GDP under the circumstances of statistics in Cuba during the 1989-93 time period. The same could be applied to the 1958-62 span, in which the statistical system of Cuba fell in total disarray. Thus, it can be concluded that the major trauma afflicting the Cuban economy during these crucial transition periods of modified export orientation have probably constituted a substantial part of the process of immiserization suffered by the economy of the Island since the late 1950s. It is

APPENDIX TABLE 9.1. Exports by Country of Destination, 1958-62
(in millions of US$)

TRADE WITH	EXPORTS				
	1958	1959	1960	1961	1962
Total	732	638	630	486	402
United States	491	445	357	35	7
Canada	16	10	7	5	3
United Kingdom	37	9	20	15	20
France	8	9	13	1	2
Germany (West)	7	14	9	2	6
Italy	1	1	1	0	0
Netherlands	16	17	12	4	4
Spain	18	6	10	9	8
USSR	14	13	104	312	234
Germany (East)	0	0	4	12	0
Poland	0	0	9	24	19
Brazil	1	3	3	0	0
Colombia	3	2	1	0	0
Mexico	1	1	1	0	0
Venezuela	3	9	1	0	0
Neth Antilles	7	6	1	0	0
Trinidad-Tobago	1	1	0	0	0
Syria	3	2	5	5	4
Morocco	12	13	19	7	22
Japan	47	28	18	24	36
China	4	0	0	0	0

Source: IMF, *Direction of Trade Statistics Yearbook*, several years.

interesting to note that the estimated shrinkages in the GDP of the country that would parallel the export drops were more serious in the 1990s. The explanation will be explored below, as it is noted that the USSR picked up an important share (almost 50 percent) of the export loss to the United States. Unfortunately for the Cuban economy, no nation could play the same role in the early nineties.

If the direction of exports depicted in Appendix Table 9.1 are considered from a geographical standpoint, it seems clear that the US market was the bread and butter of Cuban exports in 1958-60. After that it practically disappeared. The other major markets, Japan and the United Kingdom, represented about 10 percent of the U.S. market. As mentioned before, the USSR geared up its agreement with the Island by 1960, taking then more than seven times the exports it had absorbed from Cuba in 1958. It should be noted that Canada and Spain (and much less Mexico and China) did not represent significant markets for Cuban exports during this time frame.

In Appendix Table 9.2 data are presented corresponding to Cuban imports from the rest of the world from 1958 to 1962. The contraction in imports is of 36 percent between these years, smaller than what it exports, but still a damaging blow to any open economy, which Cuba clearly was then.[14] The rate of decline of U.S. imports to the nation was more or less in line with what happened on the export side. But with respect to the USSR, the build up of imports was even faster than what happened on the other side of the ledger. The former Soviet Union had nil imports into the Cuban economy in 1958 and 1959, and by 1961 was supplying more imports to the Island than the latter imported from the United States in 1960, when political ties had not yet been broken. By 1962 it was shipping $371 million in goods to Cuba.

The principal sources of goods to the economy of Cuba before the advent of Castro communism, of course after the United States by far, were Venezuela, the United Kingdom, and West Germany. It is interesting to note that the former country, a Latin American one, was the second largest trading partner of Cuba, representing 12 percent of total U.S. supplies to Cuba in that year, basically in terms of oil imports. These countries rapidly vanished toward zero by the end of 1962 (with East Germany substituting its inferior exports for those previously supplied by Bonn). It is also noteworthy that Poland had become a significant trader with Cuba, actually its second largest source of imports by 1962. Again the major exporters to Cuba in the 1990s— Mexico, Canada and Spain—were not significant ones in the early 1960s, and suffered severe contractions in their Cuban imports during the earlier period (particularly noticeable with Spanish imports). Which suggests that these countries have built a trade relationship with Cuba on the basis of opportunism, and not in terms of being natural trading partners with the Island (which, in contrast, Venezuela could easily be).

Unfortunately the IMF statistical sources, which internationally are considered the most reliable, do not provide a breakdown of foreign trade by type of good. The next alternative source providing these data are the United Nations various *Year-*

APPENDIX TABLE 9.2. Imports by Country of Origin, 1958-62
(in millions of US$)

TRADE WITH	IMPORTS				
	1958	1959	1960	1961	1962
Total	777	692	470	514	496
United States	543	437	223	14	13
Canada	18	16	13	32	11
United Kingdom	22	43	21	13	7
France	7	14	11	6	2
Germany (West)	24	30	15	12	6
Italy	11	8	5	4	1
Netherlands	7	8	8	11	8
Spain	13	8	10	4	1
USSR	0	0	71	276	371
Germany (East)	0	0	3	28	0
Poland	0	0	4	23	20
Brazil	2	0	0	0	1
Colombia	0	2	0	0	0
Mexico	5	2	1	3	1
Venezuela	67	56	28	1	3
Neth Antilles	3	9	5	4	5
Morocco	0	2	0	3	5
Japan	5	10	6	12	11
China	0	0	0	0	0

Source: IMF, *Direction of Trade Statistics Yearbook*, several years.

book of International Trade Statistics published during the years 1958 to 1962. The problem with the latter source mainly stems from the acceptance of statistical data supplied by the member countries, without adjusting and checking them to assure consistency with the flows reported by their trade partners. It is here that the *Direction of Trade* statistics stand out.

Nevertheless, in Appendix Tables 9.3 and 9.4 an attempt is made to provide orders of magnitude of the patterns of commodity exports and imports in the Island. The relative shares in question are less affected by the distortions in the absolute numbers that the *Yearbooks* probably bear. Turning first to exports, it is evident that Appendix Table 9.3 depicts a country that is a textbook case of a monoculture. If anything, the traditional dependence on sugar and its by-products for Cuba's foreign exchange earnings was exacerbated somewhat by 1962, with almost 83 percent of exports attributable to these items. In contrast with other developing countries of the world, by 1989 the nation's export earnings were still so heavily concentrated on sugar products (73.4 percent according to Table 9.3) that the economy of Cuba had to be considered one of the most dependent on a single product export, and a relatively low priced one at that. So much can be said of an economy by examining its structure of commerce, that it is clear that the diversification, industrialization, and branching into services characteristic of economic growth had not occurred in the Cuban economy just before the demise of the Soviet communist bloc.

Turning now to imports, shown in Appendix Table 9.4, it can be seen that the importation of machinery was about as important in 1962 as in 1958. The same was the case for transport equipment. In contrast to the transition from a market-oriented to a command economy between 1958 and 1962, on which the share of investment in importation did not suffer, the most recent reversal from the communist system to free world trade has seen a plunge in the participation of capital goods imports to levels about half those of 1989 in machinery, and even less than that for transports. (According to Table 9.4, imports of machinery in 1995 represented only 12.74 percent of total imports, and imports of transport equipment only 3.54 percent. Both shares were down from their 1989 levels of 23.6 and 7.49 percent, respectively.) Thus it is evident that the disruption suffered by the economy in question in its recent transition has been more damaging than the one in the early 1960s, and that after several years of low investment this will compromise its ability to grow for the next seven or eight years. Unless, of course, there are substantial amounts of aid and subsidized lending that would come forth.

APPENDIX TABLE 9.3. Commodity Exports, 1958 and 1962
(in percentages*)

	1958	1962
Sugar/molasses and honey	80.1	82.9
Fruits and vegetables	0.0	1.2
Tobacco	6.7	4.8
Nickel and other metals	3.8	7.3
Textiles and apparel	1.2	0.8
Other	7.9	0.3

*Percentages may not add to 100.0 because of rounding.
Source: United Nations, *Yearbook of International Statistics.*

APPENDIX TABLE 9.4. Commodity Imports, 1958 and 1962
(in percentages*)

	1958	1962
Food	14.4	23.3
Raw materials	9.6	5.7
Fuels	12.9	11.6
Chemical products	4.8	9.5
Semifinished goods	10.5	21.9
Machinery	19.2	16.7
Transport equipment	6.9	9.5
Consumer and other goods	21.7	2.0

*Percentages may not add to 100.0 because of rounding.
Source: United Nations, *Yearbook of International Statistics.*

NOTES

1. It came to seven in the case of the Soviet Union before its demise.
2. Consult Jorge Salazar-Carrillo (1986).
3. See Banco Nacional de Cuba, *Economic Report, 1994* p.3.
4. Refer to Central Intelligence Agency, *Cuba: Handbook of Trade Statistics, 1996* p. iii.
5. This information was supplied by the Bureau of Labor Statistics, Consumer Index section, in Washington D.C.
6. In 1992 Russia was by far the major importer of Cuban wares.
7. As recent as 1993 Russia was still the principal exporter to Cuba.
8. For evidence along these lines, see Jorge Salazar-Carrillo (985).
9. In 1989 this ratio represented close to 24 percent of total imports.
10. Western sources in the Island and multinational companies abroad have not confirmed the claims of Cuba that significant amounts of foreign direct investments have trekked in.
11. The straits faced by Cuba in attracting foreign indirect investment flows stem from its high foreign indebtedness and the fact that most of it is now on default. This is why it is restricted to very short term suppliers credit or cooperative arrangements by Cuban export buyers, at usury like interest rates.
12. As recent as 1993 Russia was still the principal exporter to Cuba.
13. See Jorge Salazar-Carrillo, "The Present Condition and the Rebuilding of the Cuban Economy" in Antonio Jorge and Jorge Salazar-Carrillo, eds., *The Economics of the Caribbean: Present and Future Trends*, Stockholm University, 1997.
14. It should be noted that the Cuban economy was as open in 1989 as it was thirty one years earlier. This is not only evident from comparing the estimates at both ends of the time span, but also realizing that Cuba became a provider of the same goods to the Soviet Union (and later the CMEA) that is used to supply to the United States, and imported practically the same goods from one and the other. The Island never embarked, unlike its Latin American sister nations, in a process of import-substituting industrialization.

REFERENCES

Banco Nacional de Cuba. (various years). *Economic Report.* Havana.

Central Intelligence Agency. (various years). *Cuba: Handbook of Trade Statistics*, Langley, Virginia.

Horowitz, Irving Louis. (1977). "Cuba 1997." In *Vital Speeches*, February 1, 1997.

International Monetary Fund. (various years). *Direction of Trade Statistics Yearbook.* Washington, D.C.

Salazar-Carrillo, Jorge. (1986). "Is the Cuban Economy Knowable?" *Caribbean Review,* Spring.

_____. (1995). "Interdependence and Economic Performance in Cuba." In Irving Louis Horowitz, (ed.), *Cuban Communism.* Sumerset, NJ: Transaction.

_____. (1997). "The Present Condition and the Rebuilding of the Cuban Economy." In Antonio Jorge and Jorge Salazar-Carrillo, (eds.), *The Economics of the Caribbean: Present and Future Trends.* Stockholm: Stockholm University Press.

United Nations. (various years). *Yearbook of International Trade Statistics.* New York.

10

DEBT AND DEVELOPMENT IN LATIN AMERICA IN THE GLOBAL ECONOMY

Antonio Jorge and Raul Moncarz

INTRODUCTION

This chapter considers the external debt crisis (which perhaps should be called the eternal debt crisis) of Latin America in four stages. First, we explore how the debt problem came to be as onerous as it is today, and what led up to this current state of affairs. Second, we discuss some reasons why advanced countries should be worried about letting Latin America stew in its own handling of foreign debt. Third, we examine what Latin America has done thus far to cope with its bourgeoning debt problem. We also look at the region's recent economic performance and what it means to the global economy. And fourth, we offer some possible solutions for avoiding or minimizing the impact of future shocks. It will be shown that as long as there is a contagion of debt, the eternalness of the debt problem should only arouse interest, not deep concern.

EVOLUTION OF THE DEBT CRISIS

The origins of the crises that erupted in 1982, and again in 1990 and 1994, can be traced back to the state of the world economy in the 1950s and earlier. What happened during the 1950s was a resumption of trade patterns that, earlier in this century, had led to successful growth—when all the worlds' economies were positively influenced by a then thriving international economy. But those trade patterns did not yield the same results, and a lot had changed in the international economy since the "good old days." The post-World War I years ushered in a restless and reckless era that led to the U.S. stock market crash of 1929 and a worldwide recession. What followed was a defensive environment that was extremely hostile to the international economy, as country after country began to erect trade barriers. Only after World War II did this attitude toward the international economy soften, and only then was it allowed to return to the relative levels once achieved in the 1910s. Slowly at first, debt ratios in Latin America began to build. From the region's indicators at the time (from this historical perspective), we can see why problems began cropping up as early as the 1960s.

While there were some similarities, the international economy after the 1950s was quite different from what it had been at the turn of the century. For one, developing countries were more actively involved in the world economy between the 1950s and 1970s, something that had not been the case earlier in the century. This meant increased competition among them. For another, there was an environment of decontrol, floating exchange rates, and other deregulating measures that were starting to take hold. This is illustrated by the emergence of the Organization of Petroleum Exporting Countries (OPEC), an oil-producing cartel—made up of mostly developing countries—that wrestled control of this crucial commodity away from the major oil companies of the West. The severe worldwide inflation and recession that followed the oil price shocks of the 1970s caused the U.S., Japan, and other major countries of the West to take counter-measures—curbing demand and increasing real interest rates—as they saw their hegemony over the international economy wane.

The 1980s and 1990s brought in a new era of rapid changes and significant transformations in national economies around the world. Under the banner of "free trade," the U.S. economy led the way in stimulating the growth of the international economy and dampening its inflationary creep. Other industrial countries followed suit. What has prevailed since is a pattern of disinflation in domestic, world, and financial markets that continues even today, to varying degrees. Another wrinkle to be added here is the breakdown of the Soviet empire in the 1990s. Its consequent move to global markets also influenced the international economy in ways that now echo the new buzz words: privatization, deregulation, and globalization.

In the specific case of Latin America, the debt crisis had both international and domestic causes rooted in the 1970s, though as mentioned earlier, the origins can be traced to the postwar years.[1] In its most direct and immediate sense, the crisis can be seen as the result of the severe worldwide recession that followed the second oil shock of 1979-80, combined with the sudden rise in real interest rates and the contraction of capital inflows which occurred again in the 1990s.[2]

IMPACT OF THE LATIN AMERICAN DEBT ON DEVELOPED ECONOMIES

Why should the debt problems of Latin America draw so much attention in the West? Why not allow these countries to solve their own problems? What payoffs can the developed countries expect if they come to the rescue? To answer these questions straightforwardly, we need to consider the current size and growth potential of these Latin economies. In 1997 the gross domestic product of Latin

America was roughly $1,400 billion, which is not insignificant when compared to the total size of the world economy. Total disbursed external debt outstanding in the region was $622 billion in 1996. As for growth potential, the region's average annual growth rate during the 1990s was around 3 percent, with wide fluctuations around this average. While not great, the performance is far better than that of the 1980s, where average annual growth rates were not even close to 1 percent. In fact, the lackluster performance of the past decade resulted in an 8.3 percent decline in per capita income throughout the region.

While the average growth rate for the 1990s has been positive, it is important to note that this regional average conceals wide differences in each country's economic performance—some have performed far better than others, according to the data collected by the Inter-American Development Bank.[3] Although these Latin countries initiated trade liberalization programs in the early 1980s with a view to opening their economies to international trade, in reality they are still relatively closed, especially when compared to the countries of the Pacific Basin and Europe. Brazil, by far the largest country in the region, is a case in point—trade with the rest of the world (exports and imports combined) represented less than 12 percent of its GDP in 1996.[4]

Another consideration here is the size of the Latin American market. By the mid-1980s, it had already achieved a market size very close to that of the then European Community in the 1960s. This makes it one of the largest untapped markets for the products, investments, technology, and know-how from the West.[5]

To those who may ask, What are Latin America's immediate prospects ?, consider this: By the year 2000, its population is expected to approach 600 million, which is more than twice that of the United States and double that of the European Union. By then, its GDP (as measured in 1985 prices) will have grown to about $1.5 trillion, or approximately half that of the U.S. GDP in 1985. This last figure is something the Western world cannot afford to ignore. On the other hand, although its total foreign debt will surpass the $700 billion mark by the end of the millennium, it will not have grown as fast in this decade as it had between 1980 and 1990. Looking into the next century, Latin America is certainly positioned to be one of the major trading blocs in the world, rivaling the European Union and the Pacific Basin in importance and of keen interest to the United States as a powerful neighbor. On the other hand, we should not lose sight of the fact that in exchange for past loans, the developed countries have extracted a series of economic concessions that are of questionable benefit to the indebted countries, yet of certain advantage to the big banks and corporations that acquired majority shares at fire-sale prices.[6]

From a political perspective, it is important to realize that while there is a multiplicity of views about the future of Central America, the Caribbean, and the Southern Hemisphere, Latin America is now beginning to speak with one voice. Consider, for example, the *Contadora Group*, a home-grown Latin-American organization that attempted to negotiate peace settlements in Nicaragua and El

Salvador in the mid-1980s, despite serious reservations and reticence on the part of the U.S. Another example of this united front is the *Cartagena Declaration,* which was signed by the heads of state of Bolivia, Colombia, Ecuador, Peru, and Venezuela in 1991 to prevent the introduction of weapons of mass destruction on Latin American and Caribbean soil. Representatives of these signatory countries still meet regularly to address security issues and to strengthen cooperation throughout the region. One of the group's objectives now is to press for a common "Latin American point-of-view" on debt-related matters.

Another important consideration is the wave of regionalism and multilateralism that is sweeping the region. There are at least 30 free-trade agreements in Latin America now, and another six regional agreements that include Latin America, Canada, and the United States.[7] Latin America will surely be playing an increasing role on the international stage. It is for this reason and all the other reasons above that Latin-America's debt crisis must become a policy priority of the industrialized countries.

SUGGESTIONS FOR IMPROVING DEBT MANAGEMENT POLICIES

How is Latin America managing its debt at the moment? Latin American exports contributed much to adjustment and growth in 1996, as it had over the last 12 years. Expansion of exports averaged around $15 billion per year from 1987 to 1996. The average annual growth rate was 4.9 percent from 1980 to 1990 and 10 percent from 1990 to 1996. Despite this impressive growth, their exports have been losing purchasing power to the tune of some 21 percent from 1980 to 1990, as a result of the deteriorating terms of trade.[8] Since 1994 through 1996, the terms of trade have improved at a decreasing rate for a total gain of 7.3 percent.

As for imports, they also increased at an annual average rate of 18.5 percent over the period 1990 to 1996 or, in absolute terms, from $144 billion to $304 billion, respectively. The commercial account, which once boasted a surplus balance of $25 billion in 1987, deteriorated to a deficit balance of $34 billion in 1996. The current account balance was also in deficit in 1996, to the tune of $37 billion, and this deficit has been increasing steadily since 1991.

At roughly $33 billion in 1996, foreign direct investment accounted for over half the net capital flows to the region, or nearly 2 percent of GDP. This compares favorably with 1992 and 1993, when foreign direct investment accounted for only about a third of total capital inflows, though the 1996 figure is somewhat lower than those recorded during 1994 and 1995.[9]

Latin America transferred resources abroad to the tune of $217 billion from 1987 to 1990. Since 1990, and until 1996, the net contribution of resources transferred to the region has been positive, amounting to $100 billion.[10] Not surprisingly, the share of real investment in GDP collapsed in the early 1980s, and only began to recover in the 1990s. Since then, the investment ratio has risen from 16.5 of GDP in 1990 to 19.2 percent in 1996.[11]

During the 1990s, the basic policy measures for managing the debt crisis in the 1980s were kept in place, such as privatization, preferences for private investment, deregulation, trade liberalization, and fiscal and monetary discipline, among others. The process has been gradual but cumulative. Today, all the countries of the region have adopted some kind of policy reform package and almost all have become more outward looking—with rising *exports-to-GDP* ratios, but also with rising *imports-to-GDP* ratios at even faster rates.[12] Associated with this outward looking trend is a gradual yet noticeable alteration in the distribution of income and pattern of growth that does not particularly favor the working class. This has prompted Boulmer-Thomas[13] among others to comment that "if the new neo-liberal paradigm in Latin American economic policymaking is to imitate the Chilean success story, then time is not on Latin America's side." In general, the consensus is that recent growth has been less than anticipated, and, as a result, increases in social expenditures have been minimal. When one looks at the trade liberalization and labor market reforms of the 1980s and 1990s, they appear to have hurt the low-skilled wage earner most. Also worth noting is that the transfer of assets, especially via privatization, has produced a sharp fall in real wages and a deterioration in the distribution of income.[14]

It can be said from this brief analysis of Latin America's recent performance in the international economy that things have not gone too badly for them, given the adverse circumstances that other countries have faced over the same time period. Nevertheless, the terms of trade for the long term have deteriorated, while protectionism and slackened growth in many countries have restricted the size and scope of their foreign markets. Given this situation, it is surprising that the region's GDP grew at all, never mind that it grew faster than the region's population (which is growing about 2.4 percent a year). What is urgently needed now is to ensure that the region's per capita GDP continues to grow and that this growth remains a foreign policy goal of the U.S., as recognized in the formulation of the Baker and Brady Plans. The concept of growth with domestic and economic adjustment is a major overall contribution to the intellectual vision and the policy approach to the debt crisis.

As to the formulation of definitive solutions to the crisis, specific proposals have never seemed truly effective thus far. Yet there are general propositions that should be considered as premises from which to derive wide-ranging policy measures. First, the close and independent relationship between debt, development, and trade should be acknowledged. Second, it should be recognized that world economic conditions, as they pertain to commerce and finance, are the principal exogenous determinants of the degree of amelioration of the debt crunch. Nothing can really help as much as a growing healthy international economy. Third, we must understand that policy coordination among the leading economies in the world is essential. Economic summits are important tools of the world economy. The Group of Seven has been leading economic coordination efforts among the Western economies, which have included monetary, fiscal, and exchange-rate policies. In order to address the problem at hand, it would appear that extending policy coordination to areas such as diminishing protectionism for debt-ridden countries' exports, and promoting acceptance of the principle of sharing the burden of relief with developing countries are indeed constructive and timely steps. Fourth, from the Latin American point of view it is important to further open the region's economies to international trade. A traditional lack of export orientation has been their Achilles' heel for most of the postwar period. In fact, Latin America has been losing its share in world exports during this period. This trend must change drastically, particularly now that developing countries are important exporters of industrial products.

Finally, the institutional way of handling the debt problem has to be modified. Instead of the IMF, the World Bank should now bear the brunt of reviving the lending policy to Latin America through the window of policy and structural loan changes recently opened up by that institution. The short-term loan conditionality that characterizes the fund would now become long-term under the new conception. Private banks and governments would not be far behind in supporting this novel approach to managing the debt. This is a welcome financial and economic innovation because it transforms the substance of the problem from short-term to long-term growth. These two objectives are incompatible and simply cannot be pursued simultaneously in Latin America. The attempt to reconcile them has already created many complications in the form of inconsistencies for the region's decision makers. The success of these developmental policies is required if voluntary lending is to return on a permanent basis, buoyed by renewed confidence in the ability of Latin America to service its debt through sustained growth.

A NEW PERSPECTIVE ON THE DEBT CRISIS

Once again, it is necessary to distinguish between the amelioration of the debt problem and its solution. Practically all of the measures adopted since the debt crisis of 1982 fall in the former category. Rescheduling, rollovers, privatization, emergency lending packages by international institutions and private bankers, the conversion of debt into equity or long-term public bonds, the reduction of interest rates, the adjustment of the outstanding debt total to actual market values, payments in kind or in currencies other than those in which obligations were contracted, and other such measures do not address the central issue: namely, the institution of a sustained process of real wealth creation in the debtors' countries. This is the fundamental basis and necessary condition on which any permanent resolution of the debt situation must rest. The alternative to development can only be, in the end, the default of debt, which can hardly be regarded as a satisfactory solution to all parties concerned. Even the partial or total assumption of the principal by international institutions, unlikely as it may be, through the floating of negotiable documents, would not constitute, properly speaking, a "solution" but rather a salvage operation beyond the normal realm of economic relations as defined at present in the international system.

It is in this context that the Brady Plan constitutes a definite advance beyond the type of ameliorative measures tried in the past. Its central thrust is directed at the reduction of the principal of the debt. It thus squarely addresses the fundamental issue of the debt problem. By reducing the weight of the debt burden itself, it frees the debtor's resources permanently for developmental purposes. In this sense, the plan constitutes a new beginning, a true qualitative change, in the approach to the solution of the problem. Once again, a true and lasting resolution of the debtor's situation requires the resumption of a high and sustained growth process. This, in turn, depends on resources and efforts becoming available to accomplish the task.

Improvements on the Brady Plan could stimulate bankers to become more heavily involved in financing the medium- and long-term needs of the region. Complementary trade liberalization and promotion steps should be promptly implemented in order to increase the commercial flow between Latin America and the developed nations' markets. The fine-tuning and tailoring of the Brady Plan to the specific needs and circumstances of each debtor nation have to be further worked out. Also, much remains to be done by way of integrating each modified or individual version of the plan with the structural and functional features of each nation's developmental blueprint.

The initiative to write off the debt of poor countries is also one that needs further implementation. In 1996 the International Monetary Fund and the World Bank started a debt-reduction initiative that appeared to mark the beginning of the end of the debt problems seriously affecting a number of the world's poorest countries. This step forward has stalled, and political leadership is now needed to restore the credibility of the initiative, which according to some, should be integrated into a coordinated strategy for poverty reduction.[15]

Undoubtedly, the debt problem has served to highlight the structural changes that have taken place in the international political and economic systems in the last half century. The less developed countries are now an integral part of those systems. Their function is no longer a peripheral and subservient one. This means that their economies and even social policies must dovetail with those of the developed world. In the course of time, these developments will inevitably lead to a complete revamping of the international economic institutions.

The institutional arrangements negotiated at Bretton Woods are now clearly *passe*. Naturally, it will take time for the full consciousness required for change to emerge and solidify. Gradual modification and evolution, rather than wholesale restructuring, will in all probability prevail. But in the end a new institutionalization of the international system, now looming on the horizon, will come into its own. This new order will not necessarily consist exclusively of new organizations but, more important, it will have to be infused of a new spirit: that is, a vivid realization that growth in developed countries and development in less advanced ones, international trade and finance, exchange rates, commercial and investment policies, along with domestic, social, and economic programs, will have to be coordinated and made compatible for the sake of stability and mutual prosperity.

In the above context, the so-called debt crises—the Mexican one of 1994 and the Asian of 1997-98, may be symptomatic of things to come and a harbinger of the new mentality and kind of perspective that seems destined to gradually gain ground in the realm of international affairs.

Just as historical evolution required the constitution of a new network of institutions and arrangements at the end of World War II, which made viable sustained growth possible in developed countries and growth through trade in poor ones, present times demand new changes and fresh views. The interdependence of the world economy and policy has reached a point where it is no longer possible to conduct compartmentalized, purely national or regional policies. These days, the almost continuous negotiations between industrialized countries and lesser developed ones vouch for the presence, in fact, of an international system quite different from the one that existed 50 years ago. Just consider that over the past decade world trade has grown twice as fast as world output.[16] Also, the volume of world trade has increased sixteenfold from 1950 to 1997. By contrast, world GDP has only grown sixfold during the same period.[17] What does not seem quite so evident to many, although it is actually the case, is that the less developed nations are already a part of this new reality, as exemplified by the global money and capital markets. In other words, compatibility, coherence, and coordination of goals and policies on the part of developed and less developed nations are now an inescapable necessity if crises of one sort or another are to be avoided in the future. A case in point from which many valuable lessons should be learned is the evolving financial and economic crisis of Southeast Asia.

CLOSING REMARKS

In closing, let it be repeated that the new perspective on solving the Latin American debt crisis calls for devising and adopting a comprehensive, domestic, and international set of policies that will result in the reinvigoration of international trade, investment, and lending policies, along with a resurgence of domestic savings and capital formation, leading to growth rates in excess of 5 percent annually, the kind that characterized the decades of the 1950s, 1960s, and 1970s. This kind of performance, if brought back, would be a lively sign of vigorous growth and long-term expansion, making the external debt less burdensome and reducing unproductive dead weight. The solution to the debt problem is not to have debt be a ballast that impedes growth, but rather, through its role in wealth creation, a stimulus that prods further growth. An increasing debt can be a healthy sign of growth, paraphrasing Adam Smith's famous statement that increasing salaries were an indication of growing wealth. On the other hand, recessionary conditions in less developed countries, induced by the policies of developed nations and organizations, will throw countless workers out of their jobs in the latter countries, depressing the wages of those who hold to theirs, even though there are alternative policies available that would prevent the outcome in question. Repeated devaluations and other contractionary policies will only add to the problems of cheap foreign labor undermining the jobs and negotiating leverage of workers in developed nations. A large and increasing Third World debt has no "solution" if it does not cease to be perceived as a regional problem in order to become part of a holistic solution to the economic issues facing developed and underdeveloped countries alike.

NOTES

1. See Oliveri (1992), pp. 1-10.
2. See Iglesias (1984), p. 12.
3. See Economic and Social Progress in Latin America, 1997 Report, p. 35.
4. Brazil's GDP in 1996 was $698,000 million while its exports and imports with the rest of the world totaled $81,283 million (in U.S. dollars).
5. See Jorge and Salazar (1992), pp. 15-18.
6. See Nader and Weissman (1998), pp. 5-6.
7. See Pettis (1996), pp. 2-7.
8. See CEPAL Reports (1987-1991).
9. See Economic and Social Progress in Latin America, 1997 Report, pp. 21-22.
10. See CEPAL Report, 1996.
11. See Economic and Social Progress in Latin America, 1997 Report, p. 9.
12. See Boulmer-Thomas (1994), pp. 405-408.
13. See Boulmer-Thomas (1996), pp. 29-64.
14. See Faux, Jeff (1997), pp. 18-22.
15. See Watkins (1998), p. 12.
16. See The Economist (1996), p. 4.
17. See The Economist (1997), p. 85.

REFERENCES

Boulmer-Thomas, Victor. (1994). *The Economic History of Latin America Since Independence*. London: Cambridge University Press.
Boulmer-Thomas, Victor, ed. (1996). *The New Economic Model in Latin America and Its Impact on Income Distribution and Poverty*. New York: St. Martin's Press.
CEPAL. (var. yrs.) *Balance Preliminar Sobre la Economia Latinoamericana*, Santiago, Chile: CEPAL, United Nations Commission for Latin America, 1986-97.
The Economist. (1996). "Survey of the World Economy." September 28.
The Economist. (1997). November 8.
Faux, Jeff. (1997). "The American Model Exposed," *The Nation*, Vol. 265, No. 13 (October 27).
Iglesias, Enrique. (1984). "Latin America: Crisis and Development Options," *CEPAL Review*, No. 23 (August).

Interamerican Development Bank (IDB). (1997). *Social and Economic Progress in Latin America: 1997 Report.* Washington, D.C.: Interamerican Development Bank.

Jorge, Antonio and J. Salazar-Carrillo. (1992). *The Latin American Debt.* London: Macmillan.

Nader, Ralph and R. Weissman. (1998). "A Letter to Robert Rubin," *The Nation*, January 26.

Oliveri, Ernest. (1992). *Latin American Debt and the Politics of International Finance.* Westport, CT: Praeger.

Pettis, Michael. (1996). "The Liquidity Trap—Latin America's Free-Market Past," *Foreign Affairs*, Vol. 75, No. 6 (November/December).

Watkins, Kevin. (1998). "Life and Debt Situation," *Financial Times*, January 23.

11

THE SOCIOECONOMIC IMPACT OF TOURISM IN BARBADOS

Irma T. de Alonso and Jorge Salazar-Carrillo

INTRODUCTION

This chapter examines the economic and social impact of a tourist-based development plan for Barbados, paying special attention to tourism's contribution to important economic indicators, such as GDP, government revenues, foreign exchange, and the development of other sectors in the economy. The social implications of tourism are then weighed against these economic impacts in an effort to balance the extent of tourism with the negative repercussions that may arise within the economy.

BACKGROUND AND INFORMATION

Barbados attracts a growing and diversified number of visitors from the United States (38 percent), the United Kingdom (22 percent), Canada (15 percent), and Caricom and other countries (19 percent). Tourism demand in Barbados is divided into two sources: cruise ship passengers whose numbers increased from about 156,500 in 1980 to 291,000 in 1988 and, more importantly from an economic standpoint, stay-over tourists whose numbers increased from about 369,900 in 1980 to 451,500 in 1988. By 1989, the ratio of cruise ship to stay-over increased to 0.64 from 0.42 in 1980. The average length of a stay decreased from 9.8 nights to 6.8 during the same period. These transformations have implications for the economy as the facilities demanded and expenditure patterns of both groups are distinctly different.

The importance of tourism in Barbados is much more evident when the number of stay-over tourists is compared to the local population. Barbados' population in 1987 was estimated at 253,500, while the number of stay-over visitors was 421,859. Based on these factors, the ratio of tourists to the population is 1.7. If cruise ship passengers are added, the ratio is increased to 2.8.

ECONOMIC IMPACT AND THE MULTIPLIER EFFECT

In order to explain the multiplier effect of tourist expenditures within the Barbadian economy, it is necessary to understand the concept that an increase in production will increase income, which, in turn, will increase spending in the economy.

Assume the construction of a hotel. This construction activity is part of the output of the economy in the form of an investment. In the construction process income is created (wages, salaries, profits, interest, etc.). The persons receiving this income will spend part of it and will save part of it. The income-generating process does not stop with the first round of spending, because those who receive the additional income spend some of it and save some of it, laying the base for successive rounds of spending and income. Production will increase in the second round to satisfy the increase in spending and will generate a like amount of income to those who produced those additional goods and services purchased.

When does the process end? Since part of the income is saved, the more income that leaks from the economy as savings, the less that remains to fuel still more spending and income.

Tracing through the rounds of spending is one way to determine the cumulative effects of a particular change in spending. For example, a Bds. $1[1] increase in construction generates Bds. $1 in spending in the first round. In the second round it generates Bds. $1 times the proportion of income that is spent, called the marginal propensity to consume (MPC). During the third round, the new spending equals the spending that arose in the second round ($1 x MPC) times the MPC. This goes on round after round, with each new round equal to the spending from the previous round times the MPC. The sum of the spending rounds will be the cumulative effect (or the multiplier effect) in the economy.

An alternative way to measure the economic impact of tourism to an economy is to use a formula to determine this multiplier effect. There is a relationship between the multiplier and the proportion of income that is spent in the economy. The smaller the saved portion of a change in income, the more spending there will be in each round, so the multiplier will be greater.

The formula for the simple multiplier is:

$$k' = 1 / (1\text{-}MPC) \tag{1}$$

Using econometric analysis, it was possible to estimate various multiplier effects for the economy of Barbados. All the calculations were based on an econometric model developed for the economy of Barbados. The purpose of this section is to explain multiplier effects in general, and the multiplier effect of tourism in particular. However, any economic model estimation in Barbados has to contend with the lack of information implicit in a limited number of observations. Even under the limiting circumstances confronted, a simple model was estimated to make possible the calculation of more robust multipliers. While the actual value of the multiplier may not be precise, certainly our attempt is one of the most serious on record.

According to the central bank of Barbados, they have been trying for the last ten years to estimate an econometric model for the Barbadian economy, and still the effort has not been completed. It is very unlikely that without the necessary statistics, and given the scope of this study, a more complete modeling of the economy could have been achieved. Nonetheless, the main goal of calculating the overall impact of tourism to the Barbadian economy is accomplished.

Table 11.1 contains some selected tourism statistics used in these equations.

DAILY TOURIST EXPENDITURES

Tourists are expected to spend money for goods and services during their vacations. These expenditures, injected into the local economy, will create income, output, employment, government revenues, and will generate foreign exchange.

Total gross tourist receipts have historically been estimated by the Barbados Statistical Service. However, these estimates were based on data which had not recently been updated. As a result, we estimated the tourism-related expenditures that may be associated with current visitors' to the Island. These estimates were based on our review of the marketplace, analysis of historic expenditure patterns, as well as our survey of overnight and stopover visitors to Barbados. In addition, the following points should be noted:

- Estimates of tourist expenditures were calculated for each development scenario by seasonal period, by country of origin, for both overnight and stopover visitors.
- These estimates are in constant 1989 U.S. dollars.
- Surveys of guest expenditures for overnight visitors were estimated based on the following categories:
  Lodging
  Food and beverage
  Local transportation
  Recreational activities
  Retail expenditures
- Surveys of guest expenditures for stopover visitors were estimated based on the following categories:
  Recreational activities
  Retail
  Local transportation
  Food and beverage expenditures

TABLE 11.1. Selected Tourism Statistics from Barbados, West Indies

Parameters	1980	1985	1986	1987
Arrivals:				
Stay-over Tourists	369,915.00	359,135.00	369,770.00	421,859.00
Cruise Ship Passengers	156,461.00	112,186.00	145,335.00	224,778.00
Cruise Ship/Stay-overs	0.42	0.31	0.39	0.53
Total Gross Tourist Re-ceipts	523.70	618.10	647.30	757.20
Daily Per Capita Receipts (Bd.s $)	144.00	273.00	271.00	276.00
Gross Tourist Receipts as % of GDP	34.10	28.30	28.20	30.30
Value Added by Tourism as % of GDP	11.90	10.30	10.10	10.80
Estimated, direct tourism employment (thousands):	7.65	6.69	6.73	7.39
% of total employment	7.70	7.30	7.00	7.50
ratio to available beds	0.67	0.48	0.48	0.53
Taxes on hotels and Res-taurants (Bds. $ M)	13.40	14.60	17.30	17.40
% of total gov't tax revenue	4.20	2.90	3.00	2.90
% of gross tourist receipts	2.60	2.40	2.70	2.30
First round tourism leakages:				
Total (Bds. $ M)	222.00	259.60	271.90	318.00
% of total gross tourist receipts	42.00	42.00	42.00	42.00
Net Tourism-foreign exchange earnings:				
Total (Bds. $ M)	303.70	358.50	375.40	439.20
% of imports less tourism exports	36.60	37.70	41.30	61.20

Sources: Barbados Statistical Service and Central Bank of Barbados.

TABLE 11.2. Estimated Average Length of Stays by Country of Origin, 1989

Country of Origin	Average Length of Stay
United States	5.0
United Kingdom	9.4
Canada	7.7
Caricom	5.8
Other	8.0
Total Market	6.8

Our estimates of tourism expenditures are based on the above noted considerations as well as the average length of stay of overnight visitors to the Island based on their country of origin as outlined in Table 11.2. These estimates are based on our review of the marketplace, historic trends, and our consumer research data.

The resultant estimates of gross tourist expenditure will be used as a basis for our determination of the economic impact of the proposed tourism development program to the Island. These estimates are presented in Table 11.3.

It should be noted, regarding the composition of tourists, that most of the tourist receipts are derived from stay-over rather than cruise ship visitors. This is due to their longer average length of stay, and their higher daily per capita spending.

Gross tourist receipts have increased from Bds. $523.7 million in 1980 to Bds. $757.2 million in 1987 according to government estimates. If most of these receipts are from stay-over visitors, controlling for their number and average length of a stay, estimates of daily per capita receipts can be obtained. In 1980, the per capita figure was estimated at Bds. $144, while by 1987 the amount had increased to Bds. $276.

TOURISM, GROSS DOMESTIC PRODUCT AND LINKAGES

To measure the impact of gross tourist receipts on GDP, two different indicators can be used. The first indicator shows the size of the gross tourist receipts as a percentage of GDP; the second is the value added by tourism to GDP, expressed as a percentage of total GDP.

In the first case, gross tourist receipts were 34.1 percent of GDP in 1980, 28.3 percent in 1985, 28.2 percent in 1986, and 30.3 percent in 1987. Total value added in tourism was a much smaller percent of GDP: 11.9 percent in 1980, 10.3 percent in 1985, 10.0 percent in 1986, and 10.8 percent in 1987. Both measures indicate the relative size of tourism in the economy and the degree of dependency

TABLE 11.3. Average Daily Expenditures by Barbados Visitors (in constant 1989 U.S. Dollars)

Type of Expenditure	Season		Off Season	
	Overnight	Cruise Passenger	Overnight	Cruise Passenger
Average daily room rate	$149.00	N/A	$124.00	N/A
Daily restaurant spending	38.95	58.57	39.81	33.71
Daily grocery spending	12.89	6.07	16.44	7.41
Daily gift spending	19.95	101.91	25.42	75.84
Daily tour spending	21.37	38.45	40.57	26.66
Daily night time entertainment	18.63	5.14	20.65	3.42
Total spending	$260.79	$210.14	$266.89	$147.04

N/A = not applicable.

on tourism, or alternatively, the degree of diversification

The fact that value added of tourism receipts was significantly less than the absolute percentage of gross tourism receipts to GDP suggests that tourism exhibits weak linkages with other sectors of the economy. According to estimates by Armstrong and Francis (1968), tourism's main linkages are with *other services* and *transport and communications*. Based on their estimates, other sectors that could be linked to tourism include *distribution, banking, insurance and real estate*, and *agriculture*.

THE GROSS DOMESTIC PRODUCT MULTIPLIER CALCULATIONS

With the purpose of estimating this multiplier effect, it was necessary first to estimate the marginal propensity to consume, or the proportion of income that is spent, which is assumed constant for the economy. Using statistics of private consumption and GDP in current prices from 1970 to 1987, this proportion was estimated to be 0.609.

The implication of this value is that if production increases by Bds. $1, income increases by Bds. $1, of which around $0.61 will be spent in the first round. This is called the impact multiplier or the first round of spending.

There will also be a second round of spending because those receiving the

Bds. $0.61 will consider it income, and spend another 61 percent, amounting to Bds. $0.37 (or 0.61 X 0.61), and so on. When the initial $1 of spending is added to the successive rounds of spending, we get, in Bds. $1 + $0.61 + $0.37 + $0.23 + ... +0. The sum of these consecutive rounds of spending equals the multiplier effect shown below:

$$k' = 1 / (1\text{-}MPC) = 1 / (1 - 0.609) = 2.56 \qquad (2)$$

According to this calculation, by the end of the year, the initial dollar of spending will have created, in Bds., a total of $2.56 in expenditures. This is called the simple multiplier because there is no allowance for leakages in the form of taxes, imports, payments to foreign owners of factors of production, and the like. In reality, the multiplier effect will be less than that indicated by the simple formula here, as will become evident later in the chapter.

INCOME MULTIPLIER CALCULATIONS

An important modification to the simple multiplier approach above takes into account personal taxes (taxes on income and profits) by subtracting them from gross income. This adjustment to income is defined as disposable income, and is a better indicator of spending potential in the private sector. Interestingly, in the case of Barbados, it was found that government relied more heavily on indirect taxes than on personal taxes, so the income adjustment did not affect the value of the multiplier to any great degree.

The proportion of disposable income that was spent was estimated at 0.611. Therefore the value of the multiplier was:

$$k' = 1 / (1\text{-}0.611) = 2.57 \qquad (3)$$

THE EMPLOYMENT MULTIPLIER ESTIMATES IN THE TOURIST SECTOR

Tourism generated direct employment of 7,650 in 1980, 6,690 in 1985, 6,730 in 1986, and 7,390 in 1987. Direct tourism employment accounted for 7.5 percent of total employment during this period. In general, the number of direct jobs generated is proportional to the number of rooms available to accommodate tourists. The ratio is approximately 0.50 to each available bed or, alternatively, one job per tourist room, if there are two beds per room.

Recent input-output data for Barbados was not available. In the absence of this data, a regression equation was used to calculate the impact of tourism on employment. The explanatory variables in the equation were GDP shares in tourism and an index of wages paid in the hotel industry. The result of this analysis suggests that each additional Bds. $1 million in the tourist sector creates

27 direct jobs, but that each additional one-unit increase in the wage index destroys about 3 jobs. Indirect jobs are also created, but without input-output data it was impossible to estimate their magnitude.

TAX IMPLICATIONS OF THE MULTIPLIER MECHANISM

Taxes are a leakage from circulating income and therefore reduce the value of the multiplier. In the presence of income taxes, the multiplier becomes:

$$k' = 1 / [1\text{-}MPC + MPC(\tau)] \tag{4}$$

where τ is the tax rate.

Taxes collected from tourism (in hotels and restaurants) do not decrease local income. Instead they increase government revenue. If government increases expenditures by the amount of these tax revenues, there will be a multiplier effect in the economy. Although government derives direct and indirect revenues from tourist spending, official statistics represent only an estimate of taxes on hotels and restaurants. From these estimates we've determined that taxes increased from $13.4 million in 1980 to $17.4 million in 1987 (in Bds.), but constituted only a minor source of government revenue. As a share of total gross tourist receipts they fell from 2.6 in 1980 to 2.3 in 1987.

An even more revealing indicator of the importance of tourist revenues to central government is the ratio of tax revenue from tourism to total tax revenue. In this respect, the share is identically low, and has declined from 4.2 in 1980 to 2.9 in 1987. Using an econometric model of the Barbadian economy, it was possible to estimate the government's tax multiplier of 2.48. In other words, every dollar spent by government generates subsequent rounds of spending that increase the value of output by approximately $2.48.

FOREIGN EXCHANGE IMPLICATIONS OF THE MULTIPLIER

Tourism brings into the local economy considerable amounts of foreign exchange. Some of this, however, leaks out of the local economy because of the import content of tourist consumption.

These imports are another leakage from the flow of income and spending in the local economy. In the presence of both income taxes and imports, the multiplier becomes:

$$k' = 1 / [1 - MPC + MPC(\tau) + m] \tag{5}$$

where m is the marginal propensity to import, or that proportion of income used to purchase imported goods. In Barbados, the marginal propensity to import was found to be very high, at 0.22, which reduces the size of the multiplier to:

$$k' = 1 / [1 - 0.65 + 0.65(.06) + 0.22] = 1.64 \tag{6}$$

The calculation in (6) is a much better estimate of the size of the multiplier in the Barbadian economy than the one first estimated in equation (2), where for simplification purposes, personal taxes and imports were not considered.

A useful measure of tourism's contribution to foreign exchange requirements is the net amount of foreign exchange that tourism earns as a percent of all imports minus tourism imports. (Tourism imports are deducted from total imports of goods because without tourism such imports would not be necessary.) In Barbados, net foreign exchange represented 36.6 percent of the cost of all imports, excluding tourism imports. The corresponding figure had increased to 61.2 percent in 1987. Thus, in spite of substantial leakages, tourism creates positive net foreign exchange that helps pay for other imports required by the local economy.

In the balance-of-payments accounts, tourist expenditures are treated as an export of a service. In the econometric model developed for this study, we estimated that the multiplier effect is about 2.48, which corresponds to the overall receipts generated by tourism. However, the tourist sector has a significant import content.

The Armstrong and Francis study mentioned earlier estimated that 40 percent of tourist expenditures leaked out of the economy to pay for goods and services consumed by tourists and as payments to foreign factors of production. Such leakages include payments for all goods and services imported to the Island for tourist consumption and expropriation of profits. Under these circumstances, the multiplier effect reduces to 1.49 (or 60 percent of 2.48). This value is consistent with the multiplier of 1.41 estimated by Armstrong and Francis back in 1968, using an input-output table.

The Armstrong and Francis study arrived at its estimates based on official statistics published by various agencies of the Barbadian government. Here we estimate that 60 percent of tourist expenditures leak out of the local economy. This estimate, based on our personal experience in the Caribbean tourist industry and the expert opinions of several prominent economists in the region, is more realistic. This is especially so in view of operating conditions of tourism-related enterprises in Barbados and the prevailing balance of foreign exchange processed through its central bank in recent years. Furthermore, various economists and representatives of the Barbados government and central bank support it. Therefore, with a 60 percent leakage, the multiplier effect is reduced to 1.00 (or 40 percent of 2.48).

THE VALUE ADDED OF TOURISM AS MULTIPLICAND

Value added is the difference, at each stage of production, between the value of products a firm sells and the cost of the materials purchased to make those products. Table 11.4 provides data on value added in tourism and compares that

TABLE 11.4. GDP at Factor Cost and the Value Added in Tourism

Year	GDP at Factor Cost	Value Added in Tourism	Value Added in Tourism as a % of GDP
1978	984.40	110.00	11.20
1979	1,196.10	143.90	12.00
1980	1,730.50	182.90	10.60
1981	1,904.60	206.50	10.80
1982	1,990.00	181.00	9.10
1983	2,112.70	186.50	8.80
1984	2,302.80	206.70	9.00
1985	2,409.90	225.00	9.30
1986	2,646.00	233.90	8.80
1987	2,913.70	270.00	9.30

Source: Central Bank of Barbados.

to GDP at factor cost. On average, value added in the tourist sector was around 9.9 percent of GDP, at factor costs, during the period 1978 through 1987.

STATISTICAL EQUATIONS AND CONSIDERATIONS

A simple Keynesian model was used to estimate various multipliers for the Barbadian economy. Here the following structural equations were estimated:

$$Y_t = C_t + I_t + G_t + X_t + M_t \tag{7}$$
$$C_t = a_o + a_1 DY_t + u_{t1} \tag{8}$$
$$I_t = b_o + b_1 Y_t + b_2 \ R_t + u_{t2} \tag{9}$$
$$M_t = c_o + c_1 Y_t + c_2 IP_t + c_3 ER_t + u_{t3} \tag{10}$$
$$Dy_t = Y_t - T_{xt} \tag{11}$$
$$T_{xt} = d_o + d_1 Y_t + u_{t4} \tag{12}$$

where:

Y_t = gross domestic product
C_t = private consumption expenditures
I_t = private investment expenditures
G_t = government expenditures
X_t = exports

Mt = imports
Dyt = disposable income
Txt = taxes on personal income
Rt = rate of interest, average prime lending rate
Ipt = index of import prices
Ert = exchange rate, in terms of SDR
ut = stochastic error term

The variables Rt, IPt, ERt, Gt, and Xt are exogenous here. To eliminate simultaneity bias, a two-stage least square (2SLS) method was used.

The estimated equations of the model, measured in current prices from 1970 to 1987, (with t-statistics in parentheses) are as follows:

$$Ct = 82.48 + 0.65\ DYt \qquad\qquad (13)$$
$$(25.86)$$

$F = 668.58 \qquad R^2 = 0.976 \qquad SE = 83.16 \qquad DW = 1.53$

$$It = -115.59 + 0.128\ Yt + 18.43\ Rt \qquad (14)$$
$$(10.33) \qquad (2.83)$$

$F= 74.50 \qquad R^2 = 0.908 \qquad SE = 41.43 \qquad DW = 1.06$

$$Mt - 371.605 + 0.22\ Yt + 12.41\ IPt - 351.09\ Ert \qquad (15)$$
$$(4.06) \qquad (6.73) \qquad (-3.67)$$

$F = 267.41 \qquad R^2 = 0.98 \qquad SE = 72.90 \qquad DW = 1.27$

$$Txt = 34.35 + 0.06\ Yt \qquad\qquad (16)$$
$$(7.89)$$

$F = 62.28 \qquad R^2 = 0.80 \qquad SE = 27.87 \qquad DW = 0.44$

The goodness of fit in all the equations is fairly high. The t-statistics show that all the explanatory variables are statistically significant, and the possibility of autocorrelation does not bias the estimated regression coefficients.

The implied reduced form solution of the model is:

$Yt = (82.48 + 0.65\ DYt) + (-115.59 + 0.128\ Yt + 18.43\ Rt)$
  $+ (Gt) + (Xt) - (371.605 + 0.22\ Yt + 12.41\ IPt - 351.09\ ERt)$

$\Rightarrow$

$Yt = (82.48 + 0.65[Yt - Txt]) + (-115.59 + 0.128\ Yt + 18.43\ Rt)$
  $+ (Gt) + (Xt) - (371.605 + 0.22\ Yt + 12.41\ IPt - 351.09\ ERt)$

$\Rightarrow$

$Yt = -1059.66 + 46.72\ Rt + 2.48\ Gt + 2.48\ Xt - 30.79\ IPt + 871.09\ ERt \quad (17)$

The partial derivative of Yt with respect to a given variable is the multiplier of that variable.

THE GROSS DOMESTIC PRODUCT MULTIPLIER CALCULATIONS

To calculate the GDP multiplier, a simple consumption function was estimated as follows:

$$Ct = a0 + al\ GDPt + u \tag{18}$$

The coefficient "al" is the average increase in consumption when GDP is increased by one unit, here, one Bds.\$million. It is the marginal propensity to consume and it is known as the impact multiplier or the marginal effect of GDP on consumption.

To calculate the interim multipliers, finding the average increase in consumption for a unit increase in GDP in past periods is necessary—that is, in periods before "t." Here, the equation to be estimated is:

$$Ct = a0 + al\ GDPt + a2\ GDPt\text{-}1 + a3\ GDPt\text{-}2 + \dots \tag{19}$$

With lagged variables, the equations were not found different from the previous one and, in particular, the lagged dependent variables were not found statistically significant. The implication is that most of the multiplier effect is achieved in the first year.

THE INCOME MULTIPLIER CALCULATIONS

The income multiplier was calculated with disposable income (DY)—that is, GDP minus personal taxes (DYt = Yt - TXt). The results are similar to those found in the previous case, and can be seen below:

$$Ct = 82.48 + 0.65\ DYt \tag{20}$$
$$(25.86)$$

$$F= 668.58 \qquad R^2 = 0.976 \qquad SE=83.16 \qquad DW=1.53$$

Therefore:

$$Ct = 82.48 + 0.65\ \{Yt - (34.35 + 0.06\ YT)$$

$$\Rightarrow$$

$$Ct = 60.15 + 0.611\ Yt \tag{21}$$

The income multiplier with tax on income was estimated as:

$$k' = 1/[1 - MPC + MPC(t)]$$
$$k' = 1/[1 - 0.65 + 0.65(0.06)]$$
$$k' = 2.57 \qquad (22)$$

Note that the size of this multiplier is quite similar to the simple one estimated for GDP.

THE EMPLOYMENT MULTIPLIER ESTIMATES IN THE TOURIST SECTOR

Using output, labor force, and employment data from Barbados, estimating an employment equation for tourism using regression analysis was possible. Specifically, employment in tourism depended on GDP in tourism (measured in thousands) and wages paid to hotel employees (measured by a wage index). The resulting equation produced significant results as seen below:

(Employment
in tourism) $= 5.53 + 0.027$ GDP. tourism $- 0.028$ wage index $\qquad (23)$
$\qquad\qquad\qquad$ (2.94) $\qquad\qquad\qquad$ (-2.01)
$\quad F = 7.95 \qquad\qquad R^2 = 0.64 \qquad\qquad SE = 0.56 \qquad\qquad DW = 1.75$

Equation (23) implies that an increase of Bds. \$1 million in tourism will generate 27 direct jobs in tourism, but a one-unit increase in the wage index will reduce employment by 2.8 jobs.

TAX IMPLICATIONS OF THE MULTIPLIER MECHANISM

Taxes generally reduce the size of the multiplier because income available for spending in the economy is smaller after the tax has been imposed. The exception is tourism-related taxes. Here, they do not decrease local income because the payers of the tax are not local. Consequently, such taxes increase government revenues and government expenditures. According to our model of Barbados, the value of its government spending multiplier is 2.48. This means that every dollar spent by government increases the value of output by \$2.48, in Bds.

FOREIGN EXCHANGE IMPLICATIONS OF THE MULTIPLIER

As previously discussed, the U.S. market, with approximately 30 percent of total visitors in 1988, represents the largest point of origin of tourism arrivals to Barbados. The official exchange rate between the U.S. and Barbados dollars has remained constant (Bds. \$2 = US\$1) since 1976. The rate used instead is the SDR/Bds.\$, which is the cross rate between the SDR/US\$ and the US\$/Bds.\$. From 1975 to 1987 this cross rate has fluctuated between 1.95 and 2.56.

In the import equation, the exchange rate has a negative value of -351.09, implying that an increase in the exchange rate will decrease imports, and as a result GDP will increase. In the reduced- form solution of the model, the exchange rate has a multiplier effect of 871.09, implying that an increase of 0.01 in the exchange rate will decrease imports and therefore GDP would increase by Bds. $8.71.

In the balance of payments, tourist expenditures are treated as an export of a service. Here exports were taken as exogenous, so that the multiplier effect of exports applies also to tourist expenditures, meaning the value of the multiplier is 2.48. Previous estimates by Armstrong and Francis suggested that 40 percent of tourist expenditures leak out of the economy to pay for goods and services consumed by tourists, capital goods used for tourist amenities, and as payments to foreign factors of production. However, for the purposes of this analysis, we have estimated that 60 percent of the expenditures leak-out, as previously discussed. Under these circumstances, the multiplier effect is reduced to 1.00 (40 percent of 2.48).

THE ECONOMIC IMPACT OF THE PROPOSED PLAN

Based on the assumptions and calculations previously discussed, we have prepared estimates of total tourism expenditures that are likely to occur under our proposed development plan. These estimates appear in Table 11.5.

It is important to note that since the multiplier effect is estimated to be 1.00, the impact on the Barbados economy is expected to equal the estimated tourism expenditures suggested in Table 11. 5. Furthermore, while the economic impact presented in this study is predicated on direct expenditures by tourists visiting Barbados, additional impact can be derived from the construction of new hotels and the upgrading and renovation of existing ones. Normally, the construction of new hotels recommended for development on the Island requires an investment ranging between $80,000 and $120,000 per room. Based on the recommended addition of 1,050 hotel rooms, the potential impact can be $84 to $126 million over the decade of the 1990s.

SOCIAL IMPACTS

The effects of tourism to an island's economy cannot be disputed. However, the extent of the effects, and their repercussions, must be balanced within the economy. Too often, the focus of most research and planning efforts is on the economic and fiscal benefits of the industry without addressing the social costs associated with developing tourism.

This section reviews the social implications of an advanced tourism industry. It should be noted that we reviewed each factor below in determining the optimal

TABLE 11.5. The Estimated Future Seasonal and Annual Expenditures of Visitors in Barbados (Rounded in 000's of Current U.S. Dollars)

Year	Season			Off-Season			Annual		
	Overnight	Cruise ship	Total	Overnight	Cruise ship	Total	Overnight	Cruise ship	Total
1990	$162,600	$30,700	$193,300	$326,800	$29,000	$355,800	$489,400	$59,700	$549,100
1991	178,300	34,500	212,800	355,400	32,300	387,700	533,700	66,800	600,500
1992	196,500	38,100	234,600	390,200	35,600	425,800	586,700	73,700	660,400
1993	216,600	43,600	260,200	425,500	40,000	465,500	642,100	83,600	725,700
1994	237,300	48,500	285,800	456,300	44,500	500,800	693,600	93,000	786,600
1995	257,700	53,000	310,700	494,600	49,000	543,600	752,300	102,000	854,300
1996	276,500	57,800	334,300	532,100	53,500	585,600	808,600	111,300	919,900
1997	296,200	62,800	359,000	572,800	58,500	631,300	869,000	121,300	990,300
1998	316,000	68,000	384,000	613,000	63,500	676,500	929,000	131,500	1,060,500
1999	334,200	73,500	407,700	651,100	69,000	720,100	985,300	142,500	1,127,800
2000	353,000	79,500	432,500	690,100	75,000	765,100	1,043,100	154,500	1,197,600

development plan for the Island. That is, a balance between the positive and negative economic and social considerations associated with the future of the Barbadian tourism industry.

Socioeconomic Considerations /Quality of Life

The development of tourism on an island nation has both positive and negative effects regarding the quality of life for that island's people. These factors include negatives such as traffic congestion; increased crime and prostitution; noise and air pollution; vandalism; increased demand on public facilities, parks, and infrastructure; overcrowding and loss of beach access; environmental destruction; increased social tension; and an influx of new values and diffusion of culture. There are some positives to consider as well, such as: improved infrastructures; increased employment opportunities; increased entertainment alternatives for locals; improved quality of education and literacy levels; increased government revenues to support better public services; and increased support of cultural and historic preservation and beautification.

Balancing both the advantageous and disadvantageous aspects of tourism development must occur before a well-planned and controlled tourism environment may be established. The following discusses these considerations in more detail.

Social Costs

Increases in tourist arrivals are said to increase criminal activity, as affluent tourists are tempting targets. In addition, the visibility of the economic gap that exists between visitors and residents may amplify grievances and racial differences. Sometimes, these issues can translate into insolence and indifferent attitudes of locals toward tourists. This is especially pronounced when sections of the local population are excluded from the area's beaches, or preferences are given to tourists in the use of its resources.

However, increases in tourism development also result in the establishment of new airport facilities, roads, restaurants, hospitals, and attractions. In addition, increases in education, training, and employment opportunities can provide lifestyle alternatives that were previously unavailable for locals.

Cultural Issues

Often the perception is that tourists are mainly responsible for the deterioration in culture and standards of an island's artisans. This stems from the theory that efforts are made to expand output of arts and cultural items to meet tourists' demands. While this may occur in many tourist destinations, well-organized tourist businesses can benefit residents through exposure to various cultural alternatives. Moreover, tourism can also benefit local craftspeople by providing an audience and market for their products, and thus keep their methods of artistry alive. Overall, tourism can contribute to cultural revival.

Environmental Factors

The beautiful natural surroundings and beaches of many Caribbean islands are part of the environmental attractions that inspire tourism. In addition the man-made environment, such as lodging accommodations and recreational attractions, contributes to the overall appeal of an island destination. The key is to create a plan for tourism development that allows for tourists and the environment to coexist.

The threat of environmental damage, pollution, and erosion has inspired programs that have restricted tourism developments in an attempt to preserve the ecosystem and surroundings of an island. This is one alternative to protect the environment. Other considerations include coastal planning, preservation of park areas, and ensuring that all beachfront properties are public and accessible by everyone. In addition, planning efforts should be expanded to include climate considerations such as establishing height restrictions on development that could potentially block an island's prevailing winds.

MEASURING SOCIOECONOMIC IMPLICATIONS

The previously noted considerations are important in tourism development planning. The key is to balance the number of visitors with capacities of the given environment. This allows for the greatest interaction with the least amount of destruction to any island's environment, its culture, and its people.

Too often, the social response to changing economic conditions in many Caribbean nations has not been properly measured and anticipated. In planning for tourism development, particular attention should be given to the effect of the industry on the social life of a country.

Barbados has an unusual position in the region. It is a relatively small island in comparison to its population and mature tourism industry. It has the highest population per square kilometer of any island in the Caribbean, and well above the average number of hotel rooms per square kilometer.

Because Barbados' tourism industry is mature and heavily concentrated in specific areas of the Island, the mass exploitation of the industry would not provide an overall well-balanced environment for Barbados.

Tables 11.6 and 11.7 provide various indicators of the social impact of tourism development on the Island. These indicators were used to estimate when the volume of visitor arrivals is likely to produce social stress in the Barbadian community.

Table 11.6 provides two such indicators, Barbados' tourism density ratio and estimates of its overnight tourist arrivals for the period 1990-2000. These social indicators illustrate the relationship between the resident and transient populations. Based on extensive research by travel experts, a ratio greater than 8:1 stay-over visitors to residents was the point when social stress and serious social tensions appeared in most island communities. For example, social problems be-

TABLE 11.6. Tourism Density Ratio in Barbados, West Indies

Year	Population *	Estimate of Future Overnight Arrivals	Tourism Density Ratio
1990	269,228.00	508,300.00	1.89
1991	274,613.00	526,400.00	1.92
1992	280,105.00	549,900.00	1.96
1993	285,707.00	573,300.00	2.01
1994	291,422.00	589,900.00	2.02
1995	297,250.00	609,100.00	2.05
1996	303,195.00	623,500.00	2.06
1997	309,259.00	638,000.00	2.06
1998	315,444.00	649,400.00	2.06
1999	321,753.00	656,000.00	2.04
2000	328,188.00	661,300.00	2.02

*Population estimated at 2 percent growth per annum.
Sources: Barbados Statistical Service.

gan in St. Maarten when its tourism density ratio exceeded ten visitors for every resident. In 1988, St. Maarten's tourism density ratio was 24:1. The average for our comparable supply for 1988 was 5.5. It should be noted that future development plans for the Island do not exceed 2.1 overnight arrivals per capita, assuming a constant 2 percent growth in population.

Table 11.7 provides data on tourist arrivals per square kilometer in Barbados during 1990-2000. The basis of these calculations was the estimated number of overnight visitor arrivals multiplied by the average length of a stay. This figure was then divided by the product of the number of square kilometers for Barbados multiplied by 365, or more formally:

$$\frac{(Number\ of\ Visitors)\ x\ (Average\ length\ of\ StayOver)}{365\ x\ 439}$$

According to this indicator, Barbados' tourism per square kilometer never exceeds 29 for the period 1990-2000. In 1988, Aruba's tourism per square kilometer ratio was approximately 25, and Bermuda's was 154.

The final social indicator includes an estimate of hotel rooms per 1,000 residents (see Table 11.8). This shows the relationship between the development

TABLE 11.7. Tourism Per Square Kilometer in Barbados, 1990-2000

Year	Estimated Over-night Arrivals	Average Length of Stay	Ratio
1990	508,300.00	6.80	22.00
1991	526,400.00	6.80	22.80
1992	549,900.00	6.80	23.80
1993	573,000.00	6.80	24.80
1994	589,900.00	6.80	25.60
1995	609,100.00	6.80	27.00
1996	623,500.00	6.80	27.60
1997	638,000.00	6.80	27.60
1998	649,400.00	6.80	28.10
1999	656,000.00	6.80	28.40
2000	661,330.00	6.80	28.70

of the tourism industry and the population. In 1987, Barbados rooms per thousand capita ratio was 26:1. Other island ratios include Antigua and Barbuda with 55:1, the Bahamas with 76:1, British Virgin Islands with 6:1, and Jamaica with 55:1. It should be noted that this indicator decreased during the observation period as the number of lodging units on the Island stabilized and the population increased.

ADDITIONAL CONSIDERATIONS

Measuring the socioeconomic environment of tourism development is beneficial to the island's overall stability; however, other programs besides planning must be established to reduce the disadvantages of tourism development.

One important program that should be set up to achieve the full benefits of the industry is tourism education. Residents must understand the importance of tourism in the economy to eliminate social tensions, crime, and other negative factors associated with increased tourism development. This education process may encompass training in the industry, increase understanding of cultural herit-

TABLE 11.8. Lodgings and Population in Barbados, 1990-2000

Year	Estimated Number of Future Lodgings	Population (in 000's)	Ratio
1990	7,042.00	269.00	26.20
1991	7,042.00	275.00	25.60
1992	7,242.00	280.00	25.90
1993	7,617.00	286.00	26.70
1994	7,967.00	291.00	26.70
1995	7,967.00	297.00	26.80
1996	8,017.00	303.00	26.40
1997	8,092.00	309.00	26.20
1998	8,092.00	315.00	25.70
1999	8,092.00	322.00	25.10
2000	8,092.00	328.00	24.70

Based on population at 2 percent growth per annum.

age, and lead to behavioral and attitudinal changes.

Another important component of socioeconomic planning is the continuation of environmental protection strategies. This may include the establishment of barriers in areas that are ecologically sensitive, such as were completed in Harrison's Caves, and the building of groins to alleviate beach erosion.

SUMMARY

This chapter has presented economic and socioeconomic considerations that may be associated with a tourist-based strategic development plan for Barbados. It was our intention to consider these impacts in the same chapter for proper balance. We found that, while tourism development plans may recommend significant growth in arrivals and tourism products for the Island, the negative social considerations suggested above could far outweigh any positive economic benefits. Our preeminent concern, therefore, was that the development path considered for Barbados take into account the overall well-being of the nation, by looking at both the negatives and the positives of tourism.

NOTE

1. Until 1976, Bds.$1 was equal to US $0.50; since then the rate has been Bds.$ = $1.00.

REFERENCES

Armstrong, D. S. and A. A. Francis. (1968). "A Structural Analysis of the Barbados Economy, 1968, with an Application to the Tourist Industry." *Social and Economic Studies*, Vol. 23, no. 4 (December).
Barbados Statistical Service.
Central Bank of Barbados.

PART IV

NEOLIBERALISM AND NEOPOPULISM: ADJUSTMENT AND STABILITY

NEOLIBERALISM VERSUS NEOPOPULISM

John Williamson

I was a student of Fritz Machlup, who devoted a substantial part of his profes-sional career to clarifying the meaning of terms that he felt were being used sloppily, thereby leading to unnecessary error. Some of this concern rubbed off on me, so when I am asked to speak about concepts like neoliberalism and neopopul-ism , concepts that strike me as ill-defined, I always begin with a short semantic exegesis.

The only person I recall having taken the trouble to define what he meant by neoliberalism was Mario Simonsen (1994), who defined it as the economics of Reagan and Thatcher. "Neoliberal" strikes me as an odd term to apply to their policies, since neither considered themselves to be liberal, but it does seem to fit with what other people mean when they use the term, so I shall adopt this definition. There is an important area of overlap between neoliberalism and classical liberalism (the liberalism of John Locke, Adam Smith, and John Stuart Mill), in that both regard the market as a constructive social institution to be used and fostered rather than derided and suppressed. But neoliberalism is also characterized by attitudes that strike a classical liberal as distinctly illiberal, notably an aggressive indifference toward income distribution and the sort of macroeconomic primitivism that can seem sophisticated only to a believer in real business cycle theory.

"Populism" is another ill-defined concept: my understanding of it is action undertaken on behalf of the masses (the popular classes), without much analysis as to whether it is really likely to end up benefitting them. Demand expansion that does not recognize supply-side constraints or redistribution without attempting to factor in a budget constraint are two paradigmatic examples. One more thing that puzzles me about the term "neopopulism" is, what is there that is "neo" about populism?

Our title seems to imply that the ideas currently in contention in Latin

America are confined to neoliberalism and neopopulism. Fortunately, I do not believe this to be true. Socialism may no longer be an active intellectual force, but classical liberalism is alive and well.

It is clear that the market economy, and therefore liberalism of either the new (conservative) or classical (progressive) variety, is a much more potent force in Latin America today than it has been for a long time. The degree of "neo-ness" clearly varies a lot (contrast Chile and Peru), but it is only in Venezuela that we are witnessing an attempt to push the clock back, and the results of that effort promise to be sufficiently bad to inoculate other countries against emulation. Progress elsewhere may be hesitant (as in Brazil) or controversial (as in Mexico), but most intellectuals consider movement toward a market economy and macroeconomic prudence to be progress, which is a big change from the past.

The fact is that the public likes price stability. People like to be able to buy imports. The new model is popular. Politicians can win elections by delivering policy reform, as that term is used today. In the sample of countries whose experiences were analyzed in the 1994 conference volume that I edited , *The Political Economy of Policy Reform*, reforming governments went on to win reelection in Australia, Colombia, New Zealand, Portugal, Spain, and Turkey. Only in Poland was a reforming government defeated at the polls. The other countries that were analyzed in that group of reforming governments, such as Chile, Indonesia, Korea, and Mexico, were at best, limited democracies. We have witnessed a series of Latin American cases where governments that have implemented policy reforms which the conventional wisdom of political science would have labeled political suicide a few years back have achieved striking electoral success. Consider, for example, Argentina, Bolivia, Brazil, Chile, Colombia, and Peru. In fact, a recent M.A. thesis by Carlos Gervasoni (1995), used econometric techniques to explore the factors that explain electoral success in Latin America over the period 1982-95, and found policy reform to be an important, statistically significant, electoral asset.

I would hypothesize that one reason why political scientists have erred in positing the political unpopularity of policy reform is that economists have erred in assuming that stabilization is typically costly. Economists of my generation learned to analyze stabilization in terms of the Phillips Curve. Even after we acknowledged that Edmund Phelps (1967) and Milton Friedman (1968) were correct in arguing that the Phillips Curve was vertical in the long run, we still believed that there was a short-run trade-off between unemployment and the change in inflation, so that a reduction in inflation required a (temporary) recession.[1] This led me, in *The Political Economy of Policy Reform*, to formulate the political problem faced by those who wished to institute modernizing reforms as one of how to get the body politic to accept costs that were immediate, concentrated, and easily identifiable in the hope of benefits that are delayed, dispersed, and hypothetical.

I am coming to the conclusion that this is too pessimistic. The Israeli stabilization of 1985 was an early case that proved to be expansionary (actually, Indonesia in 1966 is an even earlier case in point). There have now been several dramatic cases of expansionary stabilization in Latin America, like Argentina and Brazil. The explanation first offered for these cases of expansionary stabilization was that they were exchange-rate-based stabilizations; it was argued that a stabilization program that used the exchange rate rather than the money supply as a nominal anchor would have an initial boom followed later by a recession, rather than vice-versa. The Israeli recession of 1989 was pointed to as providing corroboration. However, no convincing reason has been offered for regarding the 1989 Israeli recession as a delayed consequence of the 1985 stabilization; the exchange-rate-based stabilization that does not allow for a flexible exchange-rate policy in time to avoid an overvaluation developing lays the seeds of a subsequent crisis that can well result in a recession; but this does not prove that any stabilization must be costly in terms of output. It seems increasingly clear that it is not true that stabilization is inherently costly.[2]

Economists are not accustomed to arguing that lunch is really free, and I still do not believe that there is no output cost to stabilization. Rather, I hypothesize that the output costs of ending a rapid inflation are prepaid. The acceleration of inflation leads to a fall in output (stagflation) as the efficiency of the economy declines because money serves its basic functions increasingly less adequately as uncertainty increases.[3] The stagflation makes economic actors understand that they cannot have income levels as high as they were demanding. The resolution of the distributive inconsistency that was driving the inflation creates the objective possibility of stopping the inflation once the political leadership can agree to forego its own excess claims— that is, until they can accept fiscal discipline, and can institute a convincing nominal anchor that coordinates the expectations of economic agents on a low rate of inflation. As that happens, inflation slows and output starts to expand again.[4]

If one accepts this view of stabilization, then it is hardly surprising that a government that succeeds in stabilizing should reap an electoral dividend. This justifies a certain degree of optimism regarding the theme of the conference. Policy reform is politically sustainable.

Of course, to sustain reform will require continuing good macroeconomic management. No one should think of reform as a once-and-for-all change. Chile and Colombia provide the examples that the rest of Latin America should seek to emulate. Their policies are broadly Keynesian, not in the populist sense of deficit spending, but in the sense that they seek to make their macropolicy anticyclical, as Keynes advocated. They run budget surpluses on average, but allow cyclical departures from the trend in order to smooth the cycle. They seek to hold an exchange rate that is consistent with long-run growth of nontraditional exports, thus avoiding the "Dutch disease[5]," even when excessive capital is flowing in. They are prepared to resort to controls on capital inflows in order to repel excessive foreign capital. They seek to reduce inflation, but, given that they are not the sort of high-inflation countries to which the foregoing analysis of costless stabilization applies, they try to do it gradually rather than insisting on German levels of inflation next year. At the same time as following these prudent policies, they eschew the simplistic macroeconomics (pick a nominal anchor and stick with it through thick and thin, balance the budget irrespective of circumstances, avoid all capital controls) that is one of the hallmarks of "neoliberalism."

In particular, one may hope that Mexico will learn from Chile as it emerges from its most recent crisis. Mexico in the early 1990s repeated much the same policy errors that Chile had made between 1979 and 1981, and which led to its collapse in 1982. It too used the exchange rate unrealistically rigidly as a nominal anchor, it too ignored a collapse in domestic saving because of foreign capital inflows, and it too failed to institute adequate prudential supervision of a newly liberalized banking system. Chile's recession in 1982 was even more severe than that of Mexico in 1995, but at least Chile learned from its mistakes and rectified its earlier errors, so that today it has the strongest economy in Latin America.

Finally, let me put on record that I see absolutely no contradiction between pressing on with policy reforms—that is, consolidating the decline in inflation, strengthening a market economy, and further integrating the region into the work economy, on the one hand, and addressing the social agenda, on the other. On the contrary, as Chile has shown, the policy reforms can lay the basis for rapid growth and provide the wherewithal for an expansion of social expenditure.

ACKNOWLEDGMENT

This chapter has been published here with permission from the Institute for International Economics, copyright 1999. All rights reserved.

NOTES

1. In fact, I still do believe this to be true for moderate rates of inflation.

2. This hypothesis looks even more convincing in light of a paper by William Easterly (1996) that came to my attention only after the conference, and which shows that (rapid) inflation systematically reduces output while its stabilization has no output cost even in the short run.

3. See the recent book by Heymann and Leijonhufvud (1995)for an interesting exploration of this theme.

4. The underlying theory of inflation here is the same theory of cost inflation that prevailed in the Anglo-Saxon world until it was obliterated by the monetarist revolution in the 1970s. The theory remained alive in Brazil, where it became formalized as the concept of inertial inflation. It has been revived in the Anglo-Saxon world by the Alesina-Drazen (1991) "war of attrition."

5. The term refers to the Netherlands' loss of relative competitiveness in its traditional industrial sector which occurred when the Dutch florin appreciated after the development of its natural gas industry.

REFERENCES

Alesina, Alberto and Allan Drazen. (1991). "Why Are Stabilizations Delayed?" *American Economic Review*, Vol. 81, no.5 (December).

Easterly, William. (1996). "When Is Stabilization Expansionary? Evidence From High Inflation." *Economic Policy*, Vol.22 (April).

Friedman, Milton. (1968). "The Role of Monetary Policy." *American Economic Review*, Vol. 58 (March).

Gervasoni, Carlos. (1995). "Economic Policy and Electoral Performance in Latin America, 1982-1995." Center for Latin American Studies, Stanford University.

Heymann, Daniel and Axel Leijonhufvud. (1995). *High Inflation*. Oxford: Clarendon Press.

Phelps, Edmund. (1967). "Phillips Curves, Expectations of Inflation, and Optimal Unemployment Over Time." *Economica*, Vol. 34.

Simonsen, Mario. (1994). *Ensaios Analíticos*. Rio de Janeiro: Editora Fundacāo Getulio Vargas.

Williamson, John. (1994). *The Political Economy of Policy Reform*. Washington, DC: Institute for International Economics.

SOME THOUGHTS ON THE ACHIEVEMENT OF SUSTAINED GROWTH WITH POVERTY REDUCTION IN LATIN AMERICA

Gustav Ranis

INTRODUCTION

We have clearly been witnessing a sea change in attitudes on development policy in Latin America over the last four or five years. Undoubtedly under the influence of the debt crisis of the early 1980s, there has been a noticeable reversal of attitudes and policies concerning the possible relevance of a more open economy setting à la East Asia, positions dismissed as irrelevant as little as a decade ago. Moreover, most Latin American decision makers now seem to realize that the avoidance of painful policy change does not guarantee developmental success; and some even recognize that the hemisphere's relatively ample natural resource endowments, previously seen as a convenient crutch, can prove to be a two-edged sword by tempting policy makers to sit tight and play for time. In a similar vein, the seductiveness of an all too-ready access to commercial bank lending in the 1970s, on top of the region's underlying relative natural resource abundance, seems to have lost some of its appeal. It is not too much to say that on the "morning after the binge," adjustment pains have generally brought a greater realization that below the surface of the debt crisis there resided a long-term development problem—that continued fascination with urban-oriented import-substituting industrialization patterns, complete with inadequate attention to agriculture, to rural industry, and to competitive exports, was not only likely to lead to diminished growth but also to a worsening of the distribution of income and the increased incidence of poverty.

In other words, what was generally true until the mid-1980s—that Latin America could continue to grow at a satisfactory rate, partly financed by its relatively ample natural resource exports and partly by commercial capital inflows, and thus permit well-known vested interests to go relatively unperturbed—ceased to be true thereafter. As the international environment worsened, the emperor's clothes came off and the underlying problems inherent in pursuing an inefficient and nonparticipatory growth path surfaced. It was indeed the ensuing debt crisis which demonstrated that the postwar Latin American "growth miracle" was ephemeral and forced a fundamental reassessment of inward looking strategies pursued too severely and for too long.

Consequently today, with a few question marks, such as Brazil and Peru, Latin America seems clearly to be en route toward a more open, East Asian type of system. Yet there are some fist-size clouds in the sky that should not be ignored. For one, while the critical macroeconomic stabilization chapter of the Washington consensus has by now been generally accepted, the performance in the realm of microeconomic structural change, being the generation and distribution of primary incomes, is still uneven and requires further attention. For another, the generation and distribution of secondary (or social) incomes—the goods and services delivered by the public sector—needs to be placed on the front burner of action, as opposed to rhetoric, really for the first time. And finally, there still exists the risk, once pressures have been sufficiently relieved, for a possible reversion to earlier modes of behavior, this time fueled by DFI and the return of flight capital. We intend to deal briefly with each of these dimensions in this chapter.[1]

At the same time, it is important to learn all the lessons of East Asia, not just those emphasized in the typical IMF or World Bank structural adjustment package—that is, to plumb the depths of what is currently being called changes in the nature of the government's role. This by no means signals a diminution of the influence of the state relative to that of the market, but it may well mean a more significant, if selective, role. Indeed, there are some lessons from the successful East Asian countries here which were not emphasized in the World Bank's East Asian Miracle study, pointing to the major critical functions which need to be carried out by the public sector in ensuring growth with poverty reduction and the improvement of the human condition in Latin America in the 21st century.

THE UNFINISHED BUSINESS OF STRUCTURAL CHANGE

By universal agreement, there exists no "typical" Latin American country, yet by equally universal practice it is permissible not to act (or write) accordingly. That there has been a major change in Latin American policy makers' views on the importance of macroeconomic balance and the inflationary threat is uncontroversial—that is, fiscal and monetary policy restraints have become part of the accepted catechism, while explanations based on structuralism and cost/push inflation have been relegated to the sidelines virtually everywhere. If there is major unfinished business in the realm of reforms today, it is much more likely to reside in two related areas: the role of the exchange rate as an anti-inflationary anchor, and the issue of how to address the varied problems of the domestic, especially the rural, economy.

With respect to exchange-rate policy, the lessons of the Southern Cone's adjustment process have still not been fully digested. For example, both Mexico and Brazil, at least up to this point, have continued to adhere to a fixed exchange-rate-based stabilization package which admittedly is helpful for a time, as long as there is confidence and the likely rising current account deficits accompanying even modest inflation and overvaluation are covered by foreign capital inflows. But, as the contrast between Chilean and East Asian experiences in the late 1980s made abundantly clear, adjusting via money-based stabilization and increased exports, rather than via additional borrowing, generates a much safer, if initially more painful, package. Once credibility is lost, the cumulative gains of almost a decade of reforms can go down the drain virtually overnight.

Turning to the required structural adjustments at the sectoral or microeconomic level, agriculture and rural nonagricultural activities continue to constitute a relatively neglected dimension of Latin American development. Much of the focus of the micro reforms to date has been on import liberalization, on restructuring and privatizing mainly urban industry, and on enhancing industrial export orientation. The importance for overall success of the complementary mobilization of the rural economy, on any of these counts, is not yet fully appreciated. While this may have been quite understandable initially, in the sense that a debt crisis is superficially perceived as an essentially external problem, the realization that it represents merely the visible tip of a development iceberg has come more slowly. Thus, while attention shifted from import substitution to how to become a competitive exporter of nontraditional commodities and on how to encourage the inflow of foreign capital, the complementary blade of the developmental scissors—balanced growth as between agriculture and rural nonagricultural activities and the encouragement of medium and small-scale urban industry—has continued to take a back seat. This becomes especially evident when we contrast Latin America with the East Asian experience, particularly Taiwan's, which had an early agricultural revolution generating both rural balanced growth as well as a burst of nontraditional agricultural exports. It is my contention that such rural dynamism, accompanied by a participatory urban development pattern, is likely to be the crucial ingredient in any primary income generation process which manages to deliver poverty reduction along with growth.

Recognizing that there exists no universal formula for success, not even a Latin American formula, the experience of the last decade encourages us to cite some of the more critical pressure points which are likely to be in need of attention if primary income generation is to become more reliable as well as equitable. First, I believe there must be some assurance of a reasonable distribution of assets and a reasonable incentive structure in place in the agricultural sector. By this I don't mean to insist that traditional land reform must necessarily constitute a first step. Where the political preconditions for ownership reform are more difficult to attain, as is generally acknowledged to be the case in Latin America, perhaps a steeply progressive land tax, requiring less involvement by the bureaucracy in land reform, along with land ceilings which take the higher land/man ratios of Latin America into account, might be a politically more feasible alternative. While some form of land redistribution would certainly be helpful, especially if accompanied by complementary institutional reforms in the allocation of rural credit infrastructure, technology information systems , and the like, even in its absence major payoffs can be obtained if the policy environment facing individual rural actors is sensitively reexamined.

For example, whether the bottleneck is farm-to-market roads, mini-irrigation facilities, or rural electrification, infrastructure allocation biases which tend to "crowd out" instead of "crowding in" private investment activity need to be corrected. It is a well-known secret that if one analyzed the allocation of physical capital as well as that of scarce organizational and institutional energies, both would continue to be heavily biased toward traditional cash-crop export or large-scale urban industry. The redirection of current R&D and extension expenditures remains a serious problem in most Latin American contexts.

The same holds for the impact of price support programs on the producers of staples. While overall budget constraints create a tendency to curtail urban consumer subsidies which so often burden treasuries, the differential impact of other interventions in commodity markets often remains to be addressed. Intersectoral commodity markets in all too many cases continue to be biased against domestic food-producing agriculture and at best exempt only the cash crop-producing subsector. Since one is realistically dealing here with the possible reallocation of given public goods and energies, rather than asking for additional dispensations from already overburdened and constrained budgets, it should not be impossible to act; but vested interests still need to be overcome. Good examples abound. For example, large irrigation projects continue to have priority over the unsilting of local waterways; superhighways crowd out feeder roads; and state-of-the-art, basic research-oriented private R&D and public science and technology institutes continue to take oxygen from adaptive research and learning-by-doing-focused plant-level innovative activities.

A closely related area of microeconomic reform which is likely to be necessary for the generation of a reasonably equitable primary income stream in Latin America is that of the patent system and of R&D incentives in general. One need only point to the large discrepancy in total factor productivity as between the Asian and Latin American systems historically to underscore the fact that an increased emphasis on indigenous applied science and technology is bound to pay off. Tax codes can be modified to encourage risk-taking, and flexibility in the legal and implementation dimensions of intellectual property rights assures that a country moves up the development ladder. The possibility of instituting a new kind of patent option—such as the utility model, with shorter protection and a lower threshold for discovery, in addition to the conventional patent—represents a related area worthy of examination. Unlike Asia, it is my impression that Latin America still relies too heavily on imported patents and imported technology and has not yet sufficiently mobilized its own adaptive or "blue collar" technological change capacity.

Much development literature and policy discourse has indeed neglected the importance of the spatial dimensions of development; and yet the reduction of rural primary income poverty depends on the generation of a development pattern which incorporates both the balanced mobilization of the hinterland and the growth of internationally competitive urban industrial output and export mixes. Given the current reality of large urban informal sectors in most of Latin America, encouraging linkages between formal and informal activities, thus enhancing the productive contribution of the latter which comprises from 20 percent to 50 percent of the urban labor force, also serves as a safety net for the growing numbers of the urban poor, given that most public-sector urban welfare programs are still in their infancy. This is of special importance for societies which are labor surplus at the outset and are at the same time in the process of privatizing their formal urban activities, often entailing an additional loss of employment, at least in the short term.

One other area of unfinished business in Latin America, perhaps the most sensitive of all, is how to render labor markets more flexible. Some things have already been accomplished in the context of the structural adjustment programs of recent years. For example, Mexico's "economic pact," permitting money wage increases to lag behind increasingly moderate inflation, has functioned remarkably well over several years now. But it remains true that, compared to Asia, Latin American labor unions and their political party connections remain relatively strong, and the recognition that the working family is not necessarily advantaged by higher individual member wages instead of higher total family wage incomes is still not fully established. As more and more Latin American economies strive for mature economy status in the years ahead, one should anticipate a shift from government-supported, production-oriented unions toward their more independent, consumption-oriented counterparts. To date, the history of relatively militant unionism in Latin America has undoubtedly been an obstacle—along with inadequate antitrust—to a really workably competitive urban industrial production structure.

In sum, primary income poverty results when the economic system's generation of primary incomes provides inadequate rewards to some households. This is most likely to occur when such households lack assets, have insufficient education, and consequently depend largely on their unskilled labor income. When incomes from low productivity, agricultural activities, supplemented by nonagricultural employment opportunities, both rural and urban, are deficient in pulling families out of poverty, even households with two or more wage earners may be classified as poor. In such a situation, macroeconomic stabilization needs to be supplemented by additional microeconomic structural reforms, yielding additional demand for labor along with the enhanced capacity of individual families to respond to any such improvements in primary income-generating opportunities.

THE ALLOCATION OF SOCIAL GOODS AND THE REDUCTION OF SOCIAL INCOME POVERTY

As already pointed out, poverty, resulting from the way primary incomes are distributed, does not tell the whole story. Both the capacity of Latin American families to take advantage of existing primary income generation, mainly via additional employment opportunities, and thus their ability to improve on such bottom-line welfare indicators as life expectancy, depend on the way the relevant overheads (mostly public goods) are allocated. What we are concerned with here is not so much the allocation of economic infrastructure or even the possible introduction of transfers/subsidies as part of a poverty alleviation program, but the distribution of education, health, potable water, and other social goods. While the family provides some of these goods informally to its members as part of the generation of the so-called full income, most are normally provided by the state.

The size of the secondary or social income to be distributed depends, of course, on the system's total resources or GNP and its willingness, via taxes and expenditures, to make such public goods available, as well as on their allocation by income class. In the presence of substantial macroeconomic stability (i.e., the absence of large-scale monetary expansion and government deficits) we must therefore focus, in the first instance, on the proportion of the GNP which is going to public expenditures (varying widely, between 15 percent and 42 percent in Latin America); in the second instance, on the proportion of such total public expenditures which is allocated to the social sectors (again varying widely, from 17 percent to 44 percent); and, in the third instance, on the proportion of social-sector expenditures which are allocated to satisfy the needs of poor households. The third calculation is the most difficult, since there is no conceptually satisfactory dividing line to help us determine the precise proportion of any social-sector expenditure pattern which benefits the poor. However, we can assume that health expenditures for preventive, rather than curative, purposes (roughly 20 percent of the total in Latin America) and education expenditures for primary and secondary rather than university purposes (roughly 75 percent) provide some indication of what we are after. We must quickly add, however, that even as we can thus derive a system's total social expenditures relative to its GNP which is aimed at the poor, we know very little about the distribution of any social priority good—say, primary education—across families.

Nevertheless, in spite of the relatively greater difficulty encountered in measuring the distribution of secondary incomes and the even greater difficulty of ascertaining how primary and secondary incomes combine most effectively to yield bottom-line improvements in welfare, such as life expectancy, for different socioeconomic groups, ignoring the need for reform in this area would be fraught with danger. The achievement of sustained growth accompanied by poverty reduction indeed requires bringing the two income-generating systems under one roof and inquiring into their joint impact on the bottom-line welfare of the population, especially the poor.

With respect to education and growth, for example, it should be recalled that primary education was the mainstay of the deployment of human capital so important to the success of agricultural and nonagricultural development among the four East Asian "tigers" in the 1960s. It should also be noted that, once labor surplus in Taiwan had come to an end (by the early 1970s), there resulted a switch from six to nine years of compulsory education. Moreover, secondary education was emphasized, heavily oriented toward the vocational and technical, as opposed to the academic, side of the ledger. By the 1980s overall education expenditures were raised to more than 5 percent of GNP, science parks were established, and other efforts expended to bring human capital back from overseas, along with the increasingly successful repatriation of financial capital. It is my impression that, while the total education expenditure/GNP ratio at 5 percent is not very different in Latin America, more attention needs to be paid to qualitative educational strategy changes over time in many country contexts. I would, moreover, surmise that the repatriation of human capital, which has still not occurred on a major scale, would be of far greater developmental significance than the simple return-of-flight capital and is indeed intertwined with it over the longer term.

Another dimension of policy advice which is relevant to the way both economic and social infrastructures are allocated relates to the extent to which the state is centralized or decentralized, as well as to the type of decentralization actually practiced. Federal states, of which there are a few major examples in Latin America, differ from unitary states in their intrinsic potential for a larger degree of decentralization. However, in both federal and unitary states, one more frequently encounters delegation or deconcentration rather than the devolution variety of decentralization, even though the latter may be essential for the success of micro-level structural reforms.

An important ingredient of effective rural mobilization, for example, may be some devolution of decision-making powers from central to local governments. Perhaps even more than in other parts of the developing world, Latin America's public sector today remains heavily centralized—that is, the decision-making process as to what to do and how to do it, in terms of both infrastructure and social sector allocations, is generally still heavily dominated by administrations working through central finance and line ministries. One does not have to be an adherent of a romantic view envisioning the absence of power elites at the local level to maintain that local officials are more knowledgeable about where the proverbial "shoe" pinches, and also more capable of translating such knowledge into effective implementation, if the resources are available, than distant central government officials operating with large "black box" projects. While there clearly exists nonfeasance and malfeasance at all levels, the capacity to set some limits through the "goldfish bowl" or relative transparency effect has special relevance at the local government level.

The usual counterargument, that local governments are not yet "ready" because of their deficient technical or administrative capacities, is painfully reminiscent of arguments of the past concerning the peasantry; in both instances, the response yielded by a more pressured environment in which actors are forced to produce and are given a chance to learn by doing (and sometimes failing) is likely to be substantial. As I see it, there really exists little alternative to devolving more functions of government to the local level, especially in the infrastructural and social sector areas—without necessarily moving from unitary to federal systems. An increased devolution of decision making on "what to do" with a given volume of available resources does not necessarily require the devolution of technical capacities on "how to do it," some of which may, from the point view of a sensible division of labor, still best be kept in the hands of some intermediate, provincial or state, level of government.

Indeed, there is little doubt that the mobilization of rural actors, both agricultural and nonagricultural, can only take place effectively with the aid of an enhanced decentralization of the public sector, removing bottlenecks in the way of private activities. It is undoubtedly also true that, as societies grow and become more complex, it is increasingly essential, not just wise, to do so, just as, in the private sector, enhanced use of the market is largely ordained by the growing complexity of modern societies increasingly defying any effort at detailed planning by the center. Decentralization by devolution, and not in the delegation sense of the old Latin American *servicio* model, is increasingly indicated.

A second important consequence of increased decentralization is the fact that additional resources can be generated in this fashion. Once the benefit principle of taxation becomes a recognized reality, it becomes far easier to raise additional revenue as well as to encourage complementary private savings in the rural areas—especially when contrasted with the present system, which all too frequently requires locally collected taxes to be passed on to the center, scarcely to be heard from again.

IS LATIN AMERICA PUTTING A PERMANENT STOP TO STOP-AND-GO?

As pointed out earlier, there can be little doubt that post-debt crisis policy mixes in Latin America have tended to converge in the general direction of the Washington Consensus, mainly in the macrostabilization arena but, to some extent, also in terms of the agenda on microeconomic structural change. Growth has gradually been resumed; protection is everywhere on the decline; privatization is the order of the day; and the concern with building safety nets for the poor— sometimes with the help of enhanced decentralization—is generally part of the dialogue. But, while highly encouraging, all this should not lead us to conclude that these changes are necessarily irreversible.

In this connection we have already noted that, historically, Latin America experienced an unusually long period of import substitution, culminating in a much fuller ossification of the interventionist habits of government, specifically much more persistent across-the-board types of interventions, than elsewhere in the developing world. This has also meant, at least in the past, that even after export orientation had become à la mode, the temptation to revert, in the face of some exogenous shock, has been strong. For example, over a typical terms of trade cycle, we have been able to observe that Latin American systems tend, in relatively "good periods," to go for more growth than is warranted by enhanced export earnings, and, in "bad periods," to try to maintain growth at all costs for as long as possible—only to be ultimately forced into crisis and a new set of restrictions.[2] This has meant a pattern of exaggerating good times by incurring additional foreign debt and trying to avoid downturns by substituting domestic credit creation for declining foreign exchange availabilities. Typically, the result has been a return to the restrictions reminiscent of the earlier import substitution era, followed by a major devaluation, possibly a new currency, and a renewed liberalization effort. Such behavior, including the continuous stop-go cycling, has been in large part made possible by the underlying ample natural resource endowment of the Latin American countries, further enhanced by their relatively easy access to foreign commercial bank capital in the 1970s and more recently to official assistance and direct foreign investment. In brief, Latin America's response to external shocks of the terms-of trade variety has led to growth activist behavior which, although temporarily successful, has always proved ultimately self-defeating.

This ability to postpone the day of reckoning with the help of natural resources and foreign capital props may be viewed as a political economy extension of the so-called Dutch disease. The question before us is whether, given the magnitude of the 1980s debt crisis and the recent groundswell for orthodox policies, the danger of a future recurrence of that disease in Latin America has passed. While one would like to think so, one cannot be completely sanguine on the subject. The previously referred to fixed exchange-rate-based stabilization strategy currently still adhered to by some important countries provides one indication of the risks ahead. The current account deficits that result from increasingly overvalued exchange rates even at relatively low rates of inflation are clearly only sustainable over the longer term as long as foreign capital continues to come in for the asking. But once credibility is damaged, the result could well be the resumed flight of the previously returned capital which is still relatively footloose, resulting in the possibility of another round in the old stop-go tradition. After all, the region does have a history of reform and relapse.

There are admittedly some other positive new configurations on the scene, including the enhanced external pressures of globalization in trade and capital as embodied in NAFTA and its potential extension into a WHFTA (Western Hemispheric Free Trade Agreement) buttressed by the ultimately successful conclusion of the Uruguay Round and the creation of the World Trade Organization. This change in the environment, more than pressure from the IMF and the

International Bank for Reconstruction and Development creates strong and persistent external pressures for the avoidance of a repeat of the oscillation pattern of the past.

It is also important to remember that the Brady Plan response to the last major crisis was accompanied by the seeds of a critical new lesson—that it is much better, indeed critical, for a country to thoroughly assess its own problems, needs, and capacities before proceeding to accept a structural reform package supported by the international community in order to ease the pain of adjustment. This stands in some contrast to the frequently encountered practice of blaming foreigners for imposing a reform program that has not yet been fully incorporated into the domestic body politic. The ultimate credibility and sustainability of any reform, not only with respect to so-called ownership by the top layers of government but also with reference to the implementation phases at its lower levels, are, of course, critical. The adherence to frequently difficult decisions, translated into self-conditionality actions, negotiated with and endorsed by the international financial community, obviously substantially enhances the chances of immunization against the recurrence of the Dutch disease once international skies have cleared and the pressure is off. Total net resource inflows into the region increased from $7.6 billion in 1989 to $39.3 billion in 1993. DFI alone has increased from $7 billion to $17.5 billion over the same period. Chile, Mexico, and Argentina seem to have definitively reentered the international capital markets, with others not far behind, with new private investment opportunities asserting themselves, contrary to what people expected a scant few years ago. The challenge is to use these resources to ease the pain of future structural change, not to permit them to take the pressure off.

Much of the returned flight capital, financial and human, remains footloose, with still only one foot in Latin American waters. Fears of a return to populism and a Keynesian type government instrumentation of growth have not died—see the recent experience of Venezuela which went from fair-haired ample of the "new Latin America" a couple of years ago to renewed stop-go candidate. In many countries reforms still remain incomplete, especially at the micro levels, as we have pointed out. Any future external shock, terms of trade or business cycle connected, could trigger another massive outflow of capital in magnitudes reminiscent of an earlier day. Latin America's savings rates remain low, at an average of 20 percent of GDP—compared to 34 percent in East Asia—and more than 30 percent of the population remains in poverty. Moreover, on the international front, while the headlines on NAFTA, GATT, as well as MERCOSUR, and other intraregional agreements are all favorable, the small print and the associated dispute settlement procedures which will get more attention down the road are more ambiguous. Moreover, the United States, whose economy is today absolutely more open on the average than in Latin America, is also less likely to reciprocate further liberalization efforts, at the margin, in the years ahead.

Given this basically optimistic but nevertheless precarious setting, it becomes all the more important that current programs focusing not only on resumed growth but also on poverty reduction in Latin America encourage the temporary ballooning of foreign capital inflows as needed to complete agreed-on microeconomic reforms affecting both the primary and social generation of income.

In the 1970s, petrodollars in the form of commercial bank capital circumvented monitoring by international financial institutions and took the pressure off Latin American reform efforts. In the 1990s it is important to remember that foreign friends—along with a good natural resource base—still represent a two-edged sword. They certainly can be deployed to ease the pain of the residual reforms required to assure poverty reduction along with resumed growth. But they also continue to represent a temptation to resume business as usual.

NOTES

1.   This chapter was prepared at the II International Economics Meeting, Córdoba, organized by the Fundación CIEC.

2.   For a more detailed discussion, see Chapter 3 of Ranis and Mahmood (1992).

REFERENCE

Ranis, G. and S. A. Mahmood. (1992). *The Political Economy of Development Policy Change*. Oxford: Basil Blackwell.

OUTLINE FOR A SOCIOECONOMIC PARADIGM FOR POST-CASTRO CUBA

Antonio Jorge

INTRODUCTION

In this chapter I present a very general outline of a strategy for the reconstruction, development, and desocialization of post-Castro Cuba and discuss the functions and role of the state in its implementation. Analogies with past strategies applied in Cuba in the pre-Castro period and at present in other rapidly industrializing nations in the Asian periphery are touched upon here to establish possible parallelisms.

I would like to begin by noting that the social system (or subsystem which we define as the economy) never functions in a totally autonomous fashion, not even in postindustrial nations that are highly modernized and secularized. In reality, the economy is always conditioned by an enormous set of noneconomic factors—historical-cultural, sociopsychological, religious, and legal, among others. These elements greatly influence the selection of our economic goals and objectives and the ways, means, and methods followed to achieve them. They frequently dictate or mold our strategies and policies, set priorities, point out prohibitions, restrictions, and limitations: and thus define our areas of freedom of action and of economic choice. The foregoing explains the decisive importance of formulating a general social model within which the economic subsystem may function in an effective and acceptable fashion. This, in turn, requires a profound understanding of the historical evolution of a people, of their beliefs, values, and motivations, as well as a correct interpretation of how the cultural medium permeates the thought and conduct of a society.

SOME CONSIDERATIONS FOR CUBA

In keeping with the above, it may be inferred in principle that there are many roads leading to development and desocialization in each particular case. That is, it may be reasonably assumed that given the flexible nature of most of the variables involved and their range of potential values, multiple stable equilibria solutions would exist to this general equilibrium system. The choice of one or the other solution is a very complicated process which definitely must be left in the hands of the people and their representatives in democratic or politically participatory systems. Thus, any suggestions made by a particular individual, even if a professional or expert in economic or political matters, must be taken only as a partial expression of a multifaceted reality.

In regard to the specific instance of Cuba, the preceding observations lead us to offer a few indications with respect to the nature of possible strategies for the reconstruction, development, and desocialization of the nation. As I envision it, viable strategies should generally conform to the spirit and purposes of the Cuban socioeconomic developmental stage which began in 1927. It is essential to the likelihood of this thesis to understand that the period which goes from the end of the 1920s to the end of the 1950s had its own identity and continuity. This was certainly the case in the economic area, independent of the vicissitudes in the political arena which seriously fragmented Cuban society during that time. A strong nationalist spirit, economic diversification, socialization and modernization, growing technological innovation in productive and administrative spheres, an accelerated movement toward social integration, legislative programs, and an institutional order oriented toward creating a more humane and close-knit society (in greater control of its own destiny), and also a more active policy of political management accompanied by vigorous entrepreneurial activity—these together constituted some of the most salient characteristics of Cuba from 1927 to 1958.

It is obvious that the future of a society cannot and should not seek to mechanically copy its past. The historical processes of evolution make this impossible, even in the absence of violent institutional ruptures or the reversal of established tendencies and secular movements. What is most feasible and desirable, nevertheless, is a creative reinterpretation of the cultural essence and national character of a people so that the latter may evolve freely in a new society without losing the sense of its own identity.

In trying to retain that cultural essence, the following conditions, parameters, and potentialities should be kept in mind by the policy maker. Cuba is a small nation with an open economy, still marked by monoculture, but with great potential for socioeconomic progress. Its people are vivacious, independent, intelligent, and alert, living in a strategically situated country with an abundant and productive environment. Cuba is a society in search of a social market economy system which will agree with its particular traits. That system should be able to maintain a dynamic balance in the macroeconomic sphere in order to pass safely over the hurdles of an international panorama in constant flux, while also promoting the sound internal development of the economy in a climate of economic efficiency and rationality. The difficult art of promoting and channeling individual and private activity in an atmosphere of constructive freedom, avoiding the extremes of excessive intervention and chaotic atomization (laissez faire), is the challenge posed by the creation of a new social and economic order in Cuba at the end of the 20th century.

This challenge is compounded by a mix of historical, cultural, and economic factors which call for a delicate and difficult blend of policies and institutions, perhaps not unlike, in its own way, the one that characterized the developmental strategies of Taiwan and South Korea. A very high foreign trade coefficient and foreign dependency, along with the perennial instability induced by an economy dominated by the production and export of a primary commodity in a declining world market, are two fundamental traits marking the Cuban economy. To this must be added its very low efficiency and productivity, at present reaching catastrophic levels and on the verge of a complete breakdown in the immediate future.

Concerning the sociocultural and sociopsychological order, not only is the Cuban society influenced (as is the case of all formerly socialist countries) by paternalistic ethos and a sort of welfarism, but it also shares elements of historical corporatism with other Ibero-American societies. In prerevolutionary Cuba this trait was reflected in a number of key institutions and policies such as: the provision of public and mutual health services, advanced labor legislation, regulation of the price of staples, and the politically determined distributional mechanism of the sugar industry, among many other instances.

Moreover, the relatively low level of Cuba's economic development and the urgent need to diversify its economy in the midst of imminent collapse, all the while warding off external shocks generated by uncontrollable exogenous forces, dictate the need for great prudence in devising an appropriate strategy for the transition from its peculiar variety of *caudillo* socialism to a full-fledged social market economy.

OUTLINE OF A STRATEGY FOR DECOLLECTIVIZING AND DESOCIALIZING CUBA

The suggestions contained in this section should be analyzed in light of all the preceding considerations. It is merely intended as a very preliminary outline, obviously incomplete, without any pretensions to finality, in a field characterized by extreme complexity and rapid change. Its purpose is, therefore, to stimulate thought and the exchange of ideas.

Let us then move on to detail at least some of the principal premises and conditions which serve as a basis, and which also frame the recommendations contained in the strategies for reconstruction and development presented here.

Those assumptions also underlie the *modus operandi* of the recommended processes of decollectivization and desocialization.

A first point of extraordinary importance is the adequate coordination of the means or instruments of structural change (organizations and institutions) with those of policy and stabilization measures (e.g., monetary and fiscal policies, and still those others related to subsidies and foreign exchange control, among others). While at the end of the restructuring period of the economy (which, according to my estimations, will last about five years), the basic structural changes and the policies of stabilization will be fully adjusted and coordinated with each other, it would be practically impossible to try to orchestrate in a parallel fashion in time both types of changes or to seek to achieve these instantly. It is in this vein, that we should consider the danger of trying overambitious solutions in the process of desocialization, often referred to in the literature as the Big Bang approach.

It should also be remarked that, as a theoretical principle, the choice of the Big Bang is a very attractive one, but it implies enormous political and social risks, while at the same time requiring administrative, economic, human, and moral resources which do not actually exist in socialist and communist societies. As a result, the gradualist position has become more popular in the former Soviet Union as well as in countries of Eastern Europe. Only Poland represented an exception to that preference, although it has now joined the gradualist camp. Clearly, the case of East Germany should be treated as a unique phenomenon without analogy in the rest of the former socialist world because of its having been integrally absorbed by West Germany.

The adoption and execution of the gradualist solution assumes the need to choose and prioritize the sequences of structural changes and economic policies to be followed, as well as the speed with which these are to be conducted. This is an enormously complex and difficult task to undertake, for which, of course, there are no historical antecedents that would serve as a guide, just as there are also none for the alternative position of the Big Bang.

It is also necessary to emphasize that not opting for the solution of the immediate transformation to a market economy (Big Bang), does not mean that the opposite choice, gradualism, is exempt from dangers of its own. This was pointed out succinctly in the reference made to the topic in question in an article of mine published in *Diario Las Americas* in its November 11, 1990 issue. In that article an attempt was made to explain in general terms the reasons for the failure of *perestroika*, anticipated by this writer as early as 1986. In strictly economic terms, these reasons were principally related to the vagueness, lack of definition, and absence of technical specifications necessary for the implementation of the reforms. The latter had been reduced to statements of purpose and lacked the ordering, continuity, and sequential character that a transition plan requires. Moreover, until a few years ago the modifications in economic policy in the former Soviet Union have taken place almost exclusively in the fiscal and monetary macroeconomic plane, having avoided the difficult structural reforms in institutions and organizations which a real change of system demands.

Thus, the Soviet experiment was doomed to fail. Lacking coherence and balance, it did not constitute a feasible option. We should keep this lesson uppermost in our minds in the case of Cuba. *Gradualism should not be confused with inertia nor with the search for halfway solutions which are not really such.* An inescapable condition of the gradualist strategy is to effect structural transformations according to a preconceived plan which will clearly outline the path to be followed in order to recreate fully and completely a social market economy. Likewise, stalling and pseudo-reforms—such as privatization patterns and radical enterprise restructuring in Russia, the Czech Republic, and former East Germany—have eventuated in stagnation or lower rates of growth in these countries at various points in time.

Having stated the basic or key premises for our analysis, let us now point to some objectives to be adopted and sequences of movements to be followed in the strategy for reconstruction and development suggested here. For the short term, there is no more expeditious, safe and effective way than to adopt (obviously bearing in mind the modifications which may have taken place in the Cuban production matrix from approximately 1961 on, as well as the political-economic conditions and restrictions arising from future international economic agreements and the availability of foreign real and financial resources) the general developmental strategy which was followed by the country during the period 1927 to 1958. In essence, that strategy constitutes the best route for the economic reconstruction of the nation as well as for the simultaneous beginning of the process of the decollectivization and desocialization of the Cuban economy.

The policies of agricultural diversification and of rational economic self-sufficiency, applied as much to the production of basic goods for general consumption as to primary activities in general, as well as to agribusiness and cattle ranching, should enjoy maximum priority in the dual programs of reconstruction and decollectivization. A second but close priority should be given to light industry for the production of consumer goods and intermediate manufacturing in general. Here we include the reconstruction and development of the broad base already existing in the 1950s in the field of semidurable consumer goods, as well as the gradual expansion of the production of industrial raw materials—the latter in close connection with the growth and needs of the national agroindustrial complex.

This succinctly formulated program would yield optimum results along a gamut of fronts and would accomplish several objectives: (1) it would serve to reestablish relatively quickly and massively personal and private initiative as well as private enterprise in society; (2) it would contribute decisively over the short period to the diversification and stability of the economy and to a greater degree of self-determination over both the national destiny and economic policy itself; and (3) it would be of great value as well in the promotion of the country's domestic and external financial stability. The first two objectives would be effected by means of the stimulation of entrepreneurial activity and the accelerated increase in the production of highly necessary consumer goods. This, in turn, would help to establish a stable equilibrium in price levels, a high level of employment, and the continued expansion of the gross national product (GNP). The third objective, financial stability, would be promoted by means of policies tending to favor a positive trade balance, or at least one which maintains equilibrium, and also by increased savings of hard foreign exchange with the consequent accumulation of reserves in convertible currency.

All of the preceding would serve to facilitate the gradual and orderly transition from a collectivist, centralized economy, to a healthy market-system economy through spontaneous natural growth and expansion. The growth of a market-system economy would primarily result from the flourishing of the personal and private initiative of the economic agents, at present repressed by the political system. In turn, the outlined program would constitute the best vehicle (and the easiest, least bureaucratic road) toward introducing free markets for goods, services, and real inputs of all kinds. It would also serve to facilitate the creation, once the process is launched, of parafinancial and credit markets in general and later on—perhaps in a period of two to four years—of the corresponding system of private institutions for their operation.

This approach would undoubtedly represent the simplest path, the one requiring least government intervention in important sectors of the economy and also the least upsetting in relation to existing economic activity, facilitating the sound organic growth of markets and the new economic institutional order. The outlined option would definitely stimulate the process of the structural evolution of the society toward a full market economy. At the same time, it would make possible the staggered introduction of highly sensitive stabilization policies, such as the withdrawal or cancellation of subsidies for production and consumption purposes and the policy limitation on salary increases, making unnecessary, after an initial period, other unpopular measures such as the freezing of savings and a drastic increase in taxation, or still other restrictions which would affect the consumption of domestic or imported goods.

Let us point out that the solution we are sketching avoids sudden breaks or discontinuities in the economic process with their deflationary aftermath in terms of production and employment. It also skirts the forced or sudden changes which inevitably lead to errors in economic and social policy, such as some of those which have been made in Eastern Europe, especially in connection with austerity and stabilization policies, and from which we surely must learn in order to avoid their repetition. Finally, this path is the one which most easily adapts to the disastrous Cuban economic situation obtaining at present: to the country's low level of development, its small market extension, scarce productive resources, limited land availability, present population, climate, topography, insufficient energy infrastructure, transportation, communications and distribution networks, as well as many other economic and social factors to be taken into consideration in the conceptualization of the best strategic approach to accomplish the task ahead. As a new social and economic reality emerges as a consequence of the process which has been thus far described, basic structures, organizations and institutions, incentives, motivations, and forms of behavior will begin to take shape. Some of these are essential and others merely supporting elements in a true, modern market economy, one whose nature would be socially compatible with the historical and cultural characteristics of Cuba and its people.

This gradualist, organic process is the only one that can solve the antinomies and contradictions which a radical change in the economic system would inevitably present. The author has often referred to this question in addressing the serious problems faced by East European countries such as Poland, and also Hungary to a lesser degree, in their attempt to institute a market-based, legitimate program of privatization without having created beforehand the conditions which could assure its success. By way of illustration, let me quote from my November 1990 article:

> Ideally, in order to privatize the means of production one must be able to first evaluate them economically. But in order to do that one must project the future yield of productive assets. However, this in turn would require the existence of a free market where supply and demand determine prices, not only of finished products or consumer goods but also of the means of production, whether in the form of physical capital, land or labor or entrepreneurial or administrative services.
>
> Free markets, in turn, require a regime of private property and the use of financial and commercial instruments or of investment credit which only private banks can facilitate. Moreover, the assessment of the financial assets of productive entities requires the existence of a stock market.
>
> In order to function effectively, all of the above requires a stable fiscal and monetary medium which, in turn, presupposes budgetary austerity and the control of the money supply. This would in turn imply the hardening of budgetary constraints and the limitation of subsidies to businesses, without which many existing enterprises would go bankrupt.
>
> Naturally, in a complex process such as this, we will run up against many obstacles, such as the relationship between the amount of free monetary reserves, the financial state of the current account balance and the balance of payments; monetary, salary, and trade policies, and the convertibility of national currency. Still another illustrative example is the interdependence between the levels of production, wage policies, the regulation of prices and foreign trade policy, and so forth *ad infinitum.*

The solution to this apparently unsolvable puzzle, which the complex interdependence of economic factors posits and which constitutes the Gordian knot of the decollectivization and desocialization processes, resides in the growth and expansion, as in concentric circles of increasing diameter, of the structural and functional network that make up the material substratum of that entity which we refer to as a social market economy.

Nonetheless, these processes of circular causation must start at some point. There must be an inception and a winding of the clock for the market mechanism to work in accordance with its basic design. If the aim is to expeditiously create a true market system with all of its normal attributes, then an entrepreneurial model of privatization should be pursued from the very beginning. Many of the problems confronted by the former Soviet Union and East European countries arise from the fact that this issue has not been straightforwardly dealt with. *A fortiori*, in the case of Cuba, entrepreneurial privatization must be vigorously and resolutely pursued *ab initio*. The country's geoeconomic and geopolitical characteristics, comparative advantage in trade and investment, supply sources of financial resources, in conjunction with its own historical or traditional economic psychology and sociology, as well as that of its immediate neighbors and natural economic partners, unequivocally dictate a pattern of economic institutionalization based on the centrality of the entrepreneurial function in society.

Once the question of property rights over the means of production has been settled in the manner just indicated, the serious difficulties to be faced in the process of implementing the reforms stem from the fact that it is necessary, when selecting a reconstruction and development strategy, to address in advance the following matters:

- The choice of key sectors or activities selected to start the process
- The nature of the legal and administrative provisions which would give viability to the establishment of the new institutional and organizational order, as well as the functional modes of administration and policy which would make possible the execution of the transformation process by stages toward a market economy
- Availability of resources and the use of them in regard to mode and manner in the introduction of the preestablished investment pattern for reconstruction and development of the economy
- Extent and form of state economic action in the promotion and guidance of the complex network of interrelations between sectors, industries, activities and projects, which will result from the new production matrix created by the emerging market economy

The most important step to be taken, however, is the following:

- Definition of long-, medium-, and short-range objectives to achieve the final goal, which is the creation of a social market economy and the corresponding, anticipated formulation of the corrective policies which should be applied in the event, which is quite likely to materialize, of deviations and nonfulfillment in substance and time of the sequence of predetermined objectives

All that has been stated thus far has had for its purpose the clarification of the essential logic of the process of decollectivization, by means of the application of an appropriate reconstruction strategy which, by making use of economic relationships and mechanisms, would serve to promote the formation of a social market economy in the particular case of Cuba.

In this short chapter—it is impossible to describe in a detailed or concrete form the policies to be employed in this intricate project and the specific results that would follow from such policies. We must limit ourselves to offer remarks on the rationality and internal logic involved in the strategic processes themselves. These must obey a double condition in their formulation: (1) a clear, precise vision of the final objective to be achieved, namely, the creation of a social market economy adapted to the specificities of the Cuban nation, and (2) the adoption of orthogenetic and epigenetic programs of decollectivization, desocialization, and reconstruction. This means that the programs in question have to reproduce mimetically the ordered, sequential, harmonic, and gradually differentiated evolution of the natural organic processes of market growth and development. That is, they must imitate the procedures and spontaneous patterns which govern the creation of the complex interrelationships that characterize biological entities in their developmental process.

If the evolutionary mechanism behaves in keeping with the norms and policies of a system of natural economics, those apparently perplexing difficulties will disappear. Among the most important norms and policies to be applied by a successful program are the following: definition of property rights; establishment of semirational price systems; designing of policies of austerity and stabilization (including tax reform, reduction in public expenditures, phasing out of subsidies, and restrictive monetary policy); implementing limited convertibility of the national currency; determination of a rate (or rates) of foreign exchange, which would correspond to the parity of the real purchasing power of domestic and foreign currencies; formulation of the patterns to follow in the interweaving of businesses, projects, activities, industries, and sectors of the economy, and in the allotment of resources to them in the process of implementing the corresponding strategies; the creation of financial, banking, and credit systems in general (in a period of two to four years); and many other issues which, due to their circular character, would seem to frustrate any rational (efficient) solution of the conundrum facing former socialist societies traveling the road to market.

From all of the above, it is evident that the emergence of rational price system(s) and truly competitive markets in the economy will not take place instantaneously. In effect, no matter how intellectually satisfying that outcome would prove to be, it is practically impossible to attempt to create rational prices and perfect markets at one fell swoop. In the same manner in which a market system cannot be constructed by the intervention of a *deus ex machina*, so competitive prices cannot be formed by the mere waving of a magic wand.

In a similar fashion, it is essential to avoid the false dilemma posed by those who argue in favor of either first instituting competitive market structures, or else bringing about immediately a complete liberalization of prices. To cast the reform of the economic system in that light is to incur in a logically fallacious, *ab ovo* or "chicken-an-egg," causal relationship. Actually, the appearance of a free price system is a process which is itself coextensive with the emergence of truly competitive market structures. The latter, in turn, are dependent upon profound societal changes which may take a long time to come about.

However, it is also crucial to realize that, ultimately, the functions of a rational price system are different in an advanced market economy from what they are in a developing marketing economy. Also, the order of the functional priorities involved will radically vary in both cases. The reason for the variation in question resides in the nature of the differing long-term goals of the developed and less developed market economies. Whereas in the former case, maximum aggregate satisfaction of the consumers is postulated as the standard goal or *raison d' être* of a modern, liberal economy; in the latter case, in an ambience characterized by poverty and acute scarcity, a more production-oriented or mercantilistic approach is called for.

That is, for advanced or relatively advanced socialist economies seeking to transform themselves into market economies, the primary goal is to substantially increase their factor productivity and overall productive efficiency. To that effect, rational prices are required to eliminate biases in factor and commodity pricing and to approximate optimal resource allocation among sectors, activities, and projects throughout the economy, as well as to attain cost-minimizing factor combinations in the relevant production functions and also in the choice of technologies. By contrast, less developed socialist economies traveling the road to market have to be mindful of other objectives, such as stimulating economic development by creating attractive investment opportunities, by reducing economic and political risks, and generally by promoting the stability of the economy and the society. Their governments have to devise diversification strategies, hedge against sharp fluctuations in world market primary commodity prices, insure continuity of a domestic flow of investment resources, induce a net inflow of external capital resources and technology, and many other related matters. In the particular case of Cuba, which, as previously described, is an impoverished and very open kind of monoculture economy, the typical difficulties of backward economies are severely compounded.

Almost by definition, less developed, open, and lopsided economies like that in Cuba, have to, with almost total single mindedness, direct their energies to a rapid acceleration of their rate of growth. This, while coextensively pursuing the diversification of production and a higher level of stability, at the same time that they must try to satisfy, even if minimally, the expectations of the population with regard to its well being. Naturally, none of this negates the importance of economic efficiency as a central goal. Quite the contrary. What it signifies, though, is that the dynamic requisites of growth are such that Pareto optimal static efficiency solutions will not be conducive to a near-optimal multiperiod dynamic growth path. It also means that social and political parametric values are to be seriously recognized as necessary conditions for a successful ride on the growth turnpike, even if this were to mean occasional detours into second-best roads.

In economic terms, the above translates, among other things, into different functions for the price system. Some of those whose fundamental importance is being increasingly realized at present are: the elimination of a pervasive antiexport bias in resource allocation; the correction of the persistent undervaluation of capital and overvaluation of labor; the use of the price system as an incentive to induce effort, and as an opportunity cost guideline in orienting public policy, in areas such as the provision of public goods and the introduction of compensatory and offsetting measures, as is the case with subsidies, tariffs, fiscal exemptions, and the like. In this regard, the experience of Asian countries, most especially that of South Korea, is extremely pertinent.

Although it goes without saying that the introduction of a larger dose of competition, the drastic reduction in overregulation, the freeing of trade, the pursuit of fiscal balance and monetary restraint—in sum, the set of measures which are encompassed in the category of austerity and stabilization policies, are highly desirable, in fact indispensable, in improving the economic efficiency of developing countries; it is also no less true that this latter group of nations, and particularly Cuba in its present situation, should not aspire in the foreseeable future to the creation of a pure and perfectly competitive market structure and a corresponding Hayekian price system, directed at providing perfect information, price fluidity, and utility-maximizing, consumer-oriented choices. Cuba is in no position to use prices as an index of preference rather than as a social cost indicator.

Finally, let us remind ourselves once more that generic terms such as competition, profit maximization, cost minimization, optimality, and so on are all culture-bound. Their meaning and content, as well as related forms of human behavior, are contingent upon cultural variation in the broad sense of the latter term. Likewise, the functions and operations of the price system will differ, as well as their relative importance, from one society to the next. Cuba is no exception to that rule.

The foregoing analysis in terms of strategic steps, sequences, and policies does not exclude, but instead is complemented, by the fostering and stimulation of certain key projects for economic maintenance and/or development in areas where Cuba enjoys a clear, comparative economic advantage at the present time or potentially. These projects can contribute to the stability and economic growth of the nation and provide substantial income in much-needed convertible currency. Among these are the sugar industry in particular, others such as tourism and mining, and, on a lesser scale, fishing. Other products for export, such as tobacco, citrus fruits, and various other fruits and vegetables, were meant to be included in the preceding considerations regarding the agricultural sector, but because of their present or future importance in the area of foreign trade, should also receive immediate and special attention in the formulation of the nation's developmental strategy.

The economic future and welfare of Cuba and the Cuban people make particular development projects such as those mentioned above not simply important but, actually, *imperative*. Therefore, the creation of developmental activities should be facilitated in every way possible and without any delay. Still, from the standpoint of the mechanics of the decollectivization and desocialization of the special projects (which constitute by virtue of their magnitude entire industries and even whole economic sectors), they are to operate, in effect, as relatively autonomous centers of economic activity which will not be initially totally integrated into the general national strategy of investment and reconstruction. The pace and means for the expanding of the development projects; their links and connections with other sectors, industries, and activities; their needs for resources, and by extension, their price systems, technologies, and use of economic factors, will not be governed at first by the discipline and norms of the general social market system. However, the latter by expanding in a gradual, measured, and consistent fashion will eventually occupy the total extent of the national economy.

How can this apparently irreconcilable conflict between the specific needs and particular mechanics of the individual development projects and the overall reconstruction processes of the national economy be solved? An efficient formula for their reconciliation in time would rely on a gradual integration of those projects, industries, or special development sectors into the general organism of the economy. Out of necessity, this should be done sensibly, through a process of iterations or successive approaches, like the smooth descent of an airplane making a perfect landing.

The prices and markets generated by those developmental projects or semiautonomous industries will gradually converge with the general systems of prices and markets of the national economy until they are completely replaced by the latter. That is, the time will arrive when those projects, industries, or special development sectors will cease to be separate entities and will become a structural part of a unitary social market system. However, until the system reaches that point of final balance, there must necessarily exist parallel systems of internal or domestic prices (so-called accounting or administrative and shadow prices) and external or foreign exchange prices. These parallel systems will, without doubt, be a source of imperfections and will detract from the ideal of static optimum economic efficiency or Pareto optimality, as the classical and neoclassical economists conceive it. Nevertheless, as has already been indicated, the imperative need to promote growth rapidly imposes a burden upon the economy in the form of a dual strategy: reconstruction on the one hand and development on the other, inevitably creating friction and diminishing the static (at each point in time) efficiency of the general economic process. The reward lies in the acceleration of economic development by the exploitation of key activities with a real or potential comparative advantage, mainly through the generation of exports to international markets.

With the passage of time—perhaps five years for decollectivization and reconstruction and ten years for the creation of a full system of social-market economy—these dualities and antinomies will disappear. At the end of the latter period a single system of internal and external prices will prevail, as well as unified, competitive markets for all the resources, goods, and services of all kinds, whether their uses are in production or consumption, in this or that sector, industry, activity or project, now or in the future.

CONCLUDING COMMENTS

A few concluding comments in connection with the role of the state during the period of desocialization, reconstruction, and development are in or order at this point. As readily apparent from the nature of the desocialization and developmental strategy advanced in this chapter, in the case of an underdeveloped, monocultural, and very open economy, which to boot is in an extremely precarious situation, the role of the state must perforce, at least initially, be a very prominent one. Especially so, if to the preceding characteristics one were to add the political and social instability which will inevitably materialize in the case of Cuba in the immediate post-Castro stage as institutional and behavioral megachanges are unleashed.

In effect, under those conditions the state is charged with the function of providing the institutional and organizational frame within which economic relations generally, and the market system in particular, are to operate. Such a state is not the liberal or benevolent one of welfare economics, nor the pluralist state of developed, modern Western democracies, but the nation-building state of old with social goals of its own.

Considerations of allocative efficiency and Pareto optimality become historically relevant only after the foundations of society are firmly established. Domestic perfect competition, rational prices, and free trade are kind of the icing on the cake. That is, albeit static efficiency is not to be underestimated as an important economic goal, it nonetheless is a contextual and not an absolute value. It certainly cannot antecede the overriding objective of creating a sound and stable society and polity.

It is of much interest to point out in this context, that there is an ample and growing body of evidence showing the absence of a clear and significant relationship between modest and even not-so-small effective protection rates and price distortion indexes, and differences in productivity and growth increments among nations. There is no decisive evidence either of a firm or strong link between competition and productivity growth, the latter being a most important (and a very large) residual in explaining differential growth rates among nations.

Managerial and organizational factors are increasingly at the forefront of explanatory attempts of dynamic efficiency, productivity advances, and secular growth. Bureaucratic control of the self-serving and asphyxiating kind existing in most less developed countries is certainly detrimental to vigorous economic growth and the sound performance of the economy. However, state guidance of the nation-building kind, geared to laying the groundwork of the economy and the proper relationship that should obtain between the public and private sectors at a given stage of socioeconomic development, is an entirely different matter. Such grand strategies and broad policy making are not to be governed by the optimization rules of microeconomic theory. In the longest of long runs, *historical sense and a correct course of social development are definitely the decisive factors in promoting sustained growth and, ultimately, a maximum benefit for society.* The developmental state, indeed, should not be dismissed as an anachronism of the mercantilist era.

It is within this universe of thought that I would like to comment on two germane questions. One, directly related to the thoughts discussed immediately above, has to do with the fascinating and relatively unexplored topic of development and growth under conditions of cultural variation and institutional and organizational diversity. This topic, one of the greatest importance, has been almost entirely left to the curiosity of social anthropologists and economic sociologists, with some interest of late being shown by those in the fields of international management and organizational theory.

One can do no more than to call attention in passing to the increasing recognition and sensitivity on the part of scholars concerned with this matter of the so-called phenomenon of functional equivalence. That is, of the observed fact that different sets of institutions, organizations, and policies may be equally efficient in the attainment of the same socioeconomic goals and objectives. The existence of a cultural indifference map, so to speak, and of an isoquant efficiency curve relating diverse cultural forms to a common level of efficiency is, perhaps, the most important insight and fruitful field of investigation to be explored in the immediate future in the entire area of social and economic development. Much is still to be learned from the examples of Japan, South Korea, and Taiwan and their organizational and institutional arrangements.

The second question pertains to the much-debated issue of the effectiveness of alterative developmental strategies in promoting their avowed goal of maximizing economic growth. It seems that as more empirical evidence becomes available for examination, the less certain appears to be the conclusion that outward-oriented or export-promotion types of strategies are superior to moderately inward-bound ones. This is especially so the poorer the country happens to be and the slower the growth of world trade during the period under investigation. As has already been observed, "getting the prices right" *a la* IMF or World Bank is not always necessarily the best policy. As a matter of fact, it can be shown that a certain degree of price distortion and a slant toward investment goods may be positively correlated with higher rates of growth. This, in turn, is related to the notion of a developmental state, as in the case of the newly industrialized countries of the Asiatic periphery, where the public sector has assumed a proactive role in leading the market, sometimes even in a big leadership kind of way, socializing the risks of investment, making resources available to some sectors or industries on preferential terms, and diminishing the impact of foreign competition.

Last, it is essential to realize that the overall efficiency of a socioeconomic system and its degree of both x and y efficiency, is related not only, perhaps not even importantly, to competitiveness in the traditional or textbook sense of a pure or perfect market but, rather, to absolute levels of effort and to the so-called traditional work ethic in a general fashion. If that is indeed the case, nation- and state-building, along with the proper set of incentives, expectations and institutions in an appropriate cultural context, is as relevant, if not more so, to development as is the accumulation of physical capital or other growth-related factors.

The preceding remarks are exceptionally pertinent in the case of Cuba. As detailed in the opening section of this chapter, the country's historicocultural and economic characteristics are such as to merit singular consideration in the formulation of its institutional, organizational, political, and socioeconomic policy context. In fact, some general similarities with the Korean and Taiwanese experiences should not be overlooked and could prove to be very intriguing in a comparative analysis of these societies.

In my opinion, the only way in which Cuba is going to be successful in reconstructing and developing its society and economy after the disaster of the last four decades is by recovering and creatively reinterpreting its historicocultural background, where its essence and national character lies, instilling into its people a new life and a renewed sense of hope and faith in the future of the society.

Carrying out that program for the new Cuba requires a remodeling of the role of the state and its relationship with the private sector, as well as a reconsideration of the specific tasks to be performed by the price system; a redesigning of the proper investment, reconstruction, and developmental strategies to be adopted by the society and also of the kind or type of market structures and financial institutions to be created and, above all, of the nature and content of the relations between the individual members of society and the state, the individual and the various social groups, and the individuals among themselves. No trivial matters, indeed. But, then, neither is the creation of a new society *ex nihilo*.

REFERENCE

Jorge, Antonio. (1990). "No Rendirán Los Frutos Deseados Las Reformas en Economicas La URSS." Diario Las Americas, November 11: 7A. (A loose translation of the title is "The Economic Reforms of the USSR will not Yield the Desired Results.")

15

ON THE POLITICAL ECONOMY OF PENSIONS AND SOCIAL SECURITY

Peter Diamond

INTRODUCTION

Governments take many actions that affect the design and execution of corporate pension plans. In this chapter I discuss exactly what it is that governments do in this respect, and some of the motivations for their actions. My focus and examples are based on U.S. experience, although I do say a few words about the Chilean system, on which I have also worked.

In considering government activities, I will invoke four motivations: (1) the short-run budget situation; (2) the long-run financial position of social security; (3) the attempt to improve the functioning of the economy, as well as the equity of income flows; (4) the government response to individual pressures to tilt resources in their direction.

The ongoing problems of U.S. budget deficits and the difficulty that Congress and the administration have faced in dealing with them are not news to anyone. That this pressure shows up in the pension area comes from the effect on the deficit of the tax treatment of pension contributions. I will return to this issue later. Similarly, it is no surprise to anyone that the United States will go through a demographic transition as the baby boom generation retires early in the next century. Each year, the Office of the Actuary of the Social Security Administration (SSA), prepares three Social Security fund projections: long-term, short-term, and intermediate, with each based on an array of demographic assumptions, in terms of aging and the pattern of those of retirement age relative to those of working age. The intermediate projection is usually considered the best guess. In addition to these demographic assumptions is a range of economic assumptions behind the financial forecasts, a critical variable here being the assumed rate of real wage growth. Unfortunately, the present combination of demographic and economic assumptions provides a somewhat unsettling picture for the trust fund: It is projected to hit zero by the year 2029. Of course problems, such as with mailing checks on time, would come sooner since a smooth cash flow requires about 14 percent of annual expenditures. The zero trust fund date has moved steadily earlier in successive projections.

As an aside, the financial difficulties of the Social Security system are swamped by the problems of medical care costs. Projecting to the year 2020, roughly one-third of the U.S. GNP will go for health care. And aging is only 10 percent of the growth in the share of GNP. This probably won't happen, but it is useful to remember when thinking of the problems associated with an aging society.

Social Security is rising rapidly in the political agenda despite the distance of the zero date. One reason is the politics of Social Security has a long tradition of paying attention to the future. Another is the recent failure to deal with health care. Political pundits conjecture that it will be easier to deal with Social Security, making it a candidate for a Congress that wants accomplishments. In any event, one party or the other is likely to seize Social Security as a good issue in the 2000 presidential election, most likely the Democrats. Since polls show that the public is already concerned with the future of Social Security, I would not be surprised to see such reform play a significant role in the 2000 Presidential campaign. This would follow a prolonged period of increased newspaper coverage of the issue, coverage which may soon begin to mount.

Now seems an appropriate time to discuss some possible directions that Social Security reform may take, and how they will impact on private pensions. I will also describe what has been happening in private pensions and some of the concerns I have in that area.[1]

SOCIAL SECURITY

Since it is a given of American politics that it is difficult-to-impossible to take benefits away from those already receiving them, it is widely recognized that the sooner this problem is addressed the better. While a crisis in 35 years does not have quite the political salience as one today, there are considerable pressures to begin addressing this problem now. First, it is easier to deal with the sooner one starts. This is simple arithmetic. But it is also true that it is easier to legislate tax increases and benefit cuts the further in the future they are scheduled to happen. And once such legislation is in place, rolling back such changes is much more difficult than blocking legislation. We saw this with the 1983 legislation that included both benefit cuts (in the form of a delayed normal retirement age) and tax increases, all of which have stayed on the books despite pressures for change. It is useful to remember the current surpluses of Social Security, and the potential for even larger ones, as a source of short-run revenue.

I expect the political process to go through two overlapping stages. The first is to decide whether to try to muddle through some mix of tax increases and benefit cuts, all disguised as much as possible—or to try a major institution reform. Then, whichever branch is followed there will be fights as to how to proceed. On the major reform branch, the two options are to imitate Chile, partially, by mandating individual savings, or to go to Mandated Universal Pensions (MUPS). The latter route has been followed by Australia, with a system that started on July 1, 1994.

Politically, a critical question is the extent to which such a change can be used to permit a significant decrease in the eventual drain on tax dollars. Many people who are intrigued by the Chilean experience know little of the details. Two elements stand out from this perspective. One is that the Pinochet government began with a major cut in the benefits promised under the old system before proceeding to introduce the new one. Reduced benefits and increased retirement ages resulted in a major drop in the cost of future promises. Second, the flow of payroll tax dollars into private accounts, as well as the reduction in the mandated tax rate, meant less revenue to finance ongoing payments, although much of the accumulated funds were invested in government debt. As Argentina has recently learned, without a drop in the tax rate there is not a great deal of immediate interest in switching from the old system to the new. Chile has run a budget surplus of roughly 4 percent of GDP to help finance this transition. Transition to a Chilean system is something that needs money, not something that generates it. Thus I think that the popularity of following Chile will fall dramatically in the United States once this lesson sinks in.

In contrast, covering a decline in Social Security benefits with mandates on private providers may look financially and politically more attractive. A number of countries mandate that firms provide pensions as a way of holding down the growth of the revenue needs of public systems. Such mandating is in place in Australia, Finland, and Switzerland, and is seriously being proposed by some groups in the United States. Mandates on business to provide health insurance were part of the failed Clinton health proposal. I think there is more scope for mandates in the pension area, since the natural mandate is a percentage of earnings, while the health mandate was a flat amount, adjusted by explicit subsidies for low earners. Percentage mandates are easier for business to adjust to.

IMPACT OF SOCIAL SECURITY REFORM ON PRIVATE PENSIONS

Any shrinking of Social Security benefits will have an immediate impact on the cost of private pensions for those pension systems that are integrated with Social Security benefits. In addition the integration rules, set by the Internal Revenue Service (IRS), may well change at the same time in reflection of this shrinkage. Also, a time of shrinking Social Security is naturally a time to reexamine the perceived problems with the private pension system.

Moreover, firms are likely to use the time of such change to rethink and renegotiate pension structures. There is a link here in that the cost of Social

Security depends on wage growth and the interest of workers in pensions rather than current income also depends on wage growth. Obviously, any mandating will also affect private pensions.

PENSION REGULATIONS

I turn now to direct regulation of pension funds. I will divide my remarks into four areas: tax treatment of pensions, regulation and insurance of pension funds, reporting of pensions, and regulation of pension rules.

Wherever there are income taxes, there are rules about the tax treatment of pension contributions, accumulations, and benefits. The United States uses preferred tax status to encourage pensions and retirement savings generally. This has two implications. One is that there is the leverage in IRS rules on the availability of preferred tax status as a device to regulate pensions. In the United States these rules have been used to press for wide coverage of pensions, against limiting them just to management of highly paid workers. The second implication is that tinkering with tax rules for pensions are another way of affecting the deficit, one that does not have much public visibility. The particular form this has taken is limiting the tax-deductible contributions to fund pension plans that the IRS rules adequately funded. Tightening the rules has noticeably decreased contributions and so increased tax revenue. Of course this has the effect of increasing the risks associated with government insurance of pension promises.

The United States has an elaborate set of rules covering both pension fund accumulation and pension application rules, such as vesting. A large part of these rules began in 1973 with the Employment Retirement Income Security Act (ERISA), which also introduced the Pension Benefit Guarantee Corporation (PBGC). In terms of political economy, both firms and unions with large underfunded pension liabilities were eager to see the government insure these liabilities, with the expectation, quite high in some cases, that these funds would be bailed out. Particularly in the early legislation, there were significant loopholes that allowed the tapping of government funds to bail out such funds, particularly for firms experiencing financial distress. This structure should have concerned other firms more than it did, since so far the cost has not fallen directly on taxpayers, but has been paid by other firms in the form of higher required insurance premiums. The rules have been significantly tightened over time.

When there is explicit government insurance of pensions, it is natural for the government to worry about the residual risks being borne by the taxpayers. Even without insurance, the presence of large pension funds probably puts the government at risk of a large bail out even without an explicit promise. The pension system as a whole is probably "too big to fail" in the face of an event like a stock market collapse that could put many pension systems at risk. Indeed a recent paper by Zvi Bodie was entitled "Lessons from FSLIC for PBGC." That is enough to scare anyone. While in principle PBGC is supposed to be self-financing, covering its losses with premiums, self-financing might not be viable. In particular, insurance only covers defined benefit pensions. Both defined contribution pensions and no pensions are allowed. Thus if there were a need for large premium increases to cover PBGC losses, we could expect a large movement of firms with healthy pension funds run out of defined benefit pensions. This resembles a bank run and is the heart of the risk the taxpayers face. As pension liabilities become more significant there has been considerable controversy over accounting reporting standards. But this point is beyond the scope of this chapter.

The 1980s and early 1990s have seen the end of the growth of pension coverage in the United States and a large swing away from defined benefit pensions to defined contribution pensions, often in the form of individual retirement savings. The distinction here is between corporate and worker management of fund accumulation. These trends have concerned some people and are part of the push toward MUPs. Part of the concern seems to me misplaced in that defined benefit plans do not seem to be a better vehicle for providing adequate retirement incomes, although they are attractive to large firms. Part of the concern is the worry about the adequacy of retirement income generally, a worry that will be exacerbated if Social Security shrinks.

Once pensions are significant sources of funds and pension promises are significant sources of liabilities for firms, one can expect regulations covering both the circumstances determining payments to workers and the reporting of both assets and liabilities to shareholders, and the capital market generally. Extensive and detailed rules on who is covered and relative pension payments to different workers are likely outcomes of the abuses that are inevitable, on the part of some firms, if there are no rules.

Pensions in the United States are subject to a large array of regulations, with heavy emphasis on vesting rules. Of increasing concern are portability issues—the implications for retirement income of repeated job switching by workers. This concern is partially related to the tendency of many workers to cash out lump-sum distributions when changing jobs. Regulations so far have tried to discourage cashing out by tax incentives. Increased pension attention will naturally result in increased regulation of this practice. Moreover, since portability is simpler with defined contribution than defined benefit plans, this concern may accelerate the move to defined contribution plans.

CAPITAL MARKETS

Pension funds play a large role in the functioning of U.S. capital markets. Over time, a country with a growth of pension funds will see a growth of pressure on government to regulate capital markets in order to provide pension funds with markets that are fairer, less risky, and less expensive to trade in.

Indeed, one of the frequently cited benefits of the Chilean Social Security reform is the political pressure coming from massive fund accumulation on the ongoing process of developing capital market regulation in Chile. Most people refer to improvement of the capital market as a benefit of the Chilean reform. I think this is backward. Improved running of the capital markets is a necessary part of a successful pension reform. And the regulations to improve running are not easy to design or implement. I was interested to see the compilation of rules of the U.S. Securities and Exchange Commission in a prominent place in government offices that I visited in Santiago. While the U.S. is just one of several models to build on, the success of the New York Stock Exchange in attracting funds worldwide suggests that this is a helpful model.

While much regulation is directed at obvious abuses of the trading process, concern naturally extends to a variety of subtle problems. In Chile, they are beginning to worry about issues of conflict of interest. If fund managers are simultaneously trading on behalf of pension funds that they manage, as well as their own account, or other funds, then there is the potential of abuse of power as trading on one account affects returns on another that is traded slightly later. Similarly, once funds have significant accumulations, there are issues of corporate governance and voting rights of shares. There are two issues here. One is identifying the group in whose interest the shares should be voted. In particular there may be conflicts between firms and workers, both of whom have interest in the pension accumulation. Second is the possibility, again, of conflict of interest as fund managers possibly use their voting power to advance other interests.

CONCLUSION

It would be hopeless to try to summarize the wide range of subjects I have touched on in a few pithy remarks. Let me close by mentioning another source of pressure on pension reform. The World Bank has published its views on pension reform. They appear eager to encourage the Chilean reform wherever they are asked or have leverage to press for it. This makes it important to recognize the complex set of linkages required to have a successful pension system.

NOTE

1. This chapter was originally presented at a seminar given at Florida International University, Miami, on October 14, 1994.

REFERENCE

Bodie, Zvio. (1993). "The PBGC: A Costly Lesson in the Economics of Federal Insurance: Commentary." In M. S. Sniderman (ed.), *Government Risk-bearing*. Proceedings of a Conference held at the Federal Reserve Bank of Cleveland, May 1991. Newell, MA: Kluwer Academic.

16

BRIEF THOUGHTS ON THE POLITICAL ECONOMY OF ADJUSTMENT: INTERNATIONAL MARKETS VERSUS NATIONAL POLITICS

Gerald M. Meier

INTRODUCTION

Long ago, when I first began teaching economic development, I believed Joan Robinson's dictum that finance is not a bottleneck to development. Recall that "where enterprise leads, finance follows"? It wasn't until later that we recognized the domestic problems that would lead to financial repression.

Now we confront international crises related to volatile international capital flows. And the new dictum may very well be, "Where policy reform leads, finance follows." Private capital flows are three times greater than official flows and it is international markets—not governments —that now dominate, especially portfolio investments in emerging markets.

This raises important issues regarding international markets and national politics. While economists applaud liberalization because it integrates economies around the world and motivates efficient resource allocations, politicians worry about their nations' increased vulnerability to external shocks. Domestic autonomy is now subordinate to international markets.

LIBERALIZATION AND OPENNESS MAY CREATE PROBLEMS

Short-term international finance can be disruptive for an number of reasons:

- Capital outflow: speculative attack on exchange rate
- may call for measures of control
- may require adjustment measures

Guillermo Ortiz Martinez, governor of Banco de Mexico (Central Bank of Mexico) since 1997, concluded in a recent article (1998) that the "current international financial system quickly exposes and punishes countries' economic weaknesses; it also facilitates the worldwide transmission of financial turmoil." His remedy calls for measures that would reduce the risks that capital flows create through "improved supervision, regulation, and transparency of financial systems" without necessarily limiting the mobility of these flows. It should be noted, however, that a development strategy that relies on foreign borrowing does not seem viable in the long run.

THE CASE OF MEXICO

A possible political economy analysis could focus on official corruption, and unresolved Indian uprisings, several unsolved killings, the election campaign—on who did what to whom. But even without these adverse political developments, would there have been economic crisis?

Policy reforms and fixed exchange rates as nominal anchors led to capital inflows (especially portfolio) which caused the exchange rate to appreciate, leading to high nominal interest rates and an increase in the current account deficit. Anti-inflationary policy lost credibility, which caused the market to place high default risk on "Tesobonos," (Mexican Treasury bills). This led to capital outflows, falling reserves, and a liquidity crisis with slow growth, high consumption, and low savings. This combination of fundamental economic disequilibria was the result of destabilizing political events and market expectations of investors.

THE NEED FOR ADJUSTMENT: POLITICAL ASPECTS AND SOCIAL STABILITY?

Labor did not gain much from capital inflows. To the contrary, it was hit hard due to the fact that these inflows mainly represented efforts at privatization, private investment in infrastructure, and the allocation of savings to investors. Under these circumstances, they can only indirectly benefit the poor unless more public spending is allocated to social services, which was not the case here.

Consequently, the distribution of income became more unequal, with GDP falling by 7 percent and public spending on education, health, food subsidies, transfers, and public employment falling by 40 percent in real terms in 1995.

As Mexico sought macroeconomic balance, with it came micro-economic hardships. Inflation that was hovering around 52 percent in 1995 was brought down to around 25 percent in 1996. At the same time, though, thousands of small and medium-sized enterprises failed while bank loans defaulted. In the labor market, hundreds of thousands of jobs were lost as unemployment reached an historic peak. Real wages also fell and consumption spending declined by 12 percent in real terms—the worst showing since 1932. Informal-sector activity grew as the formal-sector activity shrank. The banking system was weak and the question of bailing out banks was a political minefield. Expectations of exports growth was dismal, with projections at 1.5 to 2 percent for 1997.

CAN POPULISM BE AVOIDED?

Consider this:

- If orthodox economic reforms are perpetuated—can there be adjustment with a human face?
- Also, undertaking political reform amounts to political liberalization from previously excessive concentrations of power in the presidency. This means political change on many levels:
    within the Institutional Revolutionary Party (PRI)
    congressional elections in 1997
    new federalism
    opposition parties
    Institutional change for new democratic political order

John Williamson and President Ernesto Zedillo may be described as "technopol s" but what they really need to be are "polycrats." Can they combine political reform with economic reform? We need to be less "techno" and more "pol" to gain public support. A quote by Novelist Carlos Fuentes (1996) sums it up nicely: "Zedillo is hidden in his office with his calculator. He has to get out and build support with the people. But his aides say: 'We will save Mexico with numbers, not politics.'"

BEYOND MEXICO: INTERNATIONAL POLICY IMPLICATIONS:

Mexico's crisis created "negative international externality" or the "tequila effect."

- How do we avoid a crisis without controlling capital inflows?
- Who should bear the risk of volatile capital flows?
- How do we restore capital flows and growth?

The answers depend on a stronger international public sector to correct international market failures and national government failures. When international markets create a liquidity crisis and fail to provide new money, we can't again rely on an ad hoc responses—as in Mexico's crisis:

Instead, we need clearer early warning signals to reduce the risk, and mechanisms to spread the risk and permit it to be borne more efficiently. The IMF needs to take the lead:

- surveillance
- expand quotas, special drawing rights (SDRs), structural adjustment facility

● cooperate with the World Bank and World Trade Organization

Michel Camdessus, the managing director of the IMF has advocated the addition of a "social pillar"—poverty-adjustment. At the Copenhagen Summit for Social Development in 1995 he said the IMF averted "the first major crisis of our new world of globalized financial markets." But certainly not the last.

What can we look forward to in the future? Are there adequate mechanisms in place to face the next crisis? With labor growth on the rise, the next crisis may be just around the corner. Consider this: the labor force in Mexico grew recently by 3.4 percent—the highest growth rate in this century. This means Mexico's GDP will have to grow by 5 to 6 percent in order to absorb all this new labor and bring the existing unemployment rate down.

Over the next 20 years, the world's labor force is expected to grow by 40 percent, with 95 percent of that growth being in developing countries accounting for less than 15 percent of the world's capital investment (in real terms). In financial terms this means we can expect to see:

● under saving
● insufficient official liquidity
● overreacting markets — as in the case of Mexico
● incomplete risk markets

If real growth is to increase, there must be more job creation, and if there is to be a reduction in poverty, then we need a more robust international public sector:

In the past we have focused on domestic governance with overextended domestic public sectors. Now it is time to focus on global governance with measures to extend the reach of the international public sector—to remedy international market failures as globalization occurs.

REFERENCES

Camdessus, Michel. (1995). Address given at the Copenhagen Summit for Social Development (March 7).

Fuentes, Carlos. (1996). *A New Time for Mexico*. Translated from Spanish by Marina Gutman Custañeda and the author. New York: Farrar, Strauss and Giroux.

Ortiz, Guillermo. (1998). "What Lessons Does the Mexican Crisis Hold for Recovery in Asia?" *Finance & Development*, Vol. 35, no. 2.

Selected Bibliography

Adams, F. G. and I. Davis. (1994). "The Role of Policy in Economic Development: Comparisons of the East and Southeast Asian and Latin American Experience." *Asian Pacific Economic Literature*, Vol. 8, no. 1(May).

Adams, F. G. and P.A. Prazmowski. (1995). "Why Are Saving Rates in East Asia So High? Reviving The Life Cycle Hypothesis." Presented at the ICSEAD Conference, Kitakyushu, Japan, July.

Alesina, Alberto and Allan Drazen. (1991). "Why Are Stabilizations Delayed?" *American Economic Review*, Vol. 81, no. 5 (December).

Amezcua, Alejandro V. (ed.). (1995). *El Financiamiento del Desarrollo en América Latina: La Movilización del Ahorro Interno*. Mexico: Centro de Estudios Monetarios Latinoamericanos, Banco Interamericano de Desarrollo.

Armstrong, D. S. and A. A. Francis. (1968). "A Structural Analysis of the Barbados Economy, 1968, with an Application to the Tourist Industry." *Social and Economic Studies*, Vol. 23, no. 4 (December).

Barro, Robert J. (1991). "Economic Growth in a Cross Section of Countries." *Quarterly Journal of Economics*, Vol. 106, no. 2: 407-43.

Bodie, Zvio. (1993). "The PBGC: A Costly Lesson in the Economics of Federal Insurance: Commentary." In M. S. Sniderman (ed.), *Government Risk-bearing*. Proceedings of a Conference held at the Federal Reserve Bank of Cleveland, May 1991. Newell, MA: Kluwer Academic.

Borrego, John, Alejandro A. Bejar, and K.S. Jomo (eds.). (1996). *Capital, the State, and Late Industrialization: Comparative Perspectives on the Pacific Rim*. Boulder, CO: Westview Press.

Boulmer-Thomas, Victor. (1994). *The Economic History of Latin America Since Independence*. London: Cambridge University Press.

____ (ed.). (1996). *The New Economic Model in Latin America and Its Impact on Income Distribution and Poverty*. New York: St. Martin's Press.

Bruton, Henry. (1998). "A Reconsideration of Import Substitution." *Journal of Economic Literature*, Vol. 36, no. 2: 903-36.

Burki, Shahid Javid and Sebastian Edwards. (1995). "Latin America After Mexico:

Quickening the Pace." Mimeo. Washington DC: World Bank Current Issues Paper, August.

Camdessus, Michel. (1995). Address given at the Copenhagen Summit for Social Development (March 7).

Casas-González, Antonio. (1997). "Oil Prices, Economic Growth, and Economic Productivity." In A. Jorge and J. Salazar-Carrillo (eds.), Price Policies and Economic Growth. Westport, CT: Praeger.

Chenery, H. B. and A. Strout. (1966). "Foreign Assistance and Economic Development." *American Economic Review*, Vol. 56: 679-733.

Chow, Gregory C. (1993). "Capital Formation and Economic Growth in China." *Quarterly Journal of Economics*, Vol. 108: 809-41.

Easterly, William. (1996). "When Is Stabilization Expansionary? Evidence From High Inflation." *Economic Policy*, Vol. 22 (April).

Faust, Joerg. (1995). "The Mexican Crisis and Its Regional Implications." *Aussenpolitik*, Vol. 4.

Faux, Jeff. (1997). "The American Model Exposed," *The Nation*, Vol. 265, no. 13 (October 27).

French-Davis, Ricardo and Stephany Griffith-Jones (eds.). (1995). *Coping with Capital Surges: The Return of Finance to Latin America*. Boulder, CO: L. Rienner Publishers.

Friedman, Milton. (1968). "The Role of Monetary Policy." *American Economic Review*, Vol. 58 (March).

Fuentes, Carlos. (1996). *A New Time for Mexico*. Translated from Spanish by Marina Gutman Custañeda and the author. New York: Farrar, Strauss and Giroux.

García, Valeriano F. (1997). *Black December: Banking Instability, the Mexican Crisis, and its Effect on Argentina*. Washington, DC: World Bank.

Gervasoni, Carlos. (1995). "Economic Policy and Electoral Performance in Latin America, 1982-1995." Center for Latin American Studies, Stanford University.

Gonzales, Anthony. (1996). "The 1996 Budget: An International Perspective." Mimeo. St. Augustine: University of West Indies, January.

Harris, Donald. (1996). "Finance, Investment and Growth: Economic Policy for Caribbean Economies in the Next (Quarter) Century." In Keith Worrell and Anthony Gonzales (eds), *Whither the Caricom Region: Whither The CDB in Its Support?* Barbados: CDB.

Heymann, Daniel and Axel Leijonhufvud. (1995). *High Inflation*. Oxford: Clarendon Press.

Horowitz, Irving Louis. (1977). "Cuba 1997." In *Vital Speeches*: February 1.

Hughes, H. (1988). *Delivering Industrialization in Asia*. Cambridge: Cambridge University Press.

Iglesias, Enrique. (1984). "Latin America: Crisis and Development Options," *CEPAL Review*, No. 23 (August).

Jorge, Antonio and J. Salazar-Carrillo. (1992). *The Latin American Debt*. London: Macmillan.

Krugman, Paul. (1994). "The Myth of Asia's Miracle." *Foreign Affairs*, Vol. 73 (November/December): 62-78.

Krueger, Anne O. (1995). *Trade Policies and Developing Nations*. Washington DC: Brookings.

Meier, Gerald. (1984). *Emerging from Poverty: The Economics That Really Matters*. New York: Oxford University Press.

_____ (ed.). (1994). *From Classical Economics to Development Economics*. New York: St. Martin's Press.

Moss, Charles and James Seale, Jr. (1997). "Import Demand and Foreign Debt: A Latent-Variable System Wide Approach." In A. Jorge and J. Salazar-Carrillo (eds.). *Price Policies and Economic Growth.*

Oliveri, Ernest. (1992). *Latin American Debt and the Politics of International Finance.* Westport, Ct: Praeger.

Ortiz, Guillermo. (1998). "What Lessons Does the Mexican Crisis Hold for Recovery in Asia?" *Finance & Development*, Vol. 35, no. 2.

Pettis, Michael.(1996). "The Liquidity Trap—Latin America's Free-Market Past." *Foreign Affairs*, Vol. 75, no. 6 (November/December).

Phelps, Edmund. (1967). "Phillips Curves, Expectations of Inflation, and Optimal Unemployment Over Time." *Economica*, Vol. 34.

Ranis, G. and S. A. Mahmood. (1992). *The Political Economy of Development Policy Change.* Oxford: Basil Blackwell.

Rojas-Suárez, Liliana and Steven R. Weisbrod. (1996). *Building Stability in Latin American Financial Markets.* Washington, DC: Inter-American Development Bank, Office of the Chief Economist.

Romer, Paul M. (1986). "Increasing Returns and Long-Run Growth." *Journal of Political Economy*, Vol. 94, no.5: 1002-37.

Salazar-Carrillo, Jorge. (1986). "Is the Cuban Economy Knowable?" *Caribbean Review*, Spring.

_____. (1995). "Interdependence and Economic Performance in Cuba." In Irving Louis Horowitz, (ed.), *Cuban Communism.* Somerset, NJ: Transaction Publishers.

_____. (1997). "The Present Condition and the Rebuilding of the Cuban Economy." In Antonio Jorge and Jorge Salazar-Carrillo (eds.), *The Economics of the Caribbean: Present and Future Trends.* Stockholm: Stockholm University Press.

Simonsen, Mario. (1994). *Ensaios Analíticos.* Rio de Janeiro: Editora Fundacão Getulio Vargas.

Sundrum, R. M. (1994). "Exports and Growth." In G. Meier (ed.), *From Classical Economics to Development Economic.* New York: St. Martin's Press.

Turner, Philip. (1995). *Capital Flows in Latin America : A New Phase.* Basle: Bank for International Settlements, Monetary and Economic Department.

Wade, Robert. (1990). *Governing the Market: Economic Theory and the Role of Government in East Asian Industrialization.* Princeton, NJ: Princeton University Press.

Watkins, Kevin. (1998). "Life and Debt Situation," Financial Times, January 23.

Williamson, John. (1994). *The Political Economy of Policy Reform.* Washington, DC: Institute for International Economics.

World Bank. (1993). *The East Asian Miracle: Economic Growth and Public Policy.* New York: Oxford University Press.

_____. (1994). *Coping with Changes in the External Environment.* Washington, DC: World Bank, Caribbean Division, Country Department. Report No. 12821 LAC, May.

Young, Alwyn. (1995). "The Tyranny of Numbers: Confronting the Statistical Realities of the East Asian Growth Experience." *Quarterly Journal of Economics*, Vol. 11, no.3.

Index

Adams, F. Gerard, 7-8
Alonso, Irma, 10
Andean Development Corporation, 73
Aspe, Pepe, 63

Baker Plan. *See* Brady Plan
Banco Latino, 79
Barbados tourism: background, 147-148; considerations, other, for, 165-166; economic impact, 148-149, 160; employment multiplier estimates, 153-154, 159; foreign exchange implications, 154-155, 159-160; GDP multiplier calculations, 152-153, 158; importance of, 147-148; income multiple calculations, 153, 158-159; introduction to, 147; linked services, 152; size of, 151-152; social impacts of, 160-163; social vs economic impacts, 147; socioeconomic measuring, 163-165; sources for, 147; statistical equations, 156-160; summary of, 166-167; tax implication, 154, 159; tourism expenditures, 149-151; value added as multiplicand, 155-156
Barbados tourism, social impacts: cultural issues, 162; economy versus, 160-162; environmental factors,

163; quality of life, 162; social costs, 162
Barbados tourist expenditures: benefits of, 149; economic impact, 151; receipt estimates, 149-151
Bodie, Zvi, 208
Brady Plan: ameliorative measures versus, 143; banking community options, 78; benefits, 79; collateral amount, 78; debt restructuring, 78-79; GDP growth, 141; improvements on, 143; Latin America economy and, 186; par bonds, 78
Bretton Woods, negotiated agreement status, 143-144

Candessus, Michel, 65
Capital markets: Chilean social security, 209-210; pension funds and, 209
Caribbean Basin Initiative (CBI), 97
Caribbean economic growth: conclusions on, 101; direct foreign investment, 95; GDP growth, 95; growth features of, 93; growth forces, 94-95; macroeconomic fundamentals, 95; Mexico's crisis and, 93, 95-100; national savings rate, 95
Caribbean and Mexico's crisis: account balance impacts, 96-97; capital markets, 95; capital types for, 95-

96; debt service ratios, 97; Eurobond market ratings, 96; external
financing, 97-98; foreign investor
expectations, 96; growth during,
95; higher growth rate attaining,
99-100; international market reforms, 96; long-term growth projections, 97; Mexico's investors, 96;
trade shock preparation, 100;
trends effecting, 98-99
Casas-Gonzalez, Antonio, 6
Castro, Fidel. *See* Post-Castro Cuba
Central Intelligence Agency (CIA): Cuban trade activity, 122; foreign
trade statistics versus, 122-123
Chile: social security and, 207; social
security reform, 209-210
Citibank, Mexico operations, 63
Colombia, economic growth: balance of
payments, 34-36; bond spreads, 31;
economic policy objectives, 36-37;
economy accelerating, 32; exchange rates, 32, 34-36; growth vs
GDP, 32; inflation, 32-33; introduction to, 31; investments, 33-34;
policy measures, 33; problems in,
31; restrictive monetary policy, 31;
savings and, 33-34; summary of,
37; value added growth, 33
Colombian balance of payments: account deficits, 35; bond spreads,
36; debts and, 36; exports and, 34-
35; foreign investment and, 34;
policy of, 34
Colombian investment: infrastructure
increasing, 33-34; savings rates, 34
Colombian macroeconomic policy: domestic credit, 37; monetary policy,
36-37; social program problems, 36
Conference on International Economic
and Financial Systems, 3
Contadora Group, 139
Cuba: cultural essence retaining, 190-
191; factors challenging, 191;
sociocultural order, 191; socioeconomic development purposes, 190;
vs historical past, 190. *See also*
Post-Castro Cuba

Cuban commerce: export activity weakness, 126; imports composition of,
126; sugar and, 126
Cuban decollectivizing strategy: "Big
Bang" vs gradualist positions, 192-
193; characteristics of, 196-197;
circular causation processes, 196;
culture-bound concepts, 199; economic advantage maintenance, 199;
goals in, 198; gradualists process
benefits, 195; imperative nature of,
199-200; market-system transi-
tions, 194-195; natural economic
norms, 197; objectives of, 193-194;
preliminary outline, 191; premises
for, 191-192; price system functions, 198-199; rational price systems, 197-198; reconstruction processes, implementing, 200-201;
strategy for, 193; strategy issues,
selecting, 196; structural change
instruments, 192
Cuban economy: commerce composition, 126; communist economy
objectives, 121-122; foreign investments, 126-128; geographic trade
characteristics, 123-125; historical
trade patterns, 129-134; international trade statistics, 122; introduction, 121-123; policy implications, 128-129; tourism and, 126-
128; trade information sources,
122-123
Cuban foreign investments: import activity, 127-128; increase in, 127;
Soviet investments, 127
Cuban geographical trade: economic
activity levels of, 123-125; export
partners, 123; import values of,
123
Cuban policy implications, economic
turnaround, 128-129
Cuban tourism, expansion of, 126-127
Cuban trade patterns: export levels, 129;
export patterns, 133; GDP and,
129-131; immiserization process
and, 129-131; publications on, 129;
statistical sources, 131-133; U. S.

market and, 131; Western imports,
131

De Quesada, Julio, 6
Debt consequences: convertibility, 23-
24; convertibility conclusions, 23-
24; crisis consequences, 22-23;
crisis management assessing, 23;
crisis, payer of, 21-22; introduction, 17; Mexican crisis, 17-21
Debt crisis evolution: "free trade" impacts, 138; international economy,
138; Latin America and, 138; origins of, 137-138
Debt crisis perspectives: amelioration vs
debt solutions, 142-143; Brady
Plan and, 143; debt write-offs, 143;
economic systems, 143; international political systems, 143;
Wood's agreement changes, 143-
144; world economy interdependence, 144
Debt management policies: foreign direct investments, 140; import activity, 140; measures for, 141; policy
measures, 141-142; short vs long-
term solutions, 142; status of, 140;
transferred resources, 140
Diamond, Peter, 12

East Asian growth: debt burdens, 108;
export growth, 108; export-oriented
industrialization, 110; GDP and,
103, 105-108; inflation rates, 108;
Latin American development versus, 103-108; Latin American
growth, 103-105; Latin American
strategies versus, 108-110; macroeconomic policy, 110; macroeconomic stability, 112; public deficit
monetarization, 110; savings rates,
108; state's role, 112
Echeverria, Luis, 64
Economic development: conclusions
about, 116, 118; democracy role in,
117; economic history, 116; facts
of, 115-117; government role in,
116-117; introduction, 118; poor

countries and, 115-116; vicious
circles, 115, 117-118; virtuous
circles, 117-118
Economic reforms, measures for, 98-99
Employment Retirement Income Security Act (ERISA), 208
European Monetary System, fixed exchange rates, 66

Fondo Latinoamericano de Reservas, 75
Friedman, Milton, 172
Fuentes, Carlos, 213

Gervasoni, Carlos, 172
Gonzales, Anthony, 7
Gregorian, Vartan, 63
Group of Seven, economic coordination
efforts, 141-142

Inter-American Development Bank, 75,
139
International market liberalization: disruption reasons, 211-212; foreign
borrowing viability, 212
International market politics: implications of, 213-214; introduction,
211; liberalization problems, 211-
212; Mexico and, 212; national
politics versus, 211-214; political
adjustments, 212-213; populism,
213; private capital flows, 211;
social stability, 212-213
International Monetary Fund: balance-
of-payment countries, 75; Cuban
statistical sources, 129, 131-133;
debt write off and, 143; poverty
adjustments for, 214; short-term
solutions as, 142; structural adjustment packages, 178; technical advice from, 81; Venezuela agreement with, 80
International policy implications: future
crisis, 214; international public
sector, 213; Mexico's crisis and,
213; warning signals, 213-214
Investment liberalization, developing
countries and, 98

Jorge, Antonio, 9, 12

Latin America: Argentina economy, 5; Colombia and, 3; Colombia economy, 5-6; debt crisis consequences, 4; growth perspectives, 4; Mexico's crisis, 6; neoliberalism, 4; tequila effect, 3; Venezuelan economy, 6-7

Latin America, debt: conclusions on, 144-145; debt crisis evolution, 137-138; debt crisis perspectives, 142-144; debt management improvements, 140-142; developed economies impacts, 138-140; economy potential and, 138-139; external debt crisis stages, 137; growth rate of, 139; market size, 139; multilateralism, 140; political unity, 139-140; regionalism and, 140

Latin America, development: Argentina and, 105; Brazil and, 105; Chile and, 105; Cuba trade flows, 9; debt crisis, 9-10; development strategies, 108-110; East Asian growth versus, 103-108; East Asian growth, 7-8; economic indicators, 10; export-oriented industrialization, 110; future of, 112-113; GDP of, 105-108; growth differences, 108-111; growth of, 103-105; introduction, 103; macroeconomic policy, 110; macroeconomic stability, 112; Mexico and, 105; NAFTA and, 7; public deficits monetarization, 110; state's role in, 112; vicious circle theory, 8-9

Latin America, economy: Brady Plan and, 186; capital flight returning, 186; current program focusing, 186-187; exchange-rate-based stabilization, 185; government interventions, 184-185; microeconomic structural changes, 184; organizations for, 185-186; petrodollars uses, 187

Latin America, structural changes: development of spatial dimensions,

181; exchange-rate policies, 179; income poverty, 181; income streams, 180-181; inflationary importance, 178; labor market flexibility, 181; macroeconomic balance importance, 178; microeconomic levels for, 179; price support programs, 180; private investment activity, 180; success formulas, 179-180

Latin America, sustained growth: attitudes changing on, 177; challenges to, 178; government's role changes, 178; growth miracle versus, 178; introduction, 17-178; poverty reductions, 182-184; social goods allocations, 182-184; stop-and-go economies, 184-187; structural changes, 178-181

Machlup, Fritz, 171
Madariaga, Pepe, 65
Mancera, Manuel, 63
Marginal propensity to consume (MPC), 148
Martinez, Guillermo Ortiz, 211
Meier, Gerald, 13
Mexican crisis: account deficits, 63-64; banking environment, 64; convertibility and, 23-24; currency devaluation, 64; exchange flexibility, 24; future of, 68; hyperinflation, 24; introduction, 63-64; market reactions, 67-68; observations on, 68; Salinas-Zedillo transition, 64-67; unrealistic expectations and, 68
Mexican crisis consequences: Argentina and, 17, 22; balance-of-trade scenarios, 19-20; banking system and, 19-21; corrective measurers, 18-19; external sector and, 19; financial organization negotiations, 17-18; magnitude of, 18; private sector and, 19; reform success, 21; unemployment, 22-23
Mexican crisis payers: fiscal side impacts, 21-22; guaranteed deposits, 21; shareholders and, 21

Mexico, international market politics: 212; policy reforms and, 212; political developments, 212

Mexico, market reactions: banking sector, 67; impact of, 68; solution theory vs practice, 67

Moncarz, Raul, 9

Multiplier calculations: employment, 153-154, 159; foreign exchange, 154-155, 159-160; income, 153, 158-159; taxation, 154, 159

Multiplier effect: Barbados economy and, 148-149; concept of, 148; formula for, 148; MPC and, 148

Neoliberalism: defined, 171; international markets, 13; Latin America and, 10-11, 171-172; macroeconomic management, 173-174; market economies, 172; Mexico's future and, 174; pension fund effects, 12-13; policy reforms with regional integration, 174; populism and, 171; post-Castro Cuba and, 12; price reforms, 172; price stability, 172; stabilization costs, 172-173; sustained growth and, 11-12

North American Free Trade Agreement (NAFTA): CBI decline and, 97; international trends from, 98; Latin American development, 7; Mexico's entry impacts, 97-98; OECD and, 63

Ocampo, Jose Antonio, 5

Organization for Economic Cooperation and Development (OECD), NAFTA and, 63

Organization of Petroleum Exporting Countries (OPEC), international economy and, 138

Pension Benefit Guarantee Corporation (PBGC), 208

Pension regulations: accumulation rules, 208; application rules, 208; benefits vs contribution pensions, 209; government bail-out risks, 208-

209; issues in, 209; tax rules, 208

Pensions: Social Security shrinking, 207; structure renegotiating, 207-208

Petrei, A. Humberto, 5

Petroleos de Venezuela, 80

Phelps, Edmund, 172

Phillips Curve, stabilization and, 172

Populism: defined, 171-172; political reform impacts, 213

Portillo, Jose Lopez: capital flight, 65-66; currency devaluation, 64; emergency program goals, 67; exchange rate widening, 65; fixed exchange rate regimes, 66; lessons from, 66; private savings, 66; problem complexity, 66; program adjustment effects, 67; Salinas handoff and, 64-65; scenario of, 64; vs adjustments, 67

Post-Castro Cuba: comments about, 201-203; considerations on, 190-191; decollectivizing strategies, 191-201; desocializing, 191-201; developmental strategies, 202-203; historicocultural background, reinterpreting, 203; introduction, 189; neoliberalism and, 12; organizational diversity, 202; protection rates vs price distortion indexes, 201-202; social system functioning, 189; state's role, 201

Ranis, Gustav, 11

Reagan, Ronald, 171

Robinson, Joan, 211

Salazar-Carrillo, Jorge, 9-10

Salinas, Carlos: economic recover under, 63-64; Portillo handoff, 64-65; reputation of, 65; WTO and, 64; Zedillo transition, 64-67

SENIAT, 80

Simonsen, Mario, 10, 171

Social income poverty: centralized vs decentralized government, 183-184; education and, 183; income size, 182; public goods allocations,

182; rural mobilization, 183; taxation, 184; two income-generating systems, 182-183

Social Security: budget deficits and, 205-206; capital markets and, 209-210; conclusions, 210; government design of, 205; introduction, 205-206; medical care costs, 206; pension regulations, 208-209; political agenda rise, 206; political process for, 206-207; private pensions reforms, 207-208; private providers mandates, 207; problems addressing, 206; tax dollar draining, 207

Social Security Administration, U.S., 205

Social stability: capital inflows, uses, 212; income distributions, 212; international market politics, 212-213; microeconomic hardships, 212-213

Thatcher, Margaret, 171

Tourism, socioeconomic implications: Barbados and, 163-164; environmental protection strategies, 166; hotel rooms, 164-165; square kilometer impacts, 164; tourist education, 165-166

Venezuela, economic outlook for, 98

Venezuelan agreement restructuring: Brady Plan and, 78-79; overseas payments effects, 77-78; public-sector debt serving, 77

Venezuelan debt crisis: impact of, 76-77; international creditor banks, 77; origins of, 76-77; post-1988 conditions, 77

Venezuelan economy: debt crisis, 76-77; foreign debt crisis, 75; foreign financing, 76; indebtedness increasing, 76; oil prices, 75-76; post-World War II and, 75; status currently of, 79-81

Venezuelan outlook: banking crisis, 79; elements influencing, 79; exchange control system, 79; foreign financing, 80; inflation and, 79; macroeconomic disequilibria, 80-81; monetary policy effectiveness, 79-80

Vicious circles: economic development, 117; growth constraints, 117; high savings countries, 117; human capital, 118; stop-go economies, 117; technology transfers, 117-118

Virtuous circles. *See* Vicious circles

Williamson, John, 10, 213

World Bank: balance-of-payment countries, 75; debt write off, 143; short-term solutions as, 142; structural adjustment packages, 178; technical advice from, 81

World Trade Organization (WTO), Salinas and, 64

Zedillo, Ernesto, 213; Salinas transition, 64-67

About the Contributors

F. GERARD ADAMS is a chaired Professor of Economics and Business at Northeastern University and formerly a Professor of Economics at the Wharton School of Business, University of Pennsylvania..

IRMA T. de ALONSO is Professor of Economics at Florida International University.

ANTONIO CASAS-GONZALEZ is President of the Central Bank of Venezuela, and previously a Director of Petroleos de Venezuela S.A., the Venezuelan petroleum company.

PETER DIAMOND is Institute Professor of Economics at the Massachusetts Institute of Technology.

ANTHONY GONZALES is Professor of International Economics at the University of the West Indies at Saint Augustine, Trinidad and Tobago.

ANTONIO JORGE is Professor of Political Economy at Florida International University and Senior Research Fellow at the University of Miami.

GERALD M. MEIER is chaired Professor of Economics and Business at Stanford University.

RAUL MONCARZ is Professor of Finance at Florida International University.

JOSE ANTONIO OCAMPO is Executive Secretary of the Economic Commission for Latin America and the Caribbean, and form Minister of Finance in Colombia.

A. HUMBERTO PETREI is   Executive Director of the Inter-American Development Bank, and former President of the Argentinean Central Bank.

JULIO A. de QUESADA is President of Citigroup in Mexico.

GUSTAV RANIS is chaired Professor of Economics at Yale University, and Director of its International Concilium.

JORGE SALAZAR-CARRILLO is Director and Professor of Economics at Florida International University, and Non-Resident Senior Fellow at the Brookings Institution.

BERNADETTE WEST is Lecturer at Florida International University and the University of Miami.

JOHN WILLIAMSON is Senior Fellow at the Institute of International Economics of Washington D.C.

ISBN 0-275-95975-9

9 780275 959753

HARDCOVER BAR CODE